After Agatha
WOMEN WRITE CRIME

Also by Sally Cline

Non-Fiction

Reflecting Men at Twice their Natural Size
Just Desserts: Women and Food
Women, Passion and Celibacy
Lifting the Taboo: Women, Death and Dying
Radclyffe Hall: A Woman Called John
Couples: Scene from the Inside
Zelda Fitzgerald: Her Voice in Paradise
Hellman & Hammett
Life Writing: Writing Biography, Autobiography and Memoir
Literary Non-Fiction
Dashiell Hammett: Man of Mystery

Fiction

One of Us is Lying
Lily and Max

After Agatha

WOMEN WRITE CRIME

Sally Cline

Leabharlanna Poiblí Chathair Baile Átha Cliath
Dublin City Public Libraries

Oldcastle Books

First edition published in 2022 by Oldcastle Books,
Harpenden, UK

oldcastlebooks.co.uk
@oldcastlebooks

A CIP catalogue record for this book is available from the British Library.

ISBN
978-0-85730-232-8 (Paperback)
978-0-85730-233-5 (Ebook)

2 4 6 8 10 9 7 5 3 1

Typeset in 11.5 on 14.75pt Minion Pro
by Avocet Typeset, Bideford, Devon, EX39 2BP
Printed and bound in Great Britain by Clays Ltd, Elcograf S.p.A.

Contents

1

Setting the Table

It is an enduring and fascinating paradox that women who spend so much of their real lives being afraid are so drawn to stories that bring those fears to life.

Most women are conditioned from childhood to have an acute awareness of the threat of violence; to understand that there are men in the world, often in *their* world, who want to damage them. Yet so many of them persist in reading – and writing – novels in which other women are stalked, raped, battered, tortured and murdered, often in graphic and brutal detail.

In the UK, crime and thriller fiction has become the most popular literary genre, accounting for one in three of all books sold. Sales of these novels rose by 19 per cent between 2015 and 2017, overtaking general fiction for the first time. According to data company Nielsen Bookscan, 18.7 million units of crime fiction were sold in 2017, compared to 18.1 million units of general and literary fiction during the same period two years earlier. That figure for crime fiction is now widely believed to have risen to around 21 million. It is no great surprise that during the Covid-19 pandemic in 2020, people in the UK spent almost twice as much time reading. A little more surprising perhaps is the fact that more of them than ever chose to find comfort and distraction in crime and thriller novels. Nearly 120,000 more books in this genre were purchased during the last two weeks of June 2020, compared to the same period the previous year. These figures reflect the scene in the US, where sales of crime and thriller fiction are now second only to those of erotica and romance, and in Canada, where crime and mystery books combined are believed to account for more than one hundred million dollars in sales each year.

Interestingly, it is women readers who are driving this boom, accounting for as much as 80 per cent of the market. There has been much debate over the last few years about the reasons for this. Women are more preoccupied than men with the fear of violence and their own vulnerability. Reading about it is one way of addressing those fears in a safe environment and thereby going some way towards overcoming them. There also appears to be a greater desire in women to understand crime, and the psychology and motivation behind it. And while crime stories are often bleak, there is something undeniably reassuring about the fact that, in most novels in this genre, crimes are resolved, perpetrators are punished, and justice is done. In female-authored crime and psychological thriller novels, it is often the women who avenge these crimes and turn the tables on the perpetrators.

It's no great surprise then that this vast audience of women readers is especially drawn to crime books and thrillers written by other women. Some of the most phenomenally successful novels over recent years are female-authored. Think Gillian Flynn's *Gone Girl*, Paula Hawkins' *The Girl on the Train*, Louise Doughty's *Apple Tree Yard*, Tana French's Dublin Murder Squad books and the Cormoran Strike series written by JK Rowling under her pseudonym of Robert Galbraith– all of which have been adapted for television or film.

Notwithstanding the fact that these writers are extremely gifted and compelling storytellers, as women they are acutely aware of and alert to their own vulnerabilities and to the potential for violence that can overshadow their everyday lives, and this sets them apart from their male counterparts. At the Bristol CrimeFest in 2014, crime writer Val McDermid said that women writers are much better at scaring other women. They understand the root and nature of their fears and can more clearly and vividly imagine what it feels like to be afraid. This gives them a better insight into the impact and aftermath of violent crime and, as a consequence, an unsettling ability to bring it to life on the page. Women writers also seem to identify more fully with their characters, and to attempt to properly understand crime, from the perspective of both victim and perpetrator. It also means they are better able to address the levels of resentment and anger this vulnerability can make women feel.

Exploring crime from a female perspective can be seen as less gratuitous; as if the writers are communicating or sharing their own fears and experiences of violence with readers, without making them feel in any way complicit in it. This in turn provides a mutual understanding and trust between an author and her audience and goes some way to explaining why there are men currently writing crime novels using a gender-neutral or female alias. SJ Watson, SK Tremayne and JP Delaney are all male authors. Writer Martyn Waites uses the pseudonym Tania Carver for the thrillers he writes with his wife Linda. Nicci Gerrard and Sean French, another husband-and-wife team, chose the female pen name Nicci French for their hugely successful standalone psychological thrillers and their Frieda Klein series. When it was revealed that Robert Galbraith was actually JK Rowling, sales of the Cormoran Strike series rose by 150,000 per cent.

In female-authored novels, women tend to be far more than a mere narrative device; a body lying in an alleyway, or on a mortuary table. And yet, somewhat paradoxically, these writers do not shy away from violence in their novels. Their portrayal of it is sometimes ruthless in its detail and brutality. So much so that, in 2007, writer Ian Rankin claimed the violence in crime books written by women was often more graphic than in those written by men. Crucially, though, these stories usually have a strong female protagonist at their centre; one who drives the plot forward and has an impact on its resolution.

So, who are these women writers? What sort of people are they to want to explore so deeply and investigate so thoroughly the darkest side of human nature? Aside from the fact the market is an increasingly lucrative one – with crime and thriller novels repeatedly dominating the bestseller lists – their reasons for writing about crime will, to a large degree, reflect the reasons so many women want to read about it. But is there something else going on here? Their audience only has to read about stalking, assault, rape, torture and murder; the writers themselves have to research it and live with it, often for years, and to lay it down on the page. Crime fiction can be hard to read – sometimes it must be hard to write.

What issues specifically preoccupy these women and what, if anything, do they hope their work might achieve, beyond making them a very good living and entertaining such a huge and appreciative audience? What sort of characters – male and female – do they create and what decisions did they have to make when conceiving them? How do their books differ from those written by their male counterparts, and why? How do *they* feel about the crimes and the level and nature of violence in the books they and their fellow women have written, and are currently writing?

These are the questions this book will attempt to answer. I have extensively interviewed women writers from the UK, the US and Canada, all of whom write crime and thriller novels in a variety of guises: puzzle, detection, private investigators, police procedurals, lesbian mysteries, forensic science thrillers and domestic noir. Their responses to these questions reveal that they are as intrigued and fascinated by them as their readers are. Because the phenomenon of women writers addressing violent crime and their own fears is not a new one. And the answer to all these questions must lie not only with today's women crime writers, but with their predecessors – and the various and conspicuous explosions in women's crime writing between the 1930s and today.

Novelists have written about crime long before they embarked on the detective story or the exploits of the private eye. In the eighteenth century, Daniel Defoe wrote many 'true crime' stories and turned several of these into what we now describe as classical literature, such as *Moll Flanders* in 1721.

In the nineteenth century, Charles Dickens, Fyodor Dostoevsky and Honoré de Balzac based the plots for their novels on harsh and terrible real-life crimes. During the same century, Edgar Allan Poe with his 'tales of ratiocination', of which the most famous *The Murders in the Rue Morgue* (1841) is today considered the first modern detective story, and Arthur Conan Doyle, with his Sherlock Holmes mysteries, originated the two main streams of detective fiction. In these, the central protagonist is the talented amateur detective. These men, for they were all men, were the forerunners of the first explosion of women's crime writing.

In the 1920s and 1930s, five bestselling, acclaimed writers of their day – all women – exploded onto the British crime scene. They would see their male rivals go out of print and out of public consciousness. They were Agatha Christie (1890-1976), Dorothy L Sayers (1893-1957), Margery Allingham (1904-1966), Ngaio Marsh (1895-1982) and Josephine Tey (1896-1952).

This small, imaginative and energetic band of British female crime practitioners was affectionately called The Golden Age Writers. What was exceptional about their success was that, in America and Canada at this time, the literary field was still largely dominated by male authors. Even more significant is that in 1930, when the male expert in the British crime field Sir Arthur Conan Doyle died, his British female successors had already made and continued to make big names for themselves.

By the time the Second World War broke out, the great names in British detective fiction were female, whereas in America critical recognition and massive sales were still reserved for men.

The striking fact about the Golden Age Writers is not merely their success at the time, but that they have continued to sell and be widely read. Margery Allingham's 1931 novel *Police at the Funeral,* Dorothy L Sayers' *Murder Must Advertise* (1933), Ngaio Marsh's *Enter a Murderer (1935),* Agatha Christie's *And Then There were None* (1939) and Josephine Tey's *Miss Pym Disposes* (1946) remain strong sellers in crime sections in major bookstores today, more than 80 years after they were first written. The explosion of women's crime writing created classics.

Headlining those five acclaimed authors was Agatha Christie, whose first novel in 1920, *The Mysterious Affair at Styles,* followed swiftly after the fourth and final Sherlock Holmes novel, *The Valley of Fear* (1915), and the collection of Holmes short stories, *His Last Bow* (1917). In *Styles,* Christie introduced Hercule Poirot, the first of her two iconic creations, to thunderous appreciation. To her own surprise, her other bizarre protagonist, Miss Jane Marple, brought further admiration and regard when she arrived in *The Murder at the Vicarage* in 1927. No one expected the elderly eccentric Marple to compete with Poirot in the public's affections, but she did. Neither Holmes nor any other crime protagonist of their period – or thereafter – was able to rival either the epochal status of Poirot and Marple, or the worldwide sales of their creator.

While this females-first revolution was happening in Britain, over the water in America we saw the new hardboiled male private investigator emerge. Dashiell Hammett, Raymond Chandler and Ross Macdonald created private investigators Sam Spade, Philip Marlowe and Lew Archer, who moved constantly and swiftly through the urban locations they inhabited. These male PIs stood for what they saw as the American ideal, but it was a male ideal; honour, decency, male bonding. This flourished in the traditional view of America as a nation founded on the pursuit of justice, equality and the right to life, liberty and the search for happiness. But in this fiction, something was wrong in the states of America; it was a world rotten and corrupt at its core. The white male private eyes could not put that right without bending or breaking the law themselves. So often they did so. Whereas the British Golden Age female detectives could guarantee a return to an orderly world, the smart American sleuths could offer no guarantees at all.

The male American sleuths were however hugely influential on crime fiction in general, by masculinising the genre. From the mid-1920s onwards, SS Van Dine, Ellery Queen and John Dickson Carr intellectualised crime fiction, presenting complex puzzles and rigorous exercises in logic, seemingly from some superior male mind. As shown in my biography *Dashiell Hammett: Man of Mystery* (2014), Hammett was the single most significant male writer of American detective fiction and foremost in the development of the genre.[1] His five major, brilliant crime novels, which were published between 1929 and 1934, all showed a tough-guy masculinity. Hammett's heroes became archetypal characters in American literary culture, establishing the ground rules and tone for a whole new tradition of hardboiled writing, specifically male writing.

In spite of the fact that Hammett's work contained some superb philosophical insights which would appeal equally to female writers' sensitivities – such as how appearance belies reality, how nothing is as it seems, how order and meaning are mere human fabrications and blind chance the only thing on which we can rely – the message the publishers elected to put across instead was the grittiness and harshness of an urban life that largely excluded women. Thus it was that Hammett was able firmly to establish the field of private eye fiction, a field in which fellow American female practitioners were not welcome and female protagonists barely existed.

It would be the 1950s before women writers became strong voices on the American crime scene, almost 30 years after their British counterparts. The gifted American women whose books started to come out in the 1940s – Margaret Millar, Dorothy B Hughes, Charlotte Armstrong and even the later, hugely successful, Patricia Highsmith – were largely ignored. The break came when Millar's *Beast in View* won the 1956 Edgar Award. After that, Highsmith's *The Talented Mr Ripley*, written in 1955, made the Edgar shortlist. Highsmith had already written *Strangers on a Train*, her first psychological thriller, in 1950. It was reasonably successful upon publication, but it was when Alfred Hitchcock adapted it for a 1951 film that her extraordinary reputation got under way.

While Highsmith continued with her Ripley thrillers, which would make up 5 of her 22 novels, her fellow Americans were catching up. Charlotte Armstrong's *A Dram of Poison* was awarded the Edgar in 1957 and was subsequently recognised as a pioneer of domestic suspense, a forerunner to the current batch of psychological mysteries known as domestic noir.

As the series of male PIs continued to win big sales throughout the 1970s, this hardboiled male world was overtaken by the next explosion of women writers, the American trio of Marcia Muller, Sue Grafton and Sara Paretsky, who can be credited with inventing the American female private investigator. Muller established the first female private eye in American crime literature when she gave us San Francisco's inimitable and outstanding sleuth Sharon McCone. Grafton's Alphabet thrillers offered the chirpy, smart investigator Kinsey Millhone, at home in her imaginary Santa Teresa, while in Chicago, Sara Paretsky created her unique and extraordinary VI Warshawski.

All three of these characters have the typical PI voice; ironic, wisecracking and self-mocking, along with the necessary PI perspective, which is anti-hierarchical, always self-employed and resolutely independent. Like the males created by Hammett and

Chandler, they are preoccupied not only with their individual cases but with the wider social issues their investigations throw up, including the murder cases connected to white collar crime that Warshawski deals with in all her novels.

The major difference between Hammett's and Chandler's founding male PIs, whose private lives and emotions were almost always left out, and the females who subsequently exploded on to the scene, was the intrusion of the personal into the public presentation of their lives. Muller's McCone, Grafton's Millhone and Paretsky's Warshawski were all given personal histories, including sexual adventures, that made them more realistic.

In classic PI fashion, all three investigators live alone, do not have pets or children and never have permanent live-in partners. But unlike the male characters who preceded them, they do have close women friends and a few selected elderly men they know well, and these act as family.

Sara Paretsky gives Warshawski a best friend, the Viennese physician Dr Lotty Herschel, who treats her various illnesses and combat-related injuries and is her practical and emotional support and, in effect, her surrogate mother. Sue Grafton gives Kinsey Millhone an extended family, starting with her octogenarian landlord Henry Pitts, a retired commercial baker who enjoys cooking, crossword puzzles, and Kinsey's delightful company. Kinsey also feels affectionate towards Henry's siblings and towards Rosie, the flamboyant Hungarian, who cooks exotic meals for them at the local tavern.

The introduction of the personal into the public roles that characterised female private eyes continued through to the next generation of female crime writers, whose focus was on women in the police force. The experiences of women joining and struggling to survive in a male-dominated force have since been thoroughly documented in fiction. An outstanding dramatic example is Lynda La Plante's *Prime Suspect*, a highly successful 1990s television show and a series of eight novels featuring Detective Chief Inspector Jane Tennison, played with grandeur and power on television by Helen Mirren. Tennison comes through the ranks the hard way, resented, patronised and bullied by her chauvinist male colleagues in Scotland Yard. Many British novels followed, again reflecting the real experiences of women working in a police force in which active bullying may have dwindled but institutionalised sexism, misogyny and discrimination continued. In Tana French's 2016 police procedural *The Trespasser*, her lead detective Antoinette Conway, who is mixed-race and the only woman in her squad, has to overcome insidious bullying and a series of cruel practical jokes played on her by male colleagues.

Many crime writers believe these realistic novels help confront and challenge the struggles British, American and Canadian law enforcement agencies have gone through to achieve gender parity, and that their protagonists do a lot to shape and alter perceptions and representations of real-life female police officers. This influence becomes more striking when their novels are adapted for television. One stylish example is Tess Gerritsen's series about detective Jane Rizzoli and medical examiner Maura Isles, now the hugely popular TV show *Rizzoli and Isles*.

Over the years, new and different female protagonists emerged; single mothers raising children while holding down demanding police jobs and officers who had mental or physical issues or were on the autism spectrum. Female-authored police procedurals especially featured strong women characters who were often flawed or damaged but were easy for readers to identify with, such as those created by British thriller writers Jane Casey, Sophie Hannah and Sarah Hilary. Hilary's DI Marnie Rome is haunted by the brutal murder of her parents. Hannah's DC Charlie Zailer has obsessive and self-destructive traits that undermine and threaten her hard-earned career.

Another significant development of women's writing – the emergence of lesbian protagonists – was much slower to materialise. Until the early 1980s, there were few lesbian characters to be found in mainstream fiction, in either America, Canada or the UK. Katherine V Forrest, who was born in Canada but is known as an American writer, filled the gap with her LAPD homicide detective, ex-marine Kate Delafield, the first lesbian detective to have her own series. When the first Delafield mystery *Amateur City* was published in 1984, lesbian crime protagonists were almost unheard of. *Murder at the Nightwood Bar* (1987), the second in the Delafield series, is now a classic in crime literature and was followed by seven more in the series, each of which was either a finalist or a winner of the Lambda Literary Award. In 1987, three years after Forrest enabled American lesbian protagonists to reach the public gaze, Scottish author Val McDermid introduced socialist, feminist, lesbian journalist Lindsay Gordon. She kept her protagonist going in six interesting mysteries until 2003. All of the fictional cases Lindsay investigates were at the time critically important; today their relevance is still spot on.

Ten years after McDermid's then bold entrance into lesbian fiction, Manda Scott, a former Scottish vet, published her first novel *Hen's Teeth*, featuring lesbian therapist Kellen Stewart. At a time when there was little lesbian fiction in the UK or US, the book was hailed by Fay Weldon as a 'new voice for a new world' and was shortlisted for the 1997 Orange Prize. Today we are not short of lesbian romances, but we are short of mainstream lesbian crime novelists and there are not enough fictional out-lesbian investigators tackling cases the way Scott's Kellen Stewart does.

There are some in the front lines, including Jody Klaire, a former police officer, and Nancy Sanra, who offers readers Tally McGinnis, a young gay heroine working in 1990s San Francisco. Cari Hunter, who has written a lesbian crime series based in the UK's Peak District, believes mainstream authors still have a tendency to sideline or closet their LGBTQ characters.

On investigation this appears to be an accurate observation. Fortunately, small presses and indie authors have stepped in to fill the void, climbing bestseller charts and proving that UK lesbian authors are writing and, more significantly, being read.

The entry of black and disabled protagonists has also been slow, partly because there are too few black and disabled women writers being published and because white and able-bodied writers often feel wary of appropriating their stories. A number of women writers are producing interesting bodies of work, however. These include African-American author Attica Locke, whose award-winning novels confront issues of race, power, prejudice and injustice, British crime writer Jane A Adams, whose ex-policewoman Naomi Blake is blind, and American Kathy Reichs, whose live-alone ex-policewoman Sunday Night has one eye and is badly disfigured.

The next explosion of female crime writing – the emergence of forensic crime writing –was dominated by four women, a healthy reminder that the Golden Age authors of the 1920s and 1930s were only five in number. The first woman crime writer to initiate it was American Patricia Cornwell, who has sold more than 100 million books and taken every possible crime novel award with her series featuring pathologist Dr Kay Scarpetta and her tech-savvy lesbian niece Lucy. Cornwell's debut novel *Postmortem* (1990) was the first genuine forensic thriller. It won the Edgar, the Creasey, the Anthony and the Macavity awards, as well as the French Prix du Roman d'Aventures Prize; the first book ever to claim all those distinctions in a single year. Cornwell's success paved the way for those who came after her, including the brilliant Kathy Reichs, whose first book *Deja Dead* (1997) introduced smart and sassy forensic anthropologist Temperance Brennan and won the Arthur Ellis Award for Best First Novel.

Chinese-American physician and crime writer Tess Gerritsen wrote her first Rizzoli and Isles medical thriller in 2001. Eight years later, British writer Elly Griffiths published *The Crossing Places* (2009), the first in her series about the delightfully unstereotypical forensic anthropologist Ruth Galloway. These forensic thriller novels, with their fascinating blend of science and fiction, explore the new and future roles of professional women in a technological age and have at their heart what it means for women to live in this era and in a particular geographical and political setting.

The next explosion, the literary phenomenon named as domestic noir by novelist Julia Crouch in 2013, has become a hugely popular sub-genre within crime fiction.[2] These psychological tales of betrayal, deceit and murder locate their stories primarily in homes, workplaces and schools, focusing on female experiences there and explicating the idea – and the unfortunate truth – that the domestic sphere is very often a threatening and dangerous place for women. Striking examples include Gillian Flynn's psychological thriller *Gone Girl* (2012), which sold more than two million copies in print and digital editions in its first year, and Louise Doughty's *Apple Tree Yard*, which has sold more than a quarter of a million copies in the UK alone and has been translated into 26 languages.

Julia Crouch, whose own novels, including the tense psychological thrillers *Every Vow You Break* (2012) and *Her Husband's Secret* (2017), are perfect examples of domestic noir, is closely involved in another recent innovation in the UK; a female collective Killer Women, which was set up in London in 2015 by journalists Melanie McGrath and Louise Millar. Killer Women is a group of mystery novelists, almost all of whom are past and present members of the media and have come into contact with the legal world. Its 19 British women members, who include bestselling writers Paula Hawkins, Sarah Hilary, Jane Casey and Erin Kelly, have a joint lineage in radio, television or digital production, scripts, magazine or newspaper features and public relations. The group organises British crime writing events for men and women and aims to amplify and support female voices in crime writing throughout the country.

A lot of women writing today have worked in the criminal justice system and therefore have first-hand knowledge of crime and its aftermath. These frontrunners in crime writing are graduates from the criminal justice system itself – experts in one field who have become experts in another. This recent explosion in women's writing brings to the page the real-life experiences of victims, and their families and friends – and the challenges faced by the women who play a part in investigating crime.

Is there a difference between crime novels written by professional women who have worked in occupations involving criminal trials and those who haven't? Has the inclusion of novels by women who have themselves been involved in the criminal justice system changed the direction of feminist crime fiction? How do these novels reflect real feminist gains in the criminal justice system?

Linda Fairstein was one of the first to tackle these questions when she began to publish her Alexandra Cooper legal thrillers, based upon her own experience as head of the Sex Crimes Unit of the Manhattan District Attorney's office. She thought there were several significant differences in the storylines of professional and non-professional narrators in the ways they use their expertise and legal jargon, and the way they depict unequal justice systems. In the real world, challenges still exist when integrating women into the criminal justice system, and these are seen clearly in several novels. But some women who have made professional gains in the legal world can now imagine protagonists who have professional independence and autonomy.

Like their forensic counterparts Cornwell and Reichs, these ex-justice professionals, who have been lawyers, police officers, probation officers, prison officers, criminal psychologists and bodyguards, bring an insider's knowledge and authority to their work. Writers in this field can more fully and authentically imagine that world in their novels and create female protagonists who have professional independence and autonomy. They can also tackle some of the challenges that still exist for real women working in the criminal justice system and reflect real feminist gains. These writers include former British police officer Clare Mackintosh, whose books have sold more than two million copies worldwide, Edgar-winning thriller writer Meg Gardiner, who practised law in Los Angeles before turning her hand to suspense novels, and Alafair Burke, a former deputy district attorney who has written 18 crime books, including the Samantha Kincaid and Ellie Hatcher series.

One element in crime fiction has not changed. Crime and psychological thriller novels continue to show almost all female victims being abused, beaten and killed at male hands. In recent years, much of this fictional abuse has become more brutal, the violence delineated sometimes pornographic in nature. And it is not only men who are pushing the boundaries with graphic and gruesome depictions of torture, rape and murder. Women writers are doing it too. One powerful example is Val McDermid's *The Mermaids Singing* (2003) with its detailed and shocking portrayal of a serial killer who tortures his victims to death using cruel and horrific medieval techniques. Another is Mari Hannah's first novel *The Murder Wall* (2012) which opens with a graphic and disturbing account of a young girl's rape.

Crime fiction is and always has been about much more than mystery and sheer entertainment. It asks difficult questions about life and death, good and evil and justice – and what might drive one human being to take the life of another. The best crime writing also reflects and engages with contemporary society and its critical issues, giving readers an insight into the world around them – both inside and outside the home – and asking moral questions of us all, as individuals and as a society in general.

These books tell us much about who and what we are. They take an unflinching look at the cracks and fissures in our countries, towns and cities and in our communities and our close relationships, and at the way we deal with those we view as outsiders. Detective novels especially provide a penetrating guide to the environments in which they are set. Though the tales they tell are dark and tense, their storylines often end optimistically. Justice is done. Criminals are caught. Safety is re-established. For readers and writers, this redemptive quality can be satisfying, reassuring and empowering.

More than ever before, crime novels have become a guide to our changing moral and social attitudes. The fiction does not necessarily reflect our attitudes. It may well modify or exaggerate our views or reject them completely. When crime fiction had only a moderate exposure to the reading public, these issues were not at the forefront of our minds. They were not essential.

Now they are.

First-class crime writing is not merely entertaining, but human and literary in its essence. Crime has always been at the very heart of human storytelling. Its themes are related to ethics and an analysis of our value systems and it is vital we take it seriously. We do not yet do so, and we must. Despite the fact that the serious subject matter of crime fiction is about morality and its shifting relationship to the law, it is still labelled as distraction and diversion by its detractors. It is *not* allotted the critical attention the best of it warrants. It deserves more review space and more public note than it has so far been given. Its status is based on the artificial line drawn between literary and crime fiction; it has too often been seen as a mere sub-genre of fiction, similar to romance or sci-fi and, in terms of cultural significance and standing, well below the category of literary fiction.

It is the women writing crime today who are tackling some of the biggest social and moral issues. In America and Canada, women's crime writing offers up both fear and satire related to the dark issues of Trump's era. In the UK, it provides a mixture of social criticism and sharp storytelling. On both sides of the Atlantic, contemporary women crime writers are drawing a caustic critique of modern society. And they are doing it differently from their male counterparts. Anger, at the extent and nature of political corruption, poverty, misogyny, sexism, discrimination and child exploitation, is often evident in these novels.

Sara Paretsky, as feisty now as she ever was, broke ground with the rigorous and exacting way she confronted issues of violence, racism and sexism in the US. While she has never once forgotten the cardinal rule of crime fiction – its page-turning qualities – she continues to address the urgent political and social problems still facing women in the country. Patricia Cornwell and Kathy Reichs take on the highly complex technological issues of tomorrow which confront professional women today.

Other writers have been unflinching in their investigations into the darkest side of society and human nature. In her 2018 novel *A Darkness of the Heart*, Canadian Gail Bowen confronts head-on the issues of poverty and child exploitation. In *The Butterfly Girl* (2019), former death penalty investigator Rene Denfeld, who lived on the streets as a child, writes about the murders of homeless children in Oregon. British writer Kate Medina explores mental illness and the darkest reaches of the human mind in her crime series featuring clinical psychologist Dr Jessie Flynn.

In crime novels written by women, it is often the strong, independent female protagonists, like Medina's Flynn, who drive the plot – insightful scientists, doctors, psychologists, lawyers and assertive and confident women police officers, whose active agency may be stronger within their fictional narratives than they are allowed in real life, and who make a significant difference in the worlds and environments they inhabit.

These women writers are changing crime fiction, creating

intricate plots and complex male and female characters – including killers – who are real and complete human beings. In Sarah Hilary's *Come and Find Me* (2018) her series detective DI Marnie Rome attempts to understand, and even to empathise with, the foster brother who brutally murdered her parents. In her bestselling novel *The Nanny* (2019), British writer Gilly Macmillan explores the guilt, pressures, fears and insecurities of motherhood.

British author Alison Joseph, who has written a series of novels about private investigator nun Sister Agnes and was Chair of the Crime Writers' Association between 2013 and 2015, spoke for many of her fellow writers when she said all her books were a mixture of crime and social commentary. 'If you are writing about crime it needs at some level to be realistic,' she said. 'It may be fiction, but I still want it to be true. When the crime is true, it comes out as a social problem.' Fellow Briton Kate Rhodes is fascinated by some of the moral issues she is able to touch on in her writing. 'It sounds reductive, but you are always talking about life and death issues,' she said. 'I think the vast majority of crime writers are trying to be realistic about the way they depict crime.'

To further understand why – and how – these crime writers are telling some of society's most significant and relevant stories, it is important to explore in greater detail why women are compelled to read crime so devotedly and in such great numbers.

2

Why Women Read Crime

The argument that so many women are drawn to reading crime novels because they provide guaranteed entertainment and escapism – along with a reassuring antidote to the harsh realities of life – is sound enough. But the women who are writing crime today understand that the question is much more complex than that.

We know that women read more fiction than men generally. Surveys have shown they account for around 80 per cent of all sales of fiction in the UK, the US and Canada, vastly outnumbering men as buyers in all categories, except science fiction, horror and fantasy. Far more women than men attend libraries, literary events and book clubs. Nevertheless, one might expect women to avoid stories that play into the fears and anxieties that have been implanted in them since childhood and that remain with them for the rest of their lives. The mainly real and occasionally imagined violence, the physical threat present in dark and lonely places and, more often, in their own homes; the potential consequences of finding themselves in the wrong place at the wrong time.

Yet it seems many women do want to read about other women being attacked and murdered and actively seek out books in which the victims are invariably female and in which the depiction of male violence against them is often brutal, explicit and excruciatingly drawn out.

Lawyer and award-winning writer Frances Hegarty, who writes most of her crime novels under the pen name Frances Fyfield, believes that, in part, the genre satisfies women's voyeuristic instincts. 'It's a bit like the kind of spectacle of women enjoying a really brutal wrestling match,' she said. 'Why should we be surprised? The enjoyment of violence and conflict has always historically been much more the hobby of men, you would have thought. Where all the way along the line, it was just as much the hobby of women.'

For Ann Cleeves, the human drama and suspense contained in a gripping crime novel provides a much needed distraction from, and antidote to, real life troubles. 'In this time of confusion and chaos, there is something very reassuring about traditional crime fiction,' she said. 'Order restored at the end.' Cleeves is the bestselling yet modest creator of Vera Stanhope, who defied all stereotypes to become one of Britain's most eccentric and beloved police detectives, both in Ann's widely successful and critically acclaimed series of novels set in Northumberland, and in the TV adaptation *Vera*. 'Certainly, the sort of crime fiction that I write, which is quiet and domestic, can be escapist,' she said. 'If there's all these dreadful things happening in the world, you can focus safely on a particular family or small community.'

British crime writer Zoe Sharp, who writes her Charlie Fox thrillers at breakneck speed, agrees. Sharp opted out of mainstream education at the age of 12 and spent most of her formative years living on a catamaran in the north of England. She turned to writing after receiving death threat letters in the course of her work as a photojournalist. This led to the creation of Charlie, a tough no-nonsense-don't-mess-with-me heroine who has earned her a Lovey Award for Best Series and nominations for Edgar, Anthony, Barry, Benjamin Franklin and Macavity Awards in the United States, as well as the CWA Dagger Award. 'The worse reality becomes around us, the more we want the certainty of a resolution,' she said. 'The more we want justice and closure. You tend to get that in fiction rather than in real life. At the end of a crime novel the bad guys will probably be caught and punished.'

Canadian mystery and thriller writer Dorothy McIntosh said: 'My favourite movies are mountaineering movies. And the reason for that is, I'm terrified of heights. So, it's maximum suspense to be able to read about people doing these extremely risky things. So, if you transfer that to crime, you have situations that are, in many cases, deadly dangerous. And yet, you're completely safe while you're reading it. And I think the sense of danger… I think women have a heightened sense of the dangers out there because, after all, they are more real for us.'

Internationally bestselling author Sophie Hannah, whose psychological thrillers include the hugely popular Zailer and Waterhouse series, believes crime and mystery books are especially popular with women readers because, like romantic fiction, they are driven by the need for answers to the questions that life throws at us, and for 'happy' endings or resolutions. Yet she understands that crime fiction – and especially crime fiction written by women – has always been about more than the lure of suspense and action, the hunger for escapism or the satisfaction of solving a mystery. It is also a way to help women deal with the horrors of life, from a safe position – a 'kind of training'.

Because the world to which women readers are escaping is not a safe and comfortable one. It is a world in which other women are regularly beaten, raped and killed and its stories tap all too vividly into very real fears. 'If we watch a horror film, if we read a scary crime novel, we are perfectly safe,' Hannah said. 'But we can practise having the feeling we might have if we were in that situation. That's probably useful for building emotional resilience. Because we want to prove to ourselves that we can handle the difficult parts of life, the horrific bits as well as the nice bits. We wouldn't rush up to a serial killer and say hi, but we can expose ourselves in a safe way to trauma. We can almost enjoy being scared knowing it will all be okay in the end. That's a way to make ourselves stronger.'

Tess Gerritsen, who wrote romantic thrillers before beginning her Rizzoli and Isles series in 2001 and has since become one of America's top crime authors, says every day in life for women is filled with suspense. 'You walk to your car at night. You walk to work in the morning. You're always aware,' she said. 'My husband even points it out. He talked about my situational awareness. He said, you act like you're a prey animal. And I said, yeah, that's because I am. So, we have a lot more to worry about, just in our everyday lives, about our own safety than men do. It's possible these books justify our fear. They make us feel, yeah, we have a right to be fearful.'

Gerritsen, whose first Rizzoli and Isles story is about a killer who breaks into women's homes and performs horrific ritualistic acts of torture on them, has had women tell her they love to read about serial killers and only want to read books in which the victims are women. 'I thought, this is so strange. What does this mean?' she said. 'Until it came to me that when children read books that are scary, they like to read books where the victims are children. So we readers, women and children, when we read books, we identify with the victims.'

Multi-prizewinning author Mari Hannah, a former probation officer whose career was cut short when she was injured in an assault while on duty, believes reading crime is a way of acknowledging and coming to terms with fear. 'What is odd is how many women read my novels and feel all the fears as if they really happen,' she said. 'I've had women write to me saying, I'm reading your novel and loving it, but the girl who is missing is blonde with green eyes and she hasn't come home yet, and my daughter is blonde with green eyes and she hasn't come home yet, and now I'm worried.' Hannah, whose partner is a former murder detective, added that in her experience as a probation officer, and in the experience of most police officers, happy endings don't happen in real life. 'Many criminals go free or are never caught,' she said. 'Women particularly read crime novels because they give a sense of safety they often don't have in real life.'

Hannah's series' protagonist Kate Daniels is a brilliant and determined Detective Chief Inspector and Hannah believes women readers like the idea that there is someone out there looking out for them and dealing with these awful problems. 'Although not all crime novels have a happy ending,' she said. 'When the book ends, the world may not necessarily seem a safer place.'

Stella Duffy, who is a theatrical producer and stage writer as well as a print author, does not think it is the place of fiction always to give reassurance or that people should expect women to shy away from reading violent crime. 'The Greeks didn't shy away from *Medea* either,' she said. 'Life is genuinely really frightening. We are the victims of violent crime, particularly in the home – and we are told that we need to be scared. All our lives we're told to be scared and then, fucking hell, things happen, like what happened on the bus in London (*the violent homophobic attack on two lesbian women in north London in May 2019*), and we are scared again, and it feels like its 1975.

'So, we go to the place where catharsis is. It's very human. And it is entirely, understandably cathartic to want to see the truth. And of course, modern crime fiction, particularly modern British crime fiction, tends not to have things wrapped up neatly at the end and the baddie getting their just deserts. And in a way I think, painful though that is, we also want to see that. We want it confirmed that we're not idiots to think people get away with it all the time. There is something about having it in print that does that. We have a sense, yeah, that is deep and uncomfortable, a lower gut sense that it is not fair and it is not right and nothing has changed in real life and that gets confirmed by the novels we are writing for each other, as well as for a wider audience.'

There might also be an element of curiosity when it comes to reading about the stalking, rape, mutilation, torture and murder of other women; a case of women wanting to see exactly what they might be up against. Reading about violent crime can also help women make sense of experiences that might otherwise be difficult to talk about or even to acknowledge. Sarah Vaughan, whose tense and thought-provoking novel *Anatomy of a Scandal* is a thriller with a rape at its heart, said crime fiction allows readers to explore their darkest fears in a sheltered setting and that the closure offered by a crime novel can be comforting, especially in current times when the world is such an uncertain and often frightening place. *Scandal*, Vaughan's first novel, was published in January 2018, a few months after the Harvey Weinstein scandal prompted the *MeToo* movement and spent ten weeks on the *Sunday Times'* bestseller list. She said many readers wrote to her to say they had experienced something similar and they found the book cathartic to read.

It is this empathy and this understanding of what the threat of violence and actual emotional and physical abuse feels like that goes some way to explain why women readers are especially drawn to crime and thriller novels written by other women. Journalist and award-winning writer Melanie McGrath has written about the role fear plays both in women's compulsion to read crime books and female authors' decisions to write them in a certain way. 'It is partly because women who live with fear know what it feels like so much better than men,' she said. 'Girls grow up inundated by messages about our vulnerability and learn to interpret the world through that lens. Women are alert to the long shadow, the unexpected turn of the door handle and the sound of boots on a lonely night-time street. In crime fiction, women can explore those feelings safely. Resolving the crime helps resolve the feelings.'

McGrath, whose crime novels include a trilogy set in the Arctic, with Inuit detective Edie Kiglatuk, and the standalone thriller *Give Me the Child* (2017), added: 'The murdered woman in a crime novel stands in for our vulnerability or for our sense of being mere meat puppets, but she also symbolises our struggle to get out from under what can sometimes feel like life-sucking roles as mothers, wives, daughters, sisters and carers, in order to claim our own identities.

'For women required in youth to be decorous and in maturity to be invisible, crime fiction gives us permission to touch on our own indecorous feelings of rage, aggression and vengefulness, sentiments we're encouraged to pack away somewhere, along with the big underwear and the tampons, where they won't offend.

'Let's not forget, either,' McGrath added, 'that much of the crime fiction popular with women features a female protagonist. She's usually strong if a little frayed around the edges; in other words, an everywoman. The reader identifies with her, as the author intended. The protagonist not only solves the crime and restores the world to its proper equilibrium, but in another, deeper, symbolic sense, through her skill and persistence and downright doggedness, she avoids the fate represented by that lifeless, bloodless female corpse lying on the path lab slab.'[3]

Within the pages of female-authored crime novels, women are often at the centre of the story, not only as victims but as crime fighters and avengers, characters who drive the plot forward and impact its resolution. These strong female protagonists are independent, able and resilient but also human and complex. In their fictional world they fight the same obstacles and challenges women in the real world face: misogyny, sexism, discrimination and betrayal as well as society's expectations of them as professionals, wives, mothers and friends. As police officers and private investigators, especially in series fiction, they are given problematic personal lives and powerful and convincing character arcs. They are often vulnerable and flawed and this makes them more compelling and easier for readers to identify with. Examples include Ann Cleeves' frumpy, lonely yet brilliant Vera Stanhope, Grafton's pragmatic and compassionate Kinsey Millhone, Susie Steiner's devoted and respected Manon Bradshaw and Katherine V Forrest's complex and determined lesbian detective Kate Delafield.

'I think women have been hungry for ever for images in print of strong, assertive women who change their environment,' Forrest said. 'Women lesbian detectives like Kate brought a modicum of justice to the world. And it was a world that we lived in back then where there really wasn't much justice. So, those portraits I think were extremely important to us.'

Scott Montgomery, the man behind MysteryPeople, the largest mystery bookstore in Austin, Texas, says writers now accept that strong female protagonists will win them readers. 'Women are now edging out men as readers and purchasers as well as crime writers,' he said. 'I have noticed that loads of women readers want to identify with female crime writers, but also more significantly with strong female protagonists.'

Sara Paretsky believes that in America, there has been an enormous sea change in the representation of women in crime and thriller fiction. 'It started in little dribbles with Amanda Cross and Lillian O'Donnell in the 1960s,' Paretsky said. 'O'Donnell had a New York City transit cop. And then when Marcia Muller published *Edwin of the Iron Shoes*, and then Sue Grafton and I followed with our books, we were the opening of the floodgate of brash, daring women. VI Warshawski represents for me women's speech or, more personally, my speech. And so, her voice is one that demands to be heard.'

Jane Casey's series character Maeve Kerrigan is an Irish policewoman whose status anxiety and professional insecurity as a woman in a sexist police force mirrors that of many young female PCs. 'When I was coming up with the character for Maeve, I knew I wanted somebody who had a double culture to cope with,' Casey said. 'The very different Irish culture that is her background and the extremely English Murder Investigation Team that she's a part of. It's how she balances those two things. She's still quite young. And she was the only woman on the team in the first books. She was on her own completely in every respect. And I thought that was an interesting sort of tension. And how she had to justify her place and work harder than everyone else.'

American writer Alafair Burke, who is also a professor of law and a legal commentator, says strong, believable women leads are a crucial element of her joy in reading. She immediately fell in love with Southern California detective Kinsey Millhone when she first came across Sue Grafton's Alphabet mysteries. 'To have this everywoman… she was the kind of person you would want to be friends with,' Burke said. 'She was also smart and hard-working, and she figured things out. And seeing the way her mind would work… She would type the clues out on her index cards. I just found that very appealing, that she was a very organised investigator. She had an edge to her.'

Burke's own series' character, young and tenacious NYPD detective Ellie Hatcher, is haunted by her father's death and this past trauma makes her character both sympathetic and memorable. 'If for an investigator, it's just a job, it's harder for the reader to care,' Burke said. 'If you give the police officer a reason their work is integral to their own identity, if you give the investigator a reason for chasing these alleys of darkness, it's more compelling.'

For Kathy Reichs, making her series character Temperance Brennan a rounded and authentic human being with significant imperfections was crucial. Brennan is more than just a brilliant forensic anthropologist. She is a divorced, recovering alcoholic who has difficulty maintaining personal relationships and this makes her more interesting. 'I wanted her to have flaws,' Reichs said. 'I didn't want her to be perfect.' Her other series' character Sunday Night, who is badly disfigured and has spent years burying secrets and running from her past, is also conflicted. 'She's got so much baggage going on, both emotionally and physically,' Reichs said. 'I think today's female heroines, they all have baggage and many of them, if not physical scars, they've got weird psychological syndromes. Even genetic or medical syndromes that they're suffering from.'

The increasing trend for women characters to be badly damaged worries Sara Paretsky. 'When we started, our characters were embracing risk – embracing life and embracing risk,' she said. 'But it seems as though today's female investigators have to have been tortured and tormented and they act out of a need to get revenge, not because they have a zest for risk-taking on their own. One striking example is (Lisbeth) Salander (from *The Girl with the Dragon Tattoo*). That change is really troubling to me. That's the change of dwelling with such loving detail on the torture that these women have endured. I'm hoping you'll see fewer damaged women and more take-charge women.'

Sarah Hilary, whose series' detective Marnie Rome maintains a tense and frightening relationship with the foster brother who murdered her parents, agrees. 'I think the whole *The Girl with the Dragon Tattoo* idea... I know several women, readers and writers, myself included, who despair when they hear her (Salander) being called a strong woman,' Hilary said. 'The idea that somebody so damaged gets strength from damaging others is extraordinarily banal to me. I just think no, no, no. A strong woman... it's a woman who is broken and has to rebuild herself. Not who remains broken and wreaks her terrible revenge in her broken state.'

Crime fiction written by women speaks not only to women's refusal to be seen only as victims but to a growing refusal to be mistreated and abused, within the home and outside it, and not only by men. 'Crime fiction written by women often reflects parts of the female experience which remain taboo and are frequently neglected, both in other genres and by male writers,' Melanie

McGrath said. 'Women have long turned to crime fiction, both as readers and writers, because it explores the place male writers and readers often fear to tread – where female power, terror and rage intersect.' And this, she said, makes reading crime fiction written by women a 'powerfully feminist act'.

'It's not that men can't write women.' she said. 'But after so many centuries of men telling women's stories, there is a particular power in women writing and reading our own. Stories where we get to be the actors, to make the decisions, to put the wrongs right and, yes, to act as bitches. There is a female solidarity in women reading crime fiction written by women. In the act of writing and reading crime, we finally get to be the villains *and* the heroes that, as human beings, we truly are.'[4]

It is also true that women will read and identify with lead protagonists who are male, as long as they exhibit the same depth and emotional complexity as their favourite female heroes, and are as capable of growth and change. This is borne out by the popularity of Elizabeth George's blond, blue-blooded and complicated Inspector Thomas Lynley, Kate Atkinson's gruff, cynical but empathetic Yorkshire private eye Jackson Brodie, Susan Hill's sensitive and honourable yet lonely Simon Serrailler, Karin Slaughter's Will Trent, who is scarred, both inside and out, and the late P D James' most famous hero, Adam Dalgliesh.

James, the very English crime writer known to the political world as Baroness James of Holland Park and to the literary world as the Queen of Crime, made her Dalgliesh a poet as well as a police officer. She described him as aloof and self-contained but also as having a 'splinter of ice' in his soul. Dalgliesh showed unusually intense emotional depths while P D James herself displayed great psychological density in all her characters and viewed criminal violence within a moral context. She indisputably surpassed all her classic models and elevated the literary status of contemporary detective fiction. She ought to be recognised too for creating the modern female private investigator, the young and feisty Cordelia Gray, who made her first appearance in *An Unsuitable Job for a Woman* (1972) and her second ten years later in *The Skull Beneath the Skin* (1982). Perhaps the fact that James had lost her heart to her poet–protagonist meant that Gray appeared to be held by her creator more in admiration than in affection. Cordelia was certainly the young competent professional woman with the independent spirit beloved of many readers who wanted to identify with her, even if their own lives were several suburbs and a dozen routine jobs away.

British poet and crime writer Kate Rhodes believes the moral issues behind the reasons women read crime written by other women are not entirely to do with gender. 'I think they are also to do with class and colour,' she said. 'We are at a turning point in our political history, a time of real uncertainty. I think people turn to crime fiction because they are going to encounter danger but within safe limits. This is as true for working class people out of their environment, and for black boys and girls, as it is for women of all colours. In fiction they can explore within relatively safe boundaries. They are able to explore moral issues within a kind of confinement, which is reassuring. These are things the media struggle to touch on but may not be able to talk about.'

The most absorbing and memorable crime fiction is that which reflects society as a whole, tackling significant contemporary issues, giving an insight into the world at large and exploring the fundamental questions about the deepest human issues: life and death, good and evil, justice and injustice. Modern women crime writers are challenging not only the expectations of gender and the genre, but a range of social and political issues that lie at the root of crime. Even in the most violent murder stories, women writers generally seem more interested in the psychology and motivation behind violence and the long-term repercussions for those affected it.

This emotional insight is true of traditional crime books and police procedurals as well as psychological thrillers in which police officers and private investigators play second fiddle to the lead characters, where the killing can be found much closer to home, and much closer to the truth: that women are much more likely to be assaulted or murdered by someone they know. Having lived in female skins, women writers know how to get under the skin of their female characters – and their readers – and how to tap into their fears, not only about who might come up behind them in a dark street at night or finding themselves trapped in an abusive relationship, but about being poor, being neglected, being an outsider, not being a good enough mother, about the cost of ambition or the lack of it, about not knowing for certain whom they can trust. There is also a deep desire not only to understand violence and trauma – what makes it happen and what we can do to avoid it – but to see and provide examples in print of how we can survive and recover from it. Women readers and writers find the redemptive aspects of crime fiction both therapeutic and liberating.

Yet it would be wrong to claim that this psychological and emotional insight is solely the territory of modern authors. This shrewd awareness and understanding of human character, of the motives behind violent crime and its aftermath, can be found in the work of women writers as far back as Agatha Christie herself. Sophie Hannah, who has to date written four continuation novels featuring Hercule Poirot, described Christie's psychological insight as 'profound'. 'I think the whole of the contemporary crime genre owes a huge debt to Agatha Christie,' she said. 'Her books are fun and enjoyable to read and at the same time, without compromising that, they contain a powerful awareness of the darkness and dangers inherent in the human psyche. I would not be the writer I am today without the influence of Agatha Christie. No way.'

A lot of the readers I talked to during the research for this book said they have loved reading crime mysteries since they were young and that they began this love affair with the genre with Agatha Christie. Many of the writers I spoke to claimed that the impetus for their writing came from reading Agatha Christie as a child. Although others claimed her work lacks depth – that it is all plot and that her characters are 'static' – her influence is still being seen in the works of women crime writers today. This influence, as much as her success, is worth further investigation.

3

Golden Age: Agatha Herself

Agatha Christie was indisputably the Queen of the Golden Age mysteries, all of which had several similar features. Typically, their plots operated inside a closed setting, such as a dining room, library, train, cruise ship, university or country manor, in milieus which had a small social range of characters, from Christie's middle class Miss Marple to Margery Allingham's aristocratic Albert Campion, to Dorothy Sayer's noble Lord Peter Wimsey. These authors were followed swiftly by Ngaio Marsh, with her gentleman Detective Inspector, Roderick Alleyn, and Josephine Tey with her dapper and intuitive Scotland Yard inspector Alan Grant.

In each case, the detective's task was to restore the social order which had been breached and often desecrated by an individual with murderous intent. This social order was an idealistic and unchanging view of a most traditional Britain. The women writers of the Golden Age would have grown up knowing that women could not vote and, if married, could not own property. Along with women in all parts of the population, they could not often nor successfully query or fight the benign or coercive social control husbands and fathers had over wives and daughters. Yet even with this background, these creative and intelligent women authors began to earn their living through writing. Despite the prejudice they encountered as professional female writers, they all succeeded in creating heroines who were able to explore possibilities for women that their own mothers had been unable to do.

Historically, that first explosion of women crime writers is important because they helped to establish acceptance of the view that literature belonged to women as much as to men. These female authors suddenly felt a sense of ownership. As did their publishers and their public. One striking piece of evidence was that, unlike their predecessors George Eliot and the Brontes, Agatha Christie, Dorothy L Sayers, Margery Allingham, Ngaio Marsh and Josephine Tey published at once under their own names. No disguises or masks for those women writers.

Agatha Christie, whose first novel *The Mysterious Affair at Styles* was published in 1920, headed the first explosion of women's crime writing. How successful was she? Mightily. Although the sales of all thrillers and crime novels have been robust for some time and are now very healthy indeed, none are more so than those of books written by Agatha Christie. The author of 66 detective novels and 14 short story collections under her own name and 6 more under the pseudonym Mary Westmacott, Christie is the bestselling novelist of all time. Her novels have sold roughly three billion copies. She is the most translated individual author, now translated into 103 languages. Her estate claims that her works rank third in the world's most widely published books, beaten only by Shakespeare and the Bible. Her bestselling novel *And Then There Were None* recently passed the 100 million sales mark, making it the world's bestselling mystery ever.

None of those stunning figures take into account the 30 feature films based on her work, nor the innumerable television adaptations and films, nor her drama *The Mousetrap*, which is the world's longest running play. The play opened in November 1952 and was still running in March 2020, when performances had to be halted because of the Covid-19 pandemic.

Christie was a classic and extraordinarily wealthy writer. Her work is an integral part of Britain's Golden Age of mysteries, which began after the First World War and ended with the outbreak of the Second World War. Sir Arthur Conan Doyle, with Edgar Allan Poe, had already established the idea of the gifted and often eccentric amateur detective, with Sherlock Holmes and C Auguste Dupin respectively. By the time the Second World War interrupted play, the great names in British detective fiction were all female.

But – and this will come as no surprise – the two people who drew up and codified a series of 'rules' for detective fiction were male: the American mystery writer SS Van Dine (the pseudonym of the art critic Willard Huntington Wright) in 1928, and the English Catholic priest and crime author Ronald Knox in 1929.

And the first woman to break those rules was Agatha Christie. She changed the way detective fiction was written by daring to add twists and turns rather than following Van Dine and Knox's standard straightforward procedures. Once she had broken the rules, she set a path other authors followed. Her unusual plotlines and curling, twirling methods are the inspiration behind many of the crime, mystery and psychological thrillers being written today.

To understand the rage that some readers and critics felt at Christie's inventiveness, especially in *The Murder of Roger Ackroyd* (1926) and *Murder on the Orient Express* (1934), we must explore why they felt cheated by the magnificent central twists. The period between the 1920s and 1930s was one in which crosswords, treasure hunts and puzzles centred on the principle of playing fair with participants. It was considered unreasonable, both in games and detective books, for the creators to conceal clues or withhold essential information. Many readers especially felt that crime authors should give them a sporting chance of working out for themselves whodunnit by sharing the detective's findings as they occurred rather than introducing surprise suspects or outrageous clues in the final chapter.

These principles became so fashionable that Knox drew up a 'Decalogue' containing Ten Commandments. Twins and doubles were banned, along with multiple secret rooms or passages, supernatural and preternatural interventions and hitherto undiscovered poisons. Knox ordained that the criminal had to work alone and could not be the narrator nor the chief detective charged with investigating the crime. Van Dine's rules were similar but he went further, saying there must also be no love interest, no secret societies, no murderers who are also domestic servants, no professional criminals, no fake séances, no code letters, no cigarette butts as evidence, no knock-out pills.

Christie knew these rules well. For ironically, she and Dorothy L Sayers were founder members of the Detection Club, which was formed in 1930 and took as its founding rule the principle that authors must play fair with readers. Unlike her colleagues, however, Christie didn't care. She began to experiment around the edges of the rules, bending and breaking them whenever she chose.

And the critics loved it. And her. Most of them were highly complimentary about her novels, in particular *The Murder of Roger Ackroyd*. They admired its plot, form and structure. Its deductive steps were singled out for literary commendation. In the United States, the *New York Times Book Review* claimed that the novel 'cannot be too highly praised' and that few other detective novels provided 'greater analytical stimulation'. The review stated that Christie was 'not only an expert technician and a remarkably good storyteller' but she also deftly provided just enough hints to the murderer's identity for the reader to work out the solution. In England, *The Observer* was highly approving of the book's 'coherence' and 'reasonableness'.

Christie's novel *Murder on the Orient Express* famously broke most of the rules of classic detective fiction. Flouting Van Dine's rule that there must be only one murderer, no matter how many dead bodies turn up, Christie had several murderers, intent on revenge, on board her *Orient Express*. Having more than one criminal on that train gave Christie the opportunity to introduce a variety of seemingly contradictory clues and red herrings to a story that has become one of her most dramatic, most popular and most often adapted for film, theatre and television. It certainly didn't play fair with the readers who, ironically, loved it. In *Three Act Tragedy*, also published in 1934, Christie ignores Van Dine's no-love-interest rule by having the murderer kill in order to cover up his existing marriage so that he can marry someone else. She did this again a year later in *Death in the Clouds* when a woman is killed for wealth and for romance. In *Five Little Pigs* (1942) Poirot investigates and solves a 16-year-old murder which appears to have no clues at all.

According to Caroline Crampton, creator of the podcast Shedunnit, readers frequently return to those books in which Christie flagrantly subverted the norms of classic detective fiction. 'Christie found a sweet spot between the familiarity of the conventions and the absurdity of wild experimentation,' Crampton said. 'In her books, there is just the right amount of rebellion.'[5]

Christie's work, especially her method of recycling plots while keeping them fresh, is used today as a teaching tool for writers who learn that her art is undeniably balanced on intricate plot construction. Some critics claim her percipient plotting comes at the expense of insightful characterisation, but on balance most literary analysts have been struck by her combination of realistic period subject matter, intense psychological understanding and a background of high-wire tension. Characters are expertly drawn against these tense and detailed plots. In many books Christie did not rely entirely or even largely on her creative plot structure. This is strikingly evident in the novel *Curtain: Poirot's Last Case*, (1975), the brilliant finale to her famous detective's career. Written long before her death and placed in a bank safe with instructions to be published only after her demise, *Sleeping Murder* is a masterpiece that exploits the best of her talents.

This case takes as its setting Styles Court, where Poirot's first murder, *The Mysterious Affair at Styles*, is set. Poirot is reunited with the recently bereaved Captain Arthur Hastings for the first time since the two men worked together in *Dumb Witness* (1937). They have arrived at Styles Court to prevent a serial killer claiming more victims. The novel was adapted for television in 2013 and Poirot's death scene was second on the list of Best TV Drama Moments of 2013. Two years later it was nominated for Outstanding Television Movie for the 67th Emmy Awards.

Today Christie's novels maintain an unparalleled popularity and continue to inspire modern writers. Sophie Hannah published her first Hercule Poirot continuation novel, *The Monogram Murders*, in 2014 and the second, *Closed Casket*, two years later. In the same year, Hodder and Stoughton published chat show host Graham Norton's Christie-style novel *Holding*, which is centred on the discovery of human remains in a small village in Ireland. In 2017, Bloomsbury published Plum Sykes' *Party Girls Die in Pearls*, the first in a new crime series billed as *Clueless* meets Agatha Christie. In 2018, theatre maker Stella Duffy successfully completed the previously unfinished Ngaio Marsh novel *Money in the Morgue* for Harper Collins. When Macmillan made a deal with bestselling journalist Tilly Bagshaw to write a new cosy crime series under the name of M B Shaw, the artist and Marple-like village sleuth Iris Grey was born. Meanwhile, reprints of 1930s and 1940s crime classics continued to sell well. In 2020, Sophie Hannah's fourth Poirot novel, *The Killings at Kingfisher Hill*, was released to coincide with Agatha Christie's birthday and to commemorate 100 years since she wrote her first published novel.

Contemporary crime writers have lauded the distinctive and addictive qualities of Agatha Christie novels. Sophie Hannah said: 'She had this knack of starting her books with mysteries that are so unreal or unlikely or weird or impossible-seeming that the reader can't actually speculate at all about why this might be happening.' Hannah gave as an example *A Murder is Announced* (1950) which begins with a local newspaper advertisement declaring the time and location a murder is going to take place. 'You have to read on to find out why it has happened because you can't even begin to hypothesise,' she said. 'I think that's one of her key ingredients. The impossible seems to be happening.

'She also manages to blend two complete opposites without either one being compromised. The darkness is definitely present, and the fun and lightness is definitely present, and neither one detracts from the other. And her books are simple enough and accessible enough that a 12-year-old can read and enjoy them, but they are complex and labyrinthine and intellectually challenging enough that clever grown-ups can be absolutely baffled by them.'

Christie's significance is that as one of the women writing in the Golden Age, her female protagonists were for the first time allowed the individual autonomy and agency their male literary counterparts had taken for granted for years. Christie herself, though she had been left a small amount of money by her father, took on paid work so that she could have financial independence, which was still seen as a rare decision for a middle-class woman. Although we see a definite emphasis on marriage and motherhood (with the consequent joys and obstacles) within the pages of her novels, we also see this new path of singlehood and professional work for women. That heroines suddenly had these options was a big shift away from the restraints their predecessors had encountered. They were suddenly open to new, modern social possibilities in British life, many of which were explored in depth in detective fiction, not least by Christie.

When we examine whether this young female writer's work was still hedged in with conservative values, overlaid with anti-Semitic and racist views, and whether we believe there is sufficient evidence to support this view, we need to remember that she was also a forerunner when it came to exploring new positive opportunities for women. Some critics who see her as narrowly nationalistic find it easy to draw examples from her work to confirm this idea. Other reviewers see her as attacking social class and the position of men, and as a defender of women who wish to step out of the old ways of being. She certainly does not take the powerful and rich at their own face value. Indeed, she takes nothing at face value. She discovers villains and evildoers among the wealthy more often than among the poor. More significantly, her books make it obvious to all her readers that nothing is what it seems.

An important issue is the extent to which Christie can be considered feminist or whether she is a writer who illustrates a deep-rooted conservatism which produces some stale gender stereotypes. An examination of her characters and dialogue must take into account both the period in which she was writing and also the many examples of how she fought Victorian literary conventions – those which saw women as frivolous and interested only in men and marriage – and how she brought to the public gaze a series of plucky, intelligent, self-sufficient and memorable females, including the shrewd and practical Lucy Eyelesbarrow and the funny and opinionated crime writer Ariadne Oliver.

Women are frequently put centre stage in Christie's books in strong and sometimes surprising roles. Christie's middle-aged women are shown to be independent, headstrong and more than capable, while her young and spunky heroines represent the spirit of a new age coming out of Victorian values and heading for a bright new world. Lady Eileen Bundle Brent, known as Bundle, appears in two of Christie's mysteries, *The Secret of Chimneys* (1925) and *The Seven Dials Mystery* (1929). Bundle is a spirited and gutsy flapper who loves to drive fast, often terrifying her male passengers, a trait that reflected Christie's own taste for fast cars and fearless driving. In *Seven Dials*, Bundle daringly investigates stolen government information and a mysterious secret society that is implicated in two deaths. Although Christie was again chastised by critics for having deserted the methodological procedure of inquiry, this novel was enormously popular.

Christie's women not only kept up with the men but in many instances outplayed them. Until Christie began writing, female characters in detective novels were virtually always there for decoration. Christie contrived cerebral female private investigators who used their intellect and ingenuity to sweep into a crime scene, solve the murders, then sweep out, leaving the male police team flummoxed. Tuppence Beresford is one half of a middle-class married couple who become private detectives. The stylish, impetuous Tuppence turns out to be a young, spirited and intuitive sleuth and always leads the way in the husband-and-wife team. Tuppence and her husband Tommy were loosely based on Christie and her first husband Archibald, and the novels featuring Tuppence have considerably more complex plots than other novels do. Tuppence narratives feature Bolsheviks intent on plunging Britain into anarchy and German fifth columnists infiltrating boarding houses on the south coast. The pair are introduced in *The Secret Adversary* (1922), the novel in which Christie for the first time uses the device of hiding the villain in plain sight, working alongside the detectives. It is a device she uses more than once. Tuppence is written with warmth, wit and a slight sense of wonderment that girls in the 1930s could be as bright and brainy as they patently were. According to Christie's grandson Max Prichard this is as close as Christie ever came to autobiography; the Tommy and Tuppence duo evoke the early years of her marriage to Archibald. As well as coming over as unusually romantic, these books also exhibited a political element that was missing in later work.

A slightly more mature and intellectual version of Tuppence is Lucy Eyelesbarrow, a 32-year-old Oxford mathematics graduate often thought to be Christie's most modern and practical female character. She is brilliant yet steady, eschewing a distinguished academic career to set herself up in a lucrative domestic household management scheme. She is called in to help Miss Marple in *4.50 from Paddington* (1957) to untangle the mystery of a body thrown from a train. In Agatha Christie's cast of characters, Lucy Eyelesbarrow is the girl of tomorrow.

Probably Christie's most likeable female is Poirot's friend Ariadne Oliver, a down-to-earth crime novelist. Ariadne is thought to be the closest Christie came to creating a doppelganger. 'I never take stories from real life,' Christie said, in a *John Bull* magazine interview in 1956. 'But the character of Ariadne Oliver does have a strong dash of myself.' We learn that, just as Ariadne became fed up with her most famous male creation, Finnish vegetarian detective Sven Hjerson, so Christie became frustrated with her egotistical detective Poirot and decided to kill him off. Although it was written in 1952, through the depiction of Ariadne's dialogue we hear some impressively forthright speech. 'You men,' she says in *Mrs McGinty's Dead*. 'Now if a woman were the head of Scotland Yard...' In the same story Ariadne grumbles: 'Men are so slow. I'll soon tell you who did it.'[6]

Christie was keen for readers to see her female characters as flawed, even evil or potentially murderous. Several whodunnits stretched this idea by featuring a female killer. Before Christie began using this strategy, women in detective literature were rarely cold-blooded murderers. However, Miss Marple's world, in the years between 1930 and 1965, progressively became a society in which women were as likely as men to be killers or to have intimate knowledge of murder.

Once women entered the world of paid work, negative as well as positive attitudes towards money became part of women's new tool kit. Money, both the desire for and lack of it, provided a powerful motive to kill. By 1922, early in Christie's career, money is a central theme in her novels. She ensures that both Marple and Poirot are aware of it as a prime motive for crime. Of Agatha's 55 full-length detective novels, murder for financial gain is at the centre of 36. It is not only sharp killers who are obsessed with money. For nice, warm-hearted girls like Tuppence, clever young women like Lucy Eyelesbarrow, and kind, compassionate old ladies like Dora Bunner in *A Murder Is Announced* (1950), not having enough money dominates their thoughts and actions.

Laura Thompson, Agatha's most recent biographer, says Agatha had a deep-rooted fear of poverty. She often recalled how money had trickled through her father's hands. She enjoyed spending but had respect for the ways in which money was spent and how it should be saved. She understood how and why money and murder become intertwined. This begins to show in all her books after 1924. It was money that changed her attitude to work. She became an absolute professional and no longer wrote merely for the love of it. Young, beautiful women still figured frequently as murder victims but, for the first time, they also appeared as murderers. Many strong women in the books written after the mid-1920s murder for money. And in so doing they become the 'heroes' of their own lives and their own narratives.

In these novels and dramas, women are equal to men in everything, including crime. A surprising example is *The Murder at the Vicarage* (1930) in which the culprit is eventually exposed as the churchwarden's disgruntled wife Anne Protheroe. This may have been surprising for the readers but not for the cynical Miss Marple.

It was as true then as it is now that women are most at risk of serious harm or death from their male husbands or partners.

Then, as now, the home is exposed as the main location in which women are killed. Early nineteenth-century fiction saw crime take place on dark and unruly city streets, but in the twentieth century, lethal criminal acts were seen to take place indoors, in the one place women are meant to feel safe. From the moment Archibald Christie went off with another woman in 1926 and her marriage broke up, Christie knew personally about how male anger could escalate and the consequences. She can be considered radical rather than conservative in the way she exposes the dangers of marriage and the domestic front. She cleverly confronts this reality by writing, in the 1940s and the 1950s, bold and extraordinary novels with the same radical messages as the contemporary domestic noir psychological thrillers being written today. Christie's novels are very often set in the home, a scene which is depicted not as a sanctuary for women and girls, but as a cage of violent interaction, a place of torment or a cell of psychological tyranny.

Miss Jane Marple, never a woman to think kindly of anyone, deals with this new situation coolly, as only the detached distrustful feminist icon that she is could do. In Christie's pantheon of characters, only Jane Marple is so sceptical and suspicious that nothing slips past her. Christie sets up this fragile elderly spinster whose mind is as sharp as razor blades and whose viewpoints range from mistrustful and disparaging to downright cynical and contemptuous.

British and international crime writer Frances Fyfield, whose prose is second only to the late P D James and whose detailed knowledge of crime comes from her work as a lawyer with the Crown Prosecution Service, said that as a young writer she was entranced by Agatha Christie. 'Thirty years ago, it was very fashionable for crime writers to sort of poke fun at Miss Marple and Agatha Christie,' she said. 'But I always had great respect for her. I think she's really canny. It's psychologically very interesting because she's just solving it all by watching loads of human nature. And she's a poke in the eye. Raising a fist for the little old lady, being self-deprecating but really knowing that she's cleverer than the rest of them.'

Miss Marple's intellect means she takes every physical and emotional detail into consideration. She focuses on the significant characteristics of human nature, whether it is revealed in dense and dirty crime-ridden urban streets or in pretty lavender-smelling rural cottages and vicarages. She watches and makes note of the gestures, facial expressions and general behaviour of the people involved in and around a crime scene. Jane Marple is rarely the primary investigator in a case, partly because she is an amateur and partly because she is a woman. Yet her ability to identify the details the men around her have ignored and her understanding of ordinary people's psychological states and intentions means she can solve a case from under their feet. Miss Marple's sweet-seeming, placid nature conceals a mind that can effortlessly reveal the hidden depths of human evil.

In *The Body in the Library* (1942) the body of a dancer called Ruby Keene is found in Colonel Bantry's library and the story engages with the search to find the murderer. In this novel Jane Marple is described as 'sharp-eyed, sharp-tongued and a vicious gossip with an incomparable information service and a desire to believe the worst'.[7] She uses these assets to talk to the gossips in the village, question their statements, and work out what is false.

Miss Marple's old-lady appearance among the younger male sleuths changes the route of each investigation. She is determined to find the truth. She not only reveals the mystery behind each crime but in each case re-establishes the order and morality in society, something the paid male detectives fail to do. Morality is the hidden theme behind all the mysteries. At the same time, Miss Marple shows that women are as reasonable and intelligent as men, a view hardly acceptable in that male-dominated era. In the fiction of Christie's day, the stereotypical role of women as passive, submissive and often sad and despairing as they await rescue by strong men prevailed. Through Marple, Christie questions and thoroughly rejects this role. In spite of her age, appearance and hesitant speech patterns, Marple is a strong professional, a powerful female detective.

Writer and theatre artist Stella Duffy also engaged with Christie and Miss Marple when young. 'I read Agatha Christie early,' she said. 'I was in a small town in New Zealand by the time I was reading for myself, a small library which was great and let me read from the adult section very early on. I desperately wanted to read women and women protagonists. I've never read a Poirot novel in my life. And I figure that's fine seeing as Christie didn't like him either. But I read all of the Miss Marples when I was probably about 13.'

Duffy directed a play called *Murder, Marple and Me,* about the relationship between Christie and the actress Margaret Rutherford, who played Miss Marple in four films in the 1960s. The production was later renamed *Murder, Margaret and Me* on the request of Christie's Estate. 'What do I think about the character of Miss Marple?' Duffy said. 'Oh, I think she's fucking amazing. I think she's such a bitch. Christie is a great plotter. I don't think she's very good at character. I think if you're comparing the Queens of Crime, Ngaio Marsh is much better at character and much better at place. But I'm certain there is no one to beat Christie for plotting. The stories are a little predictable. If someone's wearing red, they're probably the baddie. And she's not very good on working-class characters.

'All of that said, in the stories, possibly more than in the novels, you can see the sharpness of Marple. She's sharp and she's mean. I think that's so interesting; to have written a protagonist that, on first glance, looks like this delicate, soft old lady who is just the epitome of the word perspicacious, and a bitch at that, I think that's a real achievement. That excites me about her work.'

Readers continued to follow this fragile fussy spinster sleuth through 12 novels and a series of short stories as she solved murders under the envious eyes of local police forces. Once Miss Marple's role as amateur consulting detective was established, her acquaintance with retired Metropolitan Police officer Sir Henry Clithering allowed her to gain official information as and when required. In *The Body in the Library*, Miss Marple admits 'I'm afraid you'll think my methods, as Sir Henry calls them, are terribly amateurish. The truth is, you see, that most people – and I don't exclude policemen – are far too trusting for this wicked world. They believe what is told them. I never do. I'm afraid I always like to prove a thing for myself.'

In *The Murder at the Vicarage*, the key characters are the sensitive and liberal vicar and his wife, who is beautiful but hopeless at domesticity. Christie shows readers that marriages can work well, even if the wife can't cook, and that male judgements can be wrong and should be challenged. Here is Miss Marple on the subject of male authority. 'He has always struck me as a rather stupid man... the kind of man who gets the wrong idea into his head and is obstinate about it.' Christie's subtle feminist agenda allowed Miss Marple covertly to query male power relations while at the same time appearing to uphold the well-established traditional male status quo.[8]

Was Jane Marple an interesting model for female crime writers of her day and is she still today? 'I think Miss Marple is a great model because she is without doubt one of the best ever fictional creations,' Sophie Hannah said. 'What's great about her is that she looks and presents so differently from how she actually is. So, she looks like this harmless fluffy elderly lady and actually she is incredibly shrewd, wise about people and misanthropic. People think she is lovely and cuddly, but actually she takes a dim view of human nature and is always telling her old lady friends that people are terrible creatures. Christie does the same thing with Poirot. Both characters are consistently dismissed by everybody and underestimated. That works well because it makes readers identify with them.'

Writer Kate Rhodes thinks Miss Marple is a 'beautiful, nuanced character'. 'I like a bit more flesh on the bones of my suspects,' Rhodes said. 'But Miss Marple is wonderful, elderly, intuitive, thoughtful and clever. I think she has a lot to say to women today.'

British human rights solicitor and novelist Anna Mazzola says that as a young reader, she loved Agatha Christie and Miss Marple. 'They were compelling novels and mysteries,' she said. 'I certainly didn't think of Miss Marple as silly when I read them. It didn't even make a huge impression on me that she was a woman. It seemed natural to me that a woman would be investigating. So, that's an achievement in itself, isn't it? To make young female minds think it's okay for a woman to be doing this.'

Miss Marple has become a transgressive force, a form of resistance against stereotypes. She constantly has to resist definitions of her as a fluffy old woman, just as Poirot has to resist descriptions of him as an eccentric foreigner. In spite of her self-deprecating manner, Miss Marple is a powerful private eye protagonist.

Agatha Christie's unique importance lay in her relationship to the global crime writing context in which she played a key part. She wrote her first Miss Marple book *The Murder at the Vicarage* in 1930, the year after Dashiell Hammett across the water wrote *Red Harvest* and *The Dain Curse* (1929) and the same year in which he brought forth his incomparable novel *The Maltese Falcon* (1930) and, with it, the start of the hardboiled era in crime. This masculinisation of American crime writing marginalised its American female practitioners until the 1950s, 30 years after Christie and her female colleagues were heading the crime field in Britain. Christie was seemingly unperturbed by the macho, male-dominated and wildly successful crime narratives being sold in the USA; with Hammett's *The Glass Key* in 1931 and *The Thin Man* in 1934 and the advent of Raymond

Chandler as he too swept across the States with *The Big Sleep* in 1939 and *The Lady in the Lake* in 1943.

In Britain, the settings Christie and her fellow authors wrote were sometimes rural, always open. By contrast, the mean streets of Hammett, Chandler and Ross Macdonald's worlds were always urban and often grimy. Following each murder, Christie, along with Margery Allingham and Dorothy L Sayers, offered readers a reassuring return to a well-ordered society. In the US, the private detectives might have had personal powerful morals, but they could not stand up to a world of corruption, where the rise of organised crime and corrupt policing had spread from city to city. As wholesale corruption extended through the States, the mainly male writers upheld the myth that it was necessary for upright detectives and private investigators to fight for decency and valour. Christie and her range of characters are sometimes mild, but they are never sentimental, and they fought to restore the social order with realism. Christie is a woman crime writer with no use for conventional male heroes. By contrast, Sam Spade, Lew Archer and Philip Marlowe may seem hardboiled and without illusions about the corruption in the social order, but at heart they are still sentimentalists. As critic Ernest Mandel puts it, they are still 'suckers for damsels in distress'.[9] Agatha Christie's Poirot might just come into this category but ultimately he is too clear sighted to stay there.

Christie was aware of the themes of social rather than individual corruption across the water, but she chose to ignore them. She concentrated instead on individuals who were evil within a society that was, if not good, then at least remediable. She coolly continued Miss Marple's low key feminist adventures with *The Moving Finger* in 1943. By 1955, she had written 53 novels featuring both Poirot and Marple along with many collections of short stories. At that time, American women crime writers like Dorothy B Hughes, Margaret Millar, Charlotte Armstrong, who all started publishing in the early 1940s, and

Patricia Highsmith, whose first novel came out in 1950, were only slowly being recognised and becoming a genuine force on the American crime scene.

It is interesting to look at the history of the Mystery Writers of America's Grand Master Award, the most prestigious and coveted prize in the field of crime writing. In 1955, the Grand Master Award went not to an American male but to Britain's Agatha Christie. It took until 1971 for that honour to be conferred on an American woman writer, Mignon Eberhart.

Meanwhile, Christie's fellow Golden Age Writers were also becoming bestsellers. Margery Allingham is best remembered for her aristocratic and unassuming sleuth Albert Campion. Readers initially believed him to be a parody of Dorothy L Sayers' Lord Peter Wimsey, but through 18 novels and many short stories, Campion slowly matured into a strongly individual character who was part adventurer and part detective.

Allingham regarded the mystery novel as a box with four sides: a killing, a mystery, an enquiry and a conclusion. A highly disciplined writer, she felt there had to be an element of satisfaction in each of the four sides. She felt the crime genre gave her the discipline she needed while allowing her imagination to flourish, as it did from her first novel in 1928 to her last in 1968.

Crime novelist Dorothy L Sayers was a student of classical and modern languages at Somerville College, Oxford, where she graduated with a first class honours degree in 1915. Women were not awarded degrees at that time but, when they were, she was one of the first to receive one. In 1920, she graduated with an MA. Initially she wrote poetry and worked in advertising. When she turned to crime writing, she described her principal character Lord Peter Wimsey as a mixture of Fred Astaire and Bertie Wooster. Sayers says she introduced the dark-eyed, husky-voiced detective novelist Harriet Vane in order to marry her off to Wimsey and then get rid of him, but she was never able to see Lord Peter 'exit the stage'.

Many of Sayers' novels dealt with social issues. In *The Unpleasantness at the Bellona Club* (1928), she explored the traumas undergone by First World War veterans. In *Murder Must Advertise* (1933), she discussed the ethics of advertising. In *Gaudy Night* (1935), a story about poison pen letters and mean practical jokes at a fictional Oxford college, Sayers advocated women's education, a most controversial topic at the time, and tackled the role of women in society in general. The book features a character attacking the Nazi doctrine of 'Kinder, Küche, Kirche' which restricted women's roles to domestic activities and has been described as the first feminist mystery.

Sayers' personal life could have been written by herself as a modern mystery. She had a secret illegitimate son she passed off as her nephew for many years but for whom she provided and of whom she was very proud. Only when he applied for his birth certificate to obtain a passport did the young man discover his real identity. He never mentioned his discovery to his aunt/ mother Dorothy L Sayers. Sayers' work has been completed and continued by the English novelist Jill Paton Walsh, who wrote and published four novels featuring Lord Peter Wimsey and Harriet Vane, including Sayers' abandoned story *Thrones, Dominations* (1998).

Dame Ngaio Marsh was a New Zealand crime writer and theatre director who lived, worked and wrote in Britain. She was appointed a British Dame Commander in 1966. Most of her novels focus on painting and the theatre and they all feature Detective Inspector Roderick Alleyn. One wet Saturday afternoon in 1934, she read a detective story by Christie and wondered if she could write something suitable for the crime genre. Patently she could. Alleyn became the hero of 32 detective novels. After graduating from Oxford, Alleyn served in the army for three years, spent a year in the British Foreign Service then joined the Metropolitan Police as a constable where he rose through the ranks. He was the younger brother of a Baronet, so clearly a member of the gentry, and his progress was speedy. In fictional terms he was not unlike contemporary writer Elizabeth George's blue-blooded Detective Inspector, Lord Thomas Lynley.

Josephine Tey's Inspector Alan Grant was also a public school entrant. After serving four years in the army as a sergeant, he enlisted in the Metropolitan Police in 1920 and rose from the rank of constable to that of detective inspector with Scotland Yard CID. Unlike several of his fictional contemporaries, he was not a gifted amateur but a hard-working professional. Tey wrote seven Inspector Grant mysteries between 1929 and 1952 and two standalone mysteries in 1946 and 1949. Of the Golden Age authors, Josephine Tey is particularly interesting because she opened the door for writers who came after her, such as Patricia Highsmith, Minette Walters and Ruth Rendell, in the way she explored the dark and the truly frightening aspects of human belief and human desire. Val McDermid believed Tey built a bridge between the Golden Age authors and contemporary crime writers. 'Tey opened up the possibility of unconventional secrets,' McDermid has said. 'Homosexual desire, cross-dressing, sexual perversion – they were all hinted at, glimpsed in the shadows… Tey was never vulgar nor titillating. Nevertheless, her world revealed a different set of psychological motivations.'[10]

Agatha Christie's legacy after her death is worth exploring. The women crime writers of the Golden Age could never have foreseen their amazing and long-standing legacies or how their work would be examined, tweaked and twisted after their deaths. In the case of Agatha Christie, there are two interesting biographies, by Janet Morgan and Laura Thompson, a PhD Thesis by James Carl Bernthal titled '*A Queer Approach to Agatha Christie 1920 to 1952*' and several novels by other writers in which Poirot's adventures are continued. These include Sophie Hannah's *The Monogram Murders, Closed Casket, The Mystery at Three Quarters* and *The Killings at Kingfisher Hill*. Writers from a different genre entirely have made Agatha the lead character in their novels. Biographer and fiction writer Andrew Wilson has extended his skills to include *A Talent for Murder* (2018), a lively tale in which Agatha Christie is the main character. His narrative reinvents the story of Christie's mysterious disappearance from society after she realises her first husband Archie is having an affair with a younger woman. This discovery prompts her sudden flight to a hotel in Harrogate, where she holes up under an assumed name. At that point Wilson's novel leaves facts behind and writes a delightful and inventive crime story. In another Christie book, *A Different Kind of Evil* (2019), he has Christie become an amateur sleuth to solve the mystery on behalf of the British Secret Service.

Several contemporary women writers are now looking back at that first explosion of women crime writers, the Golden Age scribes, and turning their work and influence into something new and zesty for today's readers. The most significant of these is eminent British crime writer and radio documentary writer Alison Joseph, who continued Christie's tradition by using Agatha as a fictional detective in a successful contemporary series. Insightful British novelist Nicola Upson has written a series of mysteries featuring a fictional Josephine Tey as detective. And Stella Duffy's *Money in the Morgue* is a seamless continuation of Ngaio Marsh's unfinished novel. This new phenomenon of writers who came after Agatha and are leaping forward by looking back deserves much closer inspection.

4

Looking Back, Leaping Forward

One way we can measure the importance and enduring influence of that first explosion of Golden Age Writers is to recognise and explore the different ways in which modern women writers are looking back at, recreating and continuing those classic works – and the challenges they face before they are able to leap forward.

English crime writer Alison Joseph is best known for two successful contemporary crime series, the first of which features Sister Agnes, a detective nun working in a homeless hostel in south London. Her second series introduces Berenice Killick, a senior woman police officer working in the leafy English county of Kent. When Alison was approached by Endeavour Press to write a third series, making Agatha Christie into a detective, she was at first reluctant.

'Initially I said no,' Joseph said. 'Partly because it seemed very difficult to get a real person right, especially in a fictional setting, and also because I hadn't yet written anything historical, and it would obviously have to be. Then I went away and thought about it. And I thought, it is *such* a good idea. It was so appealing.

'I love Agatha Christie. She was a fantastically interesting person. Life was not kind to her. Everybody has that image of that very successful elderly lady in beautiful fur coats going to the opera and ballet, when actually she struggled. Her husband announced he was going to leave her in the 1920s. It was a terrible thing to happen to her. I told her grandsons I wouldn't write anything about the flight to Harrogate, so I won't, but that flight was another terrible thing to happen to her. It was appalling for her to be on the front pages of the newspapers. She was such a private person. People say she did it to teach her husband a lesson, but this is so unlike what she would have been like. So, I try to be respectful to her.'

Getting to know Agatha and then turn her into a character she could work with, to write fiction about someone who had actually existed, who was so well known and so well loved, was a real challenge. 'I thought about it and tried to fit it into the ideas I have about my own work,' Joseph said. 'I have for years debated and discussed the idea of the "real" within fiction. In the end, I agreed. Writing the novellas has given me the opportunity to explore the relationship between real life and the fictional world and how we all tell stories as a way to create order out of chaos.'

Joseph admits that getting at the truth of what Christie was writing, and what she herself would be writing with Christie as her detective, was a test. Her fictional detective understood, as the great writer herself did, that readers wanted stability, calm and justice after the horrors and upheaval of the First World War. In the three Christie novellas to date – *Murder Will Out* (2014), *Hidden Sins* (2015) and *Death in Disguise* (2017) – these elements prevail. Joseph also tried to recall the writer's natural intelligence, her instinctive grasp of human nature, and her powerful observations of how people behave and, at the same time, to pay homage to Christie's craft and her deceptively simple and elegant style.

Crime writer Sophie Hannah, who to date has written four continuation novels featuring Christie's world-famous Belgian detective Hercule Poirot, said there are so many ideas in Christie's fiction that it is hard to know which were *her* ideas. 'At the very end of *Evil Under the Sun* (1941) for instance, there is a couple who have not been together up to that point,' Hannah said. 'Suddenly they get together romantically. The last line has the woman basically saying, "Oh good. Now I can give up working and stay in and keep house for ever and that is all I have ever wanted". And some of Agatha's books seem to suggest that she does think that is important: family, being a wife and mother. But at other times, she writes books that definitely say it is good for women to go to work, to be independent. It is hard to say which were her personal views. Obviously, she herself did both. She was a full-time writer and enormously successful and took very good care of her business interests, but she was also a devoted wife and mother.'

Many reviewers of Christie have suggested that her work often emphasises the foolishness of men who don't recognise women's competence, but Sophie sees it differently. 'I don't think Christie saw gender in that way,' she said. 'She liked writing about characters of all kinds who were underestimated, men and women. Poirot was constantly underestimated because he was funny looking and a foreigner; Marple was underestimated because she was an elderly woman. Through Christie's work, servants are constantly ignored, their testimonies and witness statements seldom taken notice of.' Hannah believes Christie was trying to say that we should always listen to everything and notice everyone, rather than fall back on lazy generalisations.

Hannah admits she had 'huge doubts' when she was first told the Christie family wanted her to take on the job of resurrecting Poirot, and that the task of giving such an iconic character a new lease of life was a daunting one. One of the biggest challenges would be to get every detail of the period right in what was to be her first historical novel. 'But I also had huge determination,' she said. 'I thought that I would rather try and fail than not try.' Her first Poirot novel *The Monogram Murders* (2014) became a *Sunday Times* bestseller and most critics agreed Hannah's intricate and ingenious plotting did justice to Christie's master detective. Writing for the *New York Times*, Alexander McCall Smith said Hannah's Poirot would live up to fans' expectations and *The Monogram Murders* was 'both faithful to the character and an entirely worthy addition to the canon' with a plot 'as tricky as anything written by Agatha Christie'.[11] Hannah published her fourth Poirot, *The Killings at Kingfisher Hill*, in 2020.

Stella Duffy's revival of Ngaio Marsh's much-loved Inspector Roderick Alleyn in *Money in the Morgue* has also been widely lauded. Sophie Hannah herself, writing in *The Guardian*, described Duffy's continuation novel as an 'exquisite reminder' of the brilliance of Marsh's beloved London detective.[12] Ngaio Marsh had written only a few chapters, around 5,000 words, and a sketchy outline of the plot before she died. Yet critics have been unable to identify the point in the narrative when Duffy took over from her. The work, shortlisted for the CWA Historical Dagger Award in 2018, has been described as 'a supreme act of ventriloquism'.[13]

Duffy, like Marsh, was born in New Zealand and shares her passion for the theatre as well as writing. Yet she also had reservations when she was first asked by HarperCollins to bring back to life Marsh's quiet, astute and romantic Chief Inspector Alleyn, 84 years after Marsh introduced him to the world in *A Man Lay Dead* (1934). 'I went to see them and told them, look, this is not what I do,' Duffy said. 'It is *so* not what I do. I hadn't read a Ngaio Marsh book since my teens and I didn't think they were amazing when I was younger. There were a couple I had enjoyed, but it wasn't as if they stayed with me.' Once she agreed, Duffy had to come up with a 12-page proposal, for the HarperCollins editorial team as well as Marsh's nephews and the lawyers for her estate.

'I had never done anything like that before,' she said. 'I didn't want to do it without their blessing and their support. I'm not sure I could have done it otherwise. And then I had to stick to it, which was terrifying.' Once she started writing though, Duffy relished the challenge. 'I enjoyed doing it,' she said. 'I have written several three-act plays; I am primarily a theatre maker. And this was much more like an acting job than anything to do with literature.'

It helped enormously that Marsh, like Duffy, was born in New Zealand and had a great love of the theatre, giving many of her novels theatrical settings. Duffy worked hard to capture the style, mood, settings and dialogue of the writer's original work, as well as taking on the puzzle element and the typical Ngaio Marsh structure. 'There's the scene with the ingenue,' she said. 'There's the love affair gone wrong, and then there's the stupid young man who's screwed up and he just needs a father figure to tell him to be better. And there's an ensemble of soldiers.'

Duffy studied every one of Marsh's first ten books – *Money in the Morgue* would likely have been around number eleven or twelve in the series – to make sure she located her detective in the right place and time. 'I did a huge amount of work on the books that came before this one, so that I wouldn't inadvertently get "present" Alleyn,' she said.

It was tricky working on a character another writer had created. Marsh had named him after the Elizabethan actor Edward Alleyn, who founded Dulwich College where her father had been a pupil. In the novels, Marsh describes him as being extremely handsome and looking like a cross between a monk and a grandee. His possibly most irritating habit, of quoting Shakespeare at any occasion he decides is relevant, runs throughout the series. In the early novels, Alleyn is single before he falls in love with Agatha Troy, a famous portrait painter, and finally persuades her to marry him. Duffy admits getting Alleyn's tone right was difficult. 'And if you go through the *Goodreads* reviews,' she said, 'you'll see that some fans of Alleyn think I've done it perfectly and I've revived him and it's amazing. And some think that I probably should be shot! And there is no one in between. It's really interesting. I've entirely divided people who say they're fans. Interestingly for me, all the mainstream press, touch wood, have really liked it, and that's never happened in my career before. It feels amazing.'

Insightful British novelist Nicola Upson has taken on the work of another Golden Age writer – Josephine Tey – in a different way, by making this important but often neglected exponent of the crime genre the lead protagonist in a series of fictional mystery thrillers. Initially, Upson set out to write a biography of Tey, after reading her 1948 novel *The Franchise Affair*, featuring Scotland Yard detective Alan Grant, and becoming intrigued by the writer's chameleon-like nature.

'I love that book,' she said. 'I think it is responsible for my writing fiction. On the one hand, it is a kind of nostalgic snapshot of an England that, for better or worse, is lost. But it also has a very dark subtext. It is about two women who are persecuted for keeping themselves to themselves, which is something Tey knew a lot about. It is also about mob violence and, curiously, that post-Second World War gothic hysteria of the "servant problem". Every time you read it you get something different out of it. Mainly I loved that book because, like her, it is a chameleon.'

Josephine Tey was one of two pen names used by Scottish-born writer Elizabeth Mackintosh. As Tey, she wrote dark and intelligent crime novels. She also wrote drama under the pseudonym Gordon Daviot, including the 1932 stage play *Richard of Bordeaux*, which was based on the life of Richard II. She divided her life into these three different spheres and seemed determined no one should know her intimately. She shunned publicity, avoided photographers, kept few photos of herself, never married and never had children. She had friends who believed they were close to her but who admitted, after she died in 1952, that they did not know exactly who she was. Mackintosh was a complex and intensely private woman and, as she researched her life and work, Upson found herself unable to pin down enough material for a biography.

'I was lucky in the sense that it was the early 1990s and lots of people who had worked with her and become lifelong friends of hers were still alive,' Upson said. 'So, I got to speak to them, mostly about her professional life. But there wasn't enough information in the public domain to make her a full character without relying over-heavily on endless analyses of her work and what it might tell you about her.'

Upson debated the problem for several weeks before her partner, writer Mandy Morton, told her: 'For God's sake, make it up!' The idea of putting the real woman into a fictional world quickly took hold. Upson borrowed Josephine's name and one of the writer's three identities – along with some of the more intriguing aspects of the writer's life – for what would become an ongoing and hugely successful series of amateur detective novels. Her first Josephine Tey mystery, *An Expert in Murder*, was published in 2008.

'I was terrified because I had never written fiction,' Upson remembered. 'And it seemed such a wonderful idea, and such a perfect idea for *her*, because the gaps had become as intriguing as the facts, and she was such a complex and often contradictory woman. To bring her to life in a single volume of biography was proving very, very difficult. But over a period of books, where you put her in different situations and shine a light through different characters' eyes on her, that just seemed such a wonderful thing to do that would suit her very well. But I *was* terrified, because I'd never written dialogue, I'd never constructed plots. Although, as I got further on through the series, I became a little more confident with that.'

It was important to Upson that her fictional amateur detective be as true as possible to the real Josephine Tey; true to her complex and contrary nature, her independence, her work, her friendships, her sexuality. Each of the books contains carefully researched and detailed aspects of Tey's actual life and work. 'I wasn't as bound by the facts,' Upson said. 'And yet strangely, in a way, my Josephine Tey started to become more truthful to the real person.

'Josephine was a chameleon,' Upson added. 'With typical self-awareness she called herself that. And it is true. Whatever identity she was using she matched it to the particular circumstances, while still being an outsider. And that is what makes Tey a great detective in the books, because she is an outsider in so many different senses.'

Upson believes it is this chameleon quality that prevents Tey being tied down to any particular style or period. Although she wrote in the same period as Ngaio Marsh, Agatha Christie and the other Golden Age artists, there is something intensely modern about her books. Her genius was to create a story which can be read on many levels and which differed according to the audience.

In all of Tey's novels, the question of female identity comes across most strongly and Upson wanted this to be true of her own work. 'I aimed to make that sense of femaleness and modernness and breaking boundaries true in all my novels,' she said. In *Two for Sorrow* (2010), the third in the Josephine Tey series, Upson's fictional detective draws on a real crime, the case of two baby farmers, Amelia Sach and Annie Walters, who were suspected of killing up to twenty babies and were executed in a double hanging in Holloway in 1903. Sach, who ran a nursing home, placed newspaper advertisements offering a place for pregnant women to go in the last weeks of their confinement. Contained in the advert was the tell-tale phrase 'baby can remain'. The women who answered the ad were usually unmarried mothers who couldn't afford to bring up a child. They would give birth in the nursing home and pay Sach a fee, believing the baby would go to an adoptive family. Instead, Sach would hand the baby over to Annie Walters, who killed it. Before she disposed of the body, Walters would walk around London holding the dead baby.

In *Two for Sorrow*, which is set in the 1930s, 30 years after Sach and Walters were hung, the fictional Tey decides to write a novel about the two women, and in doing so raises huge psychological questions about what might have happened to Annie Walters in her past life. Had Annie suffered a grief of her own? More significantly, had Josephine? 'If she had,' Upson said, 'no one in either Inverness or London knew or would talk about it. *Two for Sorrow* looks at those issues, and at the life and choices available for privileged women set against those available for poor desperate women in London,' Upson said. 'Both sets of women had had to reshape and remould their lives as a result of the losses and the opportunities of the First World War.'

Upson sees Josephine Tey very much as a woman of her time. 'She was very much a product of her exact period, living between those two world wars,' she said. 'Like many of her generation, she was someone who benefitted from that huge loss, the so-called surplus generation of women who were no longer expected to marry and have children because there weren't enough available men. In a way, the war gave her a get-out-of-jail-free card – as well as the grief and personal loss which she shared with hundreds of other women.'

For Upson, setting is always as important as the story. She retraced Walters' footsteps on the day she was eventually caught holding the dead baby. Walters had lived in Danbury Street, a sordid, shabby place full of transient boarding houses, a sharp contrast to the beautiful homes that occupy it today. 'I shall never forget standing outside that house – now a happy family home, with a mother downstairs making pastry with her little daughter – and realising that, in those rooms, at least two babies had been killed,' Upson said. 'If I hadn't gone there, I wouldn't have had the atmosphere. I wouldn't have known how claustrophobically desperate it had been. It's so important.'

Upson saw *Two for Sorrow* as a very dark book. As well as the baby farming issue, it contained what she believes is her best murder, the violent killing of a young seamstress. But it also features the beginning of Tey's love affair with another woman,

Marta. 'We crime writers are all very competitive about murder,' she said. 'I think we are great at violence but rubbish at love. I wanted in that book to counteract the darkness; a relationship of tenderness, somebody to reach out and touch somebody else, for it to be about love and not power or control or hate.' Upson feared she might have gone too far with her seamstress murder, that she would receive complaints. 'It never ceases to amaze me,' she said, 'that the only complaint I have had was about the love scene between the two women, rather than the really vicious murder of a woman.'

The fact that Upson's Tey is a lesbian has been controversial, but the writer is convinced the real Tey was gay and that the writer, who was typical of her period with its lack of sexual outlets and its punitive attitude towards women who were 'different', would be pleased with the response Upson has had to the aspects of her work that make Tey's sexuality more explicit.

'I realise how important it is when readers tell me what they have found in my novels,' she said. 'I am always very pleased when somebody tells me my Tey novels give a voice to a generation of gay women who didn't have a voice. I feel it is truly important. Since the series started, I have had lots of letters from people who tell me about their grandmothers or great aunts or parents, or sometimes even themselves, who have made choices in their lives that they wouldn't have made if they had lived in different times, in a more tolerant society. It is important to keep that to the fore in the books, obviously because of who Josephine Tey was and because of who I am.'

When she began writing *An Expert in Murder*, Upson thought of herself as someone writing a book about Josephine Tey, but just doing it in a slightly different way. 'It's only subsequently that I thought – and still think to this day – that her ongoing journey through the series, and the lives of the series' characters that I've made up, are worth caring about,' she said. 'I am finding people are coming to care about Josephine very much. That is just as important to me in each novel as the crime strand, although I do love the crime strand.'

Tey herself did not always have a murder at the heart of her novels. In *The Franchise Affair*, there is only the mystery of a teenage girl who claims she was kidnapped. Throughout her career, she broke almost all Knox's and Van Dine's rules of detective fiction. In *Brat Farrar* (1949) she has an imposter posing as a missing twin so that he can steal an inheritance. She was a strange, beguiling and rebellious crime writer. 'I think I have felt validated by Tey herself in doing something differently in my own work,' Upson said. 'In my first three books, I was feeling my way into the whole idea of using Josephine Tey as a character in separate detective stories. I think that the more time went on, the more I understood a lot of things about Josephine Tey, which people who know her work and her career as a playwright will appreciate.

'By the time I got to the fifth book in the series, *The Death of Lucy Kyte* (2013), I was very conscious of the real person. This made it easier for me to make decisions about that story. I was determined to set it in Suffolk, because I wanted to write about the place where I was born, where my family still live, and where I feel very close to them. Josephine was going there for the first time in her life, so I had to try to recreate those first impressions of a place that I knew very well.'

Upson wanted to set *The Death of Lucy Kyte* in her home town because the novel focuses on the first crime story she ever heard: the killing of Maria Marten by William Corder, which is known as the Red Barn Murder and has been turned into a host of melodramas, on stage and film. Upson's family used to take her for walks near the crime scene. 'We would go to Polstead and look at Maria Marten's house and William Corder's house, and so little had changed,' she said. 'I remember thinking, even as a child, what that must have been like, what those real people were like behind the legend of the Red Barn Murder.

'For a while after Maria's body was found, Polstead was the crime capital of the world. But the story of the real people behind that was not known. I wanted to know who the real Maria was. My Mum or Dad took me to Moyse's Hall Museum, which has a wonderful collection of artefacts of the murder. It has a copy of the trial bound in Corder's own skin and it has his scalp and the pistols he allegedly shot Maria with. All those things, when you're very small, are fascinating and grisly, but when I went back to Moyse's Hall as a grown woman, knowing that I was going to write about this story, the thing that moved me most was the pair of flat irons Maria had used when she was alive. And that got me thinking about how, when women are the victims of murder – and although it happens to men as well, it happens particularly and intensely with women – we lose sight of who they were before their death brought them to our attention.'

Upson did not want to know about the corpse discovered in the Red Barn, she wanted to know about the girlfriend and mother that Maria Marten had been before she died. Like Josephine Tey herself, she is passionately interested in female identity. 'It is very important to me in all these books because it is the chance to stand up for the victim,' she said. 'Female victims of crime lose their identity. It is, after all, called a whodunnit. We are far more fascinated by the people who did it, than the people it was done to. Maria, when she was killed, became either a victim at one extreme or a whore at the other. There was no real living, breathing woman in between. So, in that book, I wanted to recreate Maria as a real woman and do it through the eyes of a fictional character, who was allegedly her best friend throughout that time. And it got me thinking that Polstead, which is the most beautiful village now, still has that kind of darkness. It still has that stain.'

Upson was very conscious of the fact that, two hundred years later, a few miles from where Maria was killed, Steve Wright killed five women in Ipswich. 'I suddenly thought, we can all bring his name to mind, probably his face, but how many of us can name all five of his victims? Maria Marten has very modern repercussions.'

Despite her devotion to the more radical of Tey's works, when Upson began writing she felt she should honour the Golden Age, at least initially. 'I tried to give readers a puzzle, a circle of suspects, some red herrings, and a mystery somewhere inside,' she said. 'But I also wanted, even in my first books, to honour Josephine and have a modern frankness and historical insight. Her books feel edgy and ahead of her time. I hope my later books do too. But for somebody like me writing crime fiction now, there really aren't any rules. Christie broke the ones that existed in her day. Christie's books are brutal, raw and tough. We no longer equate the Golden Age with cosy. It is important to me that my books aren't seen as cosy.'

Like Tey, Upson is fascinated by the characters, the sense of place and the psychology behind crime – and its aftermath – rather than the puzzle alone. 'Putting character first is what the best crime writers have been doing for a very long time,' she said. 'That was Margery Allingham's strength. Also, Dorothy Sayers. It was certainly Josephine Tey's strength. When the novel was at a crossroads in the late 1950s, early 1960s, when it could easily have become an outdated mode that merely focused on the puzzle, people like P D James and Ruth Rendell took the character-based psychological fiction on board and created novels that were living, breathing reflections of the society they lived in. That was an important turning point. The best crime fiction does tend to put character first.'

Josephine Tey left her legacy as ordered and tidy as she could, her final book *The Singing Sands* (1952) neatly finished and ready to be published. 'Nobody could have finished that novel,' Upson said. 'So, it's a good job Tey did it for us. Although Jill Paton Walsh emulated Dorothy Sayers brilliantly, I don't think anyone could have done that with Josephine Tey, because it is not about her style and elegance, although she has all of that. It's about her voice: the warmth, the intelligence, the wryness, the wit. It's about the personal thing. You pick up a Josephine Tey novel and you feel the sun on your face, and you want to get to know her better. And then you start to see the darkness and the complexities and ironies.'

That joyous idea of picking up a book and feeling the sun on your face is what many contemporary women crime writers have been striving for by returning again and again to the classics in order to move forward with their own novels.

5

Private Eyes

The private eye is the most emblematic element in the crime and mystery genre, certainly in America. It is almost as popular in British crime.

An early prototype of the American male private eye was the rough and ready Race Williams, created by pulp magazine writer Carroll John Daly. Race jumped from the pages of *Black Mask* magazine in the early 1920s but was soon overtaken by a more serious and sophisticated breed of fictional private eye, all of them male. As my recent biography *Dashiell Hammett: Man of Mystery* (2014) shows, Hammett was the single most significant male writer of American detective fiction, foremost in the development of the genre. His five brilliant major crime novels, published between 1929 and 1934, all showed a tough-guy masculinity. The now famous Hammett narratives, *Red Harvest* (1929), *The Dain Curse* (1929), *The Maltese Falcon* (1930), *The Glass Key* (1931) and *The Thin Man* (1934), were all known for realism and had an authenticity built on Hammett's life as a Pinkerton Operative. Hammett's heroes are no nonsense, hard-drinking men who move casually, sometimes ruthlessly, through life, unencumbered by anything other than their personal sense of morality and code of honour. Today we can think about Hammett's successor Lee Child and his hero Jack Reacher.

Hammett's heroes – the anonymous Continental Op, the

boozy, married sleuth Nick Charles, the easy, assured gambler Ned Beaumont and his corrupt political boss Paul Madvig – all portrayed the importance of male friendship. Most memorable is Sam Spade in *The Maltese Falcon*. He became a symbol of the American private eye (with big thanks to Humphrey Bogart, who played Spade in the 1941 film). They were all men's men and they became archetypal characters in American literary culture, establishing the ground rules and tone for a whole new tradition of hardboiled writing. And it was specifically male writing, in a male culture that largely excluded women and in which female protagonists were either victims in need of a male hero's help or femme fatales whose appeal was sexual rather than cerebral. There was no room on Hammett and Chandler's mean streets for smart, savvy women who wanted to investigate crime. For decades, Spade and Marlowe were the yardstick by which other private eyes were measured.

Then, in 1977, the hard-nosed, level-headed and savvy private eye Sharon McCone made her first appearance in Marcia Muller's *Edwin of the Iron Shoes*. Five years later, Sue Grafton's former police officer and rebellious loner Kinsey Millhone arrived in *A for Alibi* (1982), the first in what would be the long-running Alphabet detective series. The same year, Sara Paretsky's *Indemnity Only* (1982) gave Chicago's crime culture the feisty, indomitable VI Warshawski.

These three authors turned out to be extraordinarily prolific. In 2017, shortly before her death, Grafton published what would be the last of her Alphabet thrillers, *Y is for Yesterday*. A year later, Marcia Muller published her 34th McCone novel, *The Breakers* (2018). In 2020, Paretsky published her 20th Warshawski novel, *Dead Land*.

How did the Big Female Trio present their private eyes at the start of their fictional careers in 1977 and 1982 and how had these much-loved characters grown and developed by the 2000s? The ways in which these influential female PIs have been described and portrayed at these two key moments in their fictional history may tell readers something significant about the evolution and expansion of female crime writing in general or it may focus in a meaningful way on the changes in the making of the new female private eye.

Sharon McCone

At the start of Muller's *Edwin of the Iron Shoes*, Sharon McCone is given her first case as staff investigator for All Souls Legal Cooperative: to find out who has been vandalising a small street of antique shops. When an elderly antique dealer is found dead, stabbed with an antique dagger, McCone is not confident in the police's ability to find out who killed her and decides to go it alone to stop the murderer striking again.

The widespread idea that it was Muller who launched the tough female private eye with her skilled and pragmatic Sharon McCone can be tempered once we look carefully at the debut heroines of Grafton's Alphabet thrillers and Paretsky's VI Warshawski. McCone is considerably milder and tamer than the two truly tough investigators who followed her and who do indeed set the standard for the first female private eyes. It was together rather than independently that the trio pushed the bar high for a genuine contemporary female private eye.

McCone does not entirely have the key attributes of a formal private eye. Although she is an investigator and does not represent the law, she is nevertheless on the All Souls payroll and her assignments come from the co-operative. This means she lacks the total autonomy of the traditional PI. To make up for this, Muller does give her heroine most of the other essentials. From the start, McCone is allotted the requisite independence by having no apparent family members. In an earlier job with a detective agency, she was fired for having an excess of independence and high moral standards and when young (she is almost 30 years old when she takes on the Edwin case) she turned down the notion of being a lady cop as they mainly typed and took shorthand.

She sees herself as courageous and assertive yet, in that first book, she falls for a self-assured detective 13 years older than she is who calls her his 'papoose'. As McCone's self-confidence increases book after book, so does her prowess, her skill and her cynicism. By the fourth book, *Games to Keep the Dark Away* (1984), she has dropped the overbearing cop and is able to reflect sensibly: 'What woman could remain in love with a man who called her by such a ridiculous nickname?'[14] As Muller allows McCone to mature and develop, she handles her protagonist with a wise but humorous eye. Her novel *Wolf in the Shadows* (1993) earned her an Edgar nomination. McCone is a slow-burning private eye, which is perhaps fitting for a debut protagonist in a new female genre. She gathers the PI characteristics she needs steadily and slowly.

Her two contemporary protagonists, however – the cheeky, smart and fierce Kinsey Millhone and the ferocious, funny and exceptional V I Warshawski – fly at us in their first books with all guns blazing, revealing a toughness, an independence, a lack of hesitation and a powerful, passionate professionalism.

Sue Grafton

Grafton's first Alphabet thriller, *A is for Alibi*, gained an immediate and extraordinary amount of positive attention and her follow-up *B is for Burglar* (1985) was awarded both the Shamus and Anthony awards for best novel. *C is for Corpse* (1986) and *G is for Gumshoe* (1990) both earned Anthony awards, while *K is for Killer* (1994) was given a second Shamus. Unlike the Sharon McCone series, the Alphabet thrillers get off to an assured start and, with each book, Grafton's protagonist becomes more confident and assertive.

The 32-year-old detective is an absolutely typical and classic private eye. Yet, because she is a woman and a feminist, she has extra, more unusual characteristics. Having been orphaned at five, she has no family, except for the aunt who brought her up after her parents were killed, although in *J is for Judgment* (1993), she discovers relatives she has never heard of living not far from her own area of Santa Teresa. Millhone has survived two marriages and two divorces, is childless and has no pets, and now lives alone. Private investigation is at the heart of her personal and professional life. She is gregarious with those of whom she is fond but she is ultimately a solitary person. The final line of this first novel sets the tone for the series. 'In the end all you have left is yourself.'[15]

A closer look reveals Millhone to be more vulnerable than the top-coat of tough-as-old-boots paint suggests. Her previous role models of male PI protagonists were often tempted by seductive female killers. Grafton cleverly inverts this misogynistic pattern by having Millhone start an affair with a man who turns out to be a killer. It doesn't take Millhone long to get a grip and, in self-defence, to kill him. But the difference between Sue Grafton and Dashiell Hammett is that, in a similar situation, Hammett's Sam Spade remains ruthlessly professional and detached, while Grafton's Kinsey is filled with remorse, guilt and self-blame. Today these qualities might be part of the contemporary private eye's character, whether male or female, but in 1993 they were always seen as exclusively female.

Although recurring themes in Grafton's storylines include consistent male abuse of female family members, she is less concerned with relevant wider patriarchal issues and social structures than the radical feminists who would follow her. The whole Alphabet series sees Millhone as a moderate, liberal feminist. During the series, she lives in a converted garage and has only one dress in her wardrobe, preferring blue jeans and blazers. She spent two years in the Santa Teresa Police

Department before quitting, after receiving too much sexist attention, and setting herself up as a private eye.

Policewomen were viewed either with contempt or curiosity and she became fed up with defending herself against so called 'good-humoured' insults. She found all police detectives worked with a leash around their necks like dogs and decided it wasn't for her. Millhone's awareness and dislike of gendered attention was new to the PI genre, although her determination to be tough and independent was not. The other feature that was new was the substitution of close friends for family (something she shared with Paretsky's Warshawski), in particular the mutual affection between Millhone and her 80-year-old landlord Henry Pitts. She claims all of Henry's large overflowing family as her own and they are as important to her as her own family might have been. She also incorporates into her large stable network the elderly and flamboyant Hungarian Rosie, who owns the restaurant where Kinsey, Henry and their friends eat many meals. It would seem Millhone has found not only good close friends but also substitute parents.

We learn a great deal about her life as a private investigator, her emotions about her job and about her friends, and her pared down and particular lifestyle. That these matter to her and count in the readers' estimation of her is another feature that is new to the PI character. In the first novel, Millhone investigates the death of prominent divorce lawyer Laurence Fife. His murder eight years earlier was blamed on his wife Nikki. Upon her release from prison, Nikki hires Millhone to find the real murderer. Millhone discovers that, not only was Laurence Fife killed with powdered oleander, but that a 24-year-old accountant in West Los Angeles died four days later of the same poison. This strange coincidence is too much for Millhone, who decides it should clear Nikki of murder. But the officer in the case, Detective Con Dolan, now believes that Nikki is guilty of not one but two murders. Millhone takes on the case and is determined to find the murderer and to solve this miscarriage of justice, although every file she looks at reveals betrayal, deception, misdirection and hostility from everyone involved.

At intervals throughout this debut novel, Kinsey emphasises how hard and tough she is. She is 'a real hard-ass when it comes to men' and she acknowledges that she has 'never been good at taking shit, especially from men'.[16] She tells readers that what she expects from her life is solitude, yet the other side of Kinsey shows a friendly, chirpy, sociable person and also some deep areas of vulnerability.

By the 1990s and *M is for Malice,* her outward appearance has hardly changed but she has managed to build up a savings account. She accepts that at heart she is 'a law-and-order type' and seems to have drifted nearer to middle-class security.[17] She has considerably more insight than in the early books (a big departure from the classic male PI) and worries about the fact that people have rejected her all her life, or so she believes. Sam Spade tells us almost nothing about his inner feelings and his independence is purposeful, whereas Millhone's autonomy appears to result from traumatic emotional issues. In Grafton's later books, the professional and personal become interwoven. Throughout each of their series, these three female PIs change and evolve in ways that their male counterparts, even the major male investigators like Sam Spade, do not. Muller, Grafton and Paretsky's books all interweave the professional and the personal, a critical departure from the classic male PI novels.

The female members of the Big Trio have been very influential on younger up-and-coming mystery writers and two of them, Paretsky and Muller, still are. Sue Grafton, right up until she died, was a profound influence on other professional writers, not only debut writers but many mature and well-established ones.

Alafair Burke is one enthusiastic example. 'I came to writing as a reader first and the Kinsey Millhone series was my favourite,' she said. 'I started reading it pretty early. I think I started with C. Those early books I read of hers I felt were like a friend coming to visit. They were warm-hearted but never soft. Sue had an edge to her. I loved that series.' Burke's own novels have a similar verve and ability to grip. The dialogue is pacy but realistic. She is less political than Sara Paretsky, another of her heroines, but her novels move almost as fast.

Sara Paretsky

Sara Paretsky's debut was a novel influenced by her own feminist perspective, her decision to have a very strong woman in the lead and several other independent female characters, as well as the authenticity lent to the book by the use of her expertise in the insurance business. VI Warshawski, Paretsky's extraordinary private eye, opened the door to a new generation of detective writing.

The plot of *Indemnity Only* (1982) is both complex and horrifying. Hired by a man who calls himself John Thayer, Warshawski's assignment is to find Thayer's son Peter's missing girlfriend Anita Hill. But when Warshawski finds young Peter's dead body instead, her client disappears. Her efforts to track him down and learn his true identity take her deep into a labyrinth of fraud and violence. Warshawski also discovers that the man who claims to be John Thayer is actually Andrew McGraw, a big labour and union leader.

Later we find out that Anita Hill had reasons for running away after Peter's murder and this leads Warshawski into a case much bigger than murder. We quickly discover that our detective knows too much as she takes a beating from a gang member. The action and plot become ever more complex, displaying unusual ambitions for a debut novel. This complexity and this moral seriousness have never left Sara Paretsky and her novels, and this is what lifts them out of the stable of more ordinary thrillers, no matter how fast-paced they are or how many devious plot traps they contain.

Paretsky's striking American novel was the inspiration for contemporary British crime writer Val McDermid to start writing crime novels of her own. At the point when she read *Indemnity Only*, McDermid hadn't written a single thriller. 'Back then, in the early 1980s, the only options in the British crime novel seemed to be the police procedural and the village mystery,' she said. 'And the detectives were either men or elderly spinsters. It took Sara Paretsky to show me that there was another set of options out there. I could try to create an independent female sleuth whose politics informed the choices she made. And I could aim to write a complex, knotty plot like Paretsky, where secrets and lies twisted round each other in a labyrinth of doubt and fear. I've followed VI Warshawski ever since.'[18]

The importance of the new novels by the ground-breaking women's trio is that they bring to the genre a powerful feminist perspective, not at that point current nor available in the detective fiction of the hardboiled era. Paretsky imbues Warshawski with the typical city spirit of most urban private eyes. As the novel is set in the centre of Chicago, this works well. Paretsky is determined to make a new, untried claim, not only for a hitherto masculine role but, in Chicago, a long-established masculine territory.

In California, where her sisters created the PIs Sharon McCone and Kinsey Millhone, other writers, readers and publishers looked on with wry amusement but not a great deal of hostility. Yet in Chicago, the resistance from publishers and agents to Paretsky's views and her proposed changes to the genre were icy stubbornness and fierce anger. She invents Warshawski, a smart, skilful lawyer who refuses to divulge her first two names because she hates to be condescended to, especially by men. She wants to investigate in a way that is not morally corrupt. She left her former job at the public defender's office because she believed the set-up was corrupt and she had found herself arguing on points of law instead of arguing for justice. Once inside the detective tradition, she is able to establish the truth in each case and then make a positive contribution.

She always remains on the side of the poor and the powerless, which puts her firmly in the tradition of Ross Macdonald's Lew Archer and Chandler's Philip Marlowe. Many times, she is there to fight the cause of women who are not always poor but are always powerless.

In that this is classic moral mission material, it does of course need an investigator who is classically independent. So Paretsky must now act more radically than Muller or Grafton. In order to establish and safeguard Warshawski's role as an independent investigator, she must be prepared to alienate if necessary the three main sets of characters in this new PI criminal world: the client Warshawski is supposed to be working for; the police, whom she often sees as another enemy; and the criminals. In the first book, Paretsky has her private eye admit: 'I seemed to be alienating everyone whose path I crossed'. Only later in the series does she realise that her short temper has begun to undermine her trustworthiness and plausibility.

Warshawski's behaviour is influenced by her preoccupation with her long dead Italian mother and, to a lesser extent, with her dead Polish father. We assume Paretsky is doing this to establish, however sketchily, a family background, something the novels by Hammett and Chandler and Macdonald all avoid. In her second novel *Deadlock* (1984), Warshawski's family life is again a subtle theme when she investigates the drowning of a cousin, and the third novel *Killing Orders* (1985) begins with her doing a favour for an aunt.

Several critics suggest that Warshawski's vivid memories of her long dead parents are an early manifestation of the huge increase in interest in family taken by many contemporary women crime writers. Certainly, the notion of family is ever prevalent. In

Warshawski's world, families can be threatening, with deadly family secrets frequently cropping up. Alongside the riveting plot lines and utterly compelling, indeed exhilarating, action, there is often a keen sense of loss. The fact that family exists in this sketchy but constantly referenced way is utterly opposed to its total absence in classic, traditional male PI narratives.

What is similar to traditional PI storylines is that, from the start, Warshawski is systematically punished in every novel. Sometimes a thug in the story tries to kill her; sometimes the punishment causes such great physical harm that she routinely visits the local hospital to be patched up. She is fortunate that her closest friend is a doctor. Dr Charlotte 'Lotty' Herschel, who is older than Warshawski, can be seen both in quasi-parental terms and also as our heroine's deepest and most emotionally sustaining relationship. Paretsky's series provides one of the best examples of women's friendship to come out of any fiction in the US during that period.

Like most of the male PIs who have gone before her, Warshawski is hard-up and has no spare cash to improve the shabby interior of her office. Most of her clients, who come from the white-collar end of financial crime, seem not to notice. Despite the fact that she has so little money, she is portrayed as a very generous woman, both emotionally and financially. The books, which began life in 1982, are as expert, compelling, clever, witty and fresh at the time of my writing this study as they were 38 years ago. They offer a sharp sense of amazement through their exhilarating action and pace and irresistible plot lines. Reviewing *Brush Back* (2015), Barry Forshaw, one of our most eminent British crime critics, said: 'Sara Paretsky's VI Warshawski remains the most distinctive female private investigator in US crime fiction, and her continuing survival after numerous pummellings, both physical and emotional, is somehow both plausible and very welcome. Paretsky's sleuth manages to rile even more people in *Brush Back* than usual and remains as bloody-minded as ever.'[19]

What is probably the most important feature of Paretsky's work is her outspoken discussion of urgent social and political issues, such as the rise of the right throughout Europe and the United States, the erosion of women's liberties and civil liberties and the cutting-edge issue of identity. Paretsky is unable to stop her tough and cocky protagonist from becoming emotionally involved in many of her cases, often causing disorder and mayhem on the way, whilst also knowing she has created the most significant private eye in the history of the genre. The female characters in Paretsky's books are highly active women. Their activity is not primarily sexual, as it had been in crime fiction by male and female writers, and during this changeover period, they are not defined by their sexuality. Warshawski defies stereotypes. She is fiercely independent, tough-minded, big-hearted, altruistic and endlessly brave; she comes out fighting for her clients and refuses to be silenced. 'For me, she represents women's speech or, more personally, my speech,' Paretsky said. 'And so, her voice is one that demands to be heard.'

Strong women protagonists in contemporary crime fiction on both sides of the water have traditionally been punished, often with increasing violence. 'To me it is a way of putting up neon warning lights to women to not take up space,' Paretsky said. 'Something I see going hand-in-hand with that is the pressure that successful women feel to be thin. You are not supposed to take up room. The less physical space you take up, the less threatening your space occupied will be.' Female detectives are, she added, almost always physically very small.

Paretsky also pointed to the idea that, for contemporary women detectives to be seen as strong, they are often also seen to be badly damaged. 'They've got to be strong, but they come out of a damaged background,' she said. 'Or they've just had terrible misadventures and been raped and brutalised and now they're being detectives.'

Even though women's voices in contemporary fiction are much stronger than they were in the past, the women in many crime books are getting killed in more gruesome ways. Paretsky's books are never like that.

'No, they aren't driven by sadism,' she said. 'I'm not willing to walk to the other side of the tightrope. I did a programme once with Gillian Flynn who said she loved being in the place where everything was unsafe – like *Sharp Objects* – with untrustworthy people. That is the space I find so terrifying. Gillian is a lovely person by the way, but I don't want to be in her head. It is important to me that, at the end of the novel, there will be some wholeness, some safe place for people. A sense of safety within a novel is important to me.

'I think we live in an age of deliberate manipulation of people's fears,' she added. 'There are horrific acts that occur every day; mass murders are a staple of American daily life. But it is possible to find islands of safety. My housekeeper is an immigrant and her family is such a little island of warmth. They've come from a difficult place, have relatives in a difficult place, but their home is like an island of warmth – a rarity in my experience of families – of cherishing each other. And I guess I think those little islands of warmth are still a place that you can go to and maybe VI's little island of warmth is her life with Mr Contreras and Lotty and Sal the bartender. Maybe not in one spot, but in one emotional place. And so, I guess what I want for myself, and maybe what readers take away, is that there is that little place. It may not exist for long, it may be unstable in some ways, but there are these little islands that you *can* inhabit.'

The Trio and followers

This fierce and feisty trio are exemplars to several significant American fellow writers, such as Meg Gardiner of Austin,

Texas, a former lawyer who is best known for her series of thrillers featuring former lawyer and freelance journalist Evan Delaney. Gardiner has written two further series, one featuring forensic psychiatrist Jo Beckett and the other introducing FBI profiler Caitlin Hendrix. She has also written three standalone titles.

Others include Laura Lippman who, in *The Girl in the Green Raincoat* (2008), did what few writers before her had dared to do. She gave her Baltimore ex-journalist private investigator Tess Monaghan a baby. Cara Black brought to life the sharp and headstrong Paris-based computer specialist investigator Aimee Leduc. Alison Gaylin has, as one of her female protagonists, 40-something missing persons private investigator Brenna Spector, who has the rare neurological disorder Hypermnesia, which gives her an astonishing autobiographical memory.

The writer who bears the most resemblance stylistically to the Big Trio is Linda Barnes, whose PI Carlotta Carlyle, a red-headed, tough-talking former cop from Boston, is very similar to Grafton's Kinsey Millhone. Carlyle, who was thrown out of the Boston police department for insubordination and also drives a taxi, strides through the pages of this series of mystery novels with her impressive six-foot stature. She is straight-talking and very funny. Barnes' first book in this series *A Trouble of Fools* (1987) won the American Mystery Award and was nominated for both the Edgar and Shamus awards. This debut book is beautifully plotted, exciting, moving and leavened with wit. Grafton hailed Carlotta as a 'true original'. Barnes' second book *The Snake Tattoo* (1989) was hailed as 'outstanding book of the year' by UK newspaper *The Times*.

English writer Liza Cody can be credited with introducing the professional female private investigator to British detective fiction with her 1980 debut novel *Dupe* and her brave and lovable former police officer Anna Lee. Michelle Spring, who was raised in Vancouver but lives in Cambridge, followed in 1994 with

Every Breath You Take, the first in a series featuring academic-turned-private eye Laura Principal.

Canadian Gail Bowen is the writer behind female private eye Joanne Kilbourn, an insightful political analyst and widowed mother, who began her creative life in 1990 and has been embroiled in one extraordinary and frightening criminal investigation after another ever since. Her seventeenth adventure *The Winners' Circle* (2017), in which Joanne investigates a triple homicide that is very close to home, was a finalist for the 2018 Arthur Ellis Award for best novel. Bowen also received the Arthur Ellis Grand Master Award, which celebrates a Canadian crime writer with a substantial body of work who has garnered national and international recognition.

Kilbourn is a political science professor and Bowen, who is also an academic, created her because she felt there were not enough women like her being represented in fiction. Kilbourn is 46 years old when the series begins and, 19 novels in, is now in her 60s, making her one of the oldest fictional sleuths. Her first husband is killed while she is trying to finish her PhD. She has three children of her own and is not financially stable. Yet Kilbourn takes in a four-year-old child, the daughter of a man she grew up with.

Kilbourn is a churchgoer and has a strong moral purpose. She has an interesting inter-racial relationship with an indigenous cop Alex Kequahtooway, and goes on to marry Zack Shreve, a paraplegic lawyer, yet she is sometimes riddled with self-doubt. 'I wanted a female protagonist and I wanted a strong protagonist, but I didn't want her to be perfect,' Bowen said. 'She is a deeply flawed character. She is not certain of herself all the time and she is not Superwoman. She has a family, she has a career, and she tries to keep all the balls in the air, but not always does it work. She makes some poor choices.'

Other fictional private investigators include Kate Rhodes' London-based psychologist Alice Quentin, Stella Duffy's sincere and dedicated lesbian Saz Martin, Alison Joseph's modern nun Sister Agnes and Zoe Sharp's ex-special forces female bodyguard Charlie Fox, all of whom are indebted to the Big Trio in differing ways.

Paretsky particularly has made it clear that central to the traditional female private eye novel is the theme that, even though the PI cannot completely destroy evil in all its shapes and forms, he or she nevertheless serves society better than any collective agent, such as the police, which might be seen as morally suspect. So how does this underpinning of private eye novels as established by the Big Trio affect the thinking of younger contemporary private eyes? Are they also believers in social justice? Is women's speech important to them? And where do they stand on issues such as safety and danger?

Risk and safety in relation to morality are high on Kate Rhodes' agenda for writing crime. 'I'm fascinated by the moral issues you are able to touch on in crime writing,' she said. 'One talks always about life and death issues. One such issue was the tainted blood scandal. That affected my husband, who was given tainted blood. I was able to write a thriller about it and people read it. Before becoming a crime writer, I was a professional poet, but if I had written a poem about it, almost no one would have read it. Crime writing gives me a little agency to write about things that matter.'

When Rhodes looks at her private eye Alice Quentin, she can see that she falls into line with Paretsky's criticisms of modern PIs as too small and taking up little space. Yet she deliberately wanted to make Alice a vulnerable-looking person in a very male-dominated world. 'I wanted to make her small, five feet tall, very slight, very petite,' Rhodes said. 'Alice is blonde, fragile looking. But she has got a warrior spirit. She runs marathons, she's personally very strong. I wanted to paint this stereotypical, tiny blonde, who is so often overlooked in society; this tiny female who has to fight for her voice to be heard. I thought that would be more interesting than writing about a male character.' Sure enough, she does have to do a lot of battling to get her voice heard in every book.

'I have to say that I like flawed characters, whether they are male or female,' Rhodes added. 'But I want the female characters that I have, in my starring roles if you like, to be strong and independent, challenging some of the accepted norms within society. Because people read these books in their thousands and become very committed to characters. It is one way of saying, as a writer, that women deserve as much as men.' Rhodes deliberately avoided making Alice a police person. 'I made her a crime psychologist, which would put her close to the crime,' she said. 'I wanted her to be fascinated by the workings of the mind. Because I am. But also, she's fascinated by everyone's mentality. Everyone she meets, she psychoanalyses to an extent, which I do as well.'

In the days before she created her strong and unusual PI bodyguard Charlie (Charlotte) Fox, Zoe Sharp worked as a photojournalist, at that time a highly male-dominated field. 'There was a certain amount of resistance to women coming in and taking things over,' she said. 'I had death threats whenever my photo appeared – proper cut outs from newspapers like a ransom note – telling me my days were numbered. Luckily the threats were sent to the magazine's London address and I was living up north at the time. So, the "we know where you are" bit was obviously slightly exaggerated. But it was scary. The police never found out who was sending them. And I thought, you know, well what would I do if they were arriving through *my* letterbox every day? The character of Charlie Fox was one I'd had kind of lying around for a while, but she really came into focus then and I started writing the first book.'

Sharp had substantial experience in action fields, such as the motor industry, the sailing and boat industry and astro-navigation, where women were rare and often scoffed at. In the motoring field, women were practically patted on the head when they turned up to talk about anything complicated, to do with remapping electronic ignition, for instance. Sharp has also been involved in boats and sailing as an astro-navigator.

'But if you were a woman on a boat, you were either the cook or the owner's girlfriend,' she said. 'You could have no other purpose. No one believed that, not only did I know that a sextant was a doubly reflecting navigation instrument that measures the angular distance between two visible objects, but that I could use it efficiently in my everyday work. I thought writing thrillers was at least going to be a level playing field.'

It wasn't of course. She feels there is a little less resistance now, but that many women still say their husbands won't read books about weaponry or anything similar written by a woman. 'People are dubious about the amount of authenticity you can get into, writing about weaponry or anything of that sort,' she said. 'And there is less leeway for women writers of crime thrillers to make mistakes.'

When Sharp began her series, there were almost no fictional female bodyguards, although women are in high demand in real life because they are less obtrusive. 'The opponent's first job is to take out the bodyguard,' she said. 'So, if the enemy can't easily identify the bodyguard that makes them very good at their job because they can't be easily spotted.' Sharp wanted to show how absolutely competent women bodyguards can be. 'I want to emphasise how women are often underestimated,' she said. 'There is no reason my people can't do a particular job based purely on the decision of gender.'

Alison Joseph, a radio dramatist and TV documentary maker, was reading radio plays part-time when she started writing her first novel. 'I happened to be reading a lot of crime at that time,' she said. 'I read Sue Grafton and Sara Paretsky and was interested in this new kind of female detective, this new wave of private investigators who were women. And I thought, Oh, a detective nun. It just came to me, this idea of doing a detective nun.'

Joseph was drawn to fictional private detectives because, with the most appealing ones, there was something archetypal about them. 'And being loners, being in some sense set apart from society,' she said. 'People that came to be like Lee Child's main character (Jack Reacher), they are often the sort of archetypal loner. And I was musing on how that quite often seems what we expect of men. We expect women to be connected, or we expect them to be responsible for family life. You know, we have expectations of what a morally good woman is. It doesn't involve that kind of lone, heroic, crossing-the-desert-on-a-motorbike thing.'

Making her lead character a nun solved a lot of problems to do with whether she should have partners or children, Joseph said. As a nun in an open order in modern everyday London, Agnes does belong, but in a quirky kind of way. Making her amateur sleuth a nun also meant that she was often privy to information not available to the police. 'In ordinary, everyday life, if someone is found dead, we call the police, because they have all that forensic knowledge,' Joseph said. 'It would be very strange and would strain readers' credibility to have an amateur person know better than the police do. And it really suited Agnes to be in a world of kids who are *not* going to talk to the police if something has happened to one of their number. They might talk to her.'

As Joseph began writing, Sister Agnes became much more than a mere literary device. 'I had no idea what a rich theme it would be to have someone who, in some sense believes in absolute good, who has that religious faith, constantly being brought up against the worst that people can do. It's really interesting for her as a character. I had no idea when I started her of the potential I would have to explore that.'

Alison Joseph's fellow crime writer Melanie McGrath has

created another even more unusual version of a private eye in a series of Arctic crime mysteries – the half-white, half-Inuit hunter and guide Edie Kiglatuk who spends her days hunting and working as a guide for tourists. In *White Heat,* (2011), the first in the chilling series, Edie turns private eye when one of her tourists is shot dead and the local Canadian Arctic Council of Elders in the tiny settlement of Autisaq seem determined to dismiss it as an accident. The headstrong Edie feels compelled to investigate the shooting and, in doing so, finds herself in terrible danger in this unforgiving landscape of rock and ice. Although she does not resemble any kind of traditional private eye, she possesses great insights and a talent for investigation.

It would be negligent to finish this chapter on private eyes without mentioning two of the finest contemporary fictional investigators, Jackson Brodie and Cormoran Strike, created by exceptional literary crime authors Kate Atkinson and Robert Galbraith, also known as JK Rowling.

I shall dwell in detail in a later chapter on disabled protagonists, on how the one-legged character Cormoran Strike is handled with vivid, realistic descriptions and affectionate wit by his creator. Here, let me say that Strike and his clever, likeable assistant Robin Ellacott have become classic private eye characters. The books are written in impeccable prose with the addictive readability which is Rowling's trademark.

Kate Atkinson's first novel *Behind the Scenes at the Museum* (1995) won the Whitbread First Novel Prize (later called the Costa). Later novels, *Life After Life* (2013) and *God in Ruins* (2015), also won the Costa Prize for Best Novel. *Life After Life* won the South Bank Sky Arts Literature Prize, was shortlisted for the Women's Prize and voted Book of the Year for the Independent Booksellers Association on both sides of the Atlantic. Around these acclaimed literary fictions, Kate Atkinson has also written a series of crime novels, the central character of which is Jackson Brodie, a former soldier and policeman. As a world-weary, lone-wolf investigator, Brodie has the classic PI's tough exterior and dark past, yet he is deeply empathetic. The first three books in the series were adapted for television, with Jason Isaacs playing the gruff but lovable amateur detective.

Writing in *The Sunday Times*, novelist and columnist Penny Perrick said: 'It doesn't really matter in which genre Atkinson chooses to write. Her subject is always the irrecoverable loss of love and how best to continue living once you have glumly recognised "that is what the world is like, things improved but they didn't get better". Her gift is presenting this unnerving and subversive philosophy as a dazzling form of entertainment.'[20] Atkinson's contribution to crime literature, and indeed to literature itself, is her exceptional writing with its emotional delicacy, her satirical dialogue and her idiosyncratic and wise voice.

I am interested in the fact that this chapter on private eyes, which started with three of our genre's ground-breaking female crime authors and protagonists, should end with two of Britain's most recent literary female writers, both of whom go beyond the label of 'crime writer' and help to abolish that imaginary line between genre and literary fiction.

6

Women in the UK Police

The police service has not been a natural home for women. Not in the UK, not in the US, not in Canada. And not in the fiction that has mirrored real events in those countries.

When women protagonists finally entered police fiction in Britain, female crime writers were keen to show how women police officers were treated by their sexist colleagues. In real life, the statistics are stark. In 1883, the British Metropolitan Police recruited its first woman and, within six years, had fourteen. They were usually the wives or relatives of male officers and their main tasks were to guard women and children. Until World War I, forces did not allow women to serve as officers. In 1910, five women formed a vociferous group to alert the police authorities to the fact that there were no women constables, although there were many female temporary prisoners in custody. It took five years before Edith Smith became the first British woman to be appointed an officer with full powers of arrest.

For many decades, the number of women in the British police continued to be severely limited. Slight increases came in the 1970s and this enabled the Equal Pay Act in 1970 and the Sex Discrimination Act in 1975. However, the belittlement and near invisibility of UK women in service continued. Until 1999, women even had their rank title prefixed with the word 'woman'. By March 2020, around one third of police officers in the UK were women, but they still make up a larger percentage of constables than of higher-ranking officers. Even today, women are generally kept in low positions; this despite the fact that the current Commissioner of the Metropolitan Police Force is the clever and redoubtable woman Cressida Dick.

Women officers are highly conscious of their low representation and many I have spoken to said they have felt isolated and have encountered sexism to a high degree. Several talked of being treated with actual cruelty. Every UK policewoman interviewed believed an endemic problem was that a 'good cop' was still seen as being a 'real man'. I noticed a profound difference between how women and men defined what it meant to be a cop. Women emphasised helping over controlling people. They regarded command actions, physical prowess, control actions, and officer safety as crucial but, unlike their male colleagues, they did not value those above other characteristics.

Competent women police officers in the UK are still obliged to prove they are as good as the men they work with, while male officers only need to be as good as one another. When a woman shows she can be aggressive, ambitious, powerful or tough she is likely to gain a reputation for being pushy or strident. When a man has those same qualities, he is likely to be promoted.

The extreme and, in many cases, unbearable situation of institutional sexism, and how it can adversely affect senior female staff, was fictionalised with enormous success by Britain's Lynda La Plante in her powerful 1990s police procedural TV drama *Prime Suspect.* In this series, Helen Mirren's Jane Tennison, one of the first female detective chief inspectors in the Metropolitan Police, shows how terrible and frightening this can be. Jane has to fight the determined discrimination and sexism of her male colleagues, along with the hostility of the upper ranks who are determined to see her fail, until finally she is promoted to Detective Superintendent.

By the 1970s, when several award-winning crime novels and television dramas appeared, readers and viewers expected women detectives to have to deal with sexism. Their Golden Age predecessors largely avoided the problem because, in the 1930s, there were so few women police officers with powers of arrest that it was logical to have as their lead protagonist an attractive, stimulating *male* inspector. Think of the series starring Detective Chief Inspector Roderick Alleyn of the Metropolitan Police which was created by Ngaio Marsh in 1934 and followed the handsome, elegant detective through 32 novels until the author's death in 1982. Alleyn is the epitome of the Golden Age gentleman detective; he is tall and elegant, was educated at Eton and trained as a diplomat before entering Scotland Yard as a constable. Marsh made him slightly unusual by giving him a humane, emotional side, which enabled him to court and eventually marry the remarkable artist Agatha Troy, who subsequently appears in 12 novels. Some readers think Alleyn lacks dynamism or verve, others consider him one of the most beloved policemen in detective fiction.

Fast forward to 1962 and Detective Chief Inspector Adam Dalgliesh, the London Metropolitan police hero of 14 successful mystery novels by PD James, the first of which was *Cover Her Face* from that year. James avoided any male stereotyping of police inspectors by making Dalgliesh an intense, frustrated poet, a cerebral and private person, and a seductively attractive man, a sensitive widower who had lost his wife in childbirth. When we meet him, he is a frustrated and insightful poet whom James uses as the vehicle for her socially conscious themes.

Like the Golden Age women writers who came before her, PD James made it easy for herself by having a male lead and therefore avoided having to draw a policewoman who would have to stand up to discrimination and demeaning sexist police banter. Several years before she died, James said that if she had written her Dalgliesh novels considerably later, she would have created a lead woman protagonist. 'If I was starting now, I would almost certainly have a woman professional police officer (as the lead character),' she said. 'And that would be perfectly logical. But when I began in the late 50s, it was a very different world. Women in the police force mostly dealt with issues concerning women and children. I don't think they were even in the detective force, so I had no choice about sex.'[21] Even when James created the bright and zesty female protagonist Cordelia Gray in 1972, she made her a private detective and not a senior member of the police force.

James had the sensitivity and insight to lay bare the human soul with penetrating psychological acuity. However, the initial crime premise meant that her early novels were set in colleges or hospitals or other locations where the main protagonists would be highly educated. I notice that she modified these settings in later books. There are several reasons she is foremost in the criminal writing stakes. One is the way in which she elevated the detective story into the realms of fine literature. Other reasons include her elegant prose, her strikingly realistic characterisation – and the way her characters are treated with incisive authority – and her determination never to write the same book twice.

A very different lead character from Adam Dalgliesh, in terms of social class, style, looks and dialogue, comes from James' friend and fellow writer Ruth Rendell, who died in May 2015. He was Detective Inspector Reg Wexford, devised in 1964 in Rendell's debut novel *From Doon with Death.*

Wexford is a middle-aged married man, a genial father, whose politics are left-leaning and who enjoys reading stimulating literature at the end of a tough police day. The Wexford novels are what readers outside of Britain would call traditionally British, but there are no signs of stodginess and a great deal of slightly cynical social criticism. What Rendell added to the crime formula that had come before her, certainly in her later books, was a rich awareness of sexism and racism. This was not true of her earliest novels, which had in their narrative several gratuitously contemptuous lines about women, many of them delivered by Wexford himself. This aspect of the narratives improved considerably as the series progressed, but it is too easy to say about the early books that Rendell was writing out of her time. Plenty of her contemporaries were never contemptible about women characters. In spite of this, Rendell, along with P D James, largely avoided writing stereotypical characters.

Contemporary crime writer Alison Bruce, a former taxi driver, dressmaker, paint sprayer, and electroplater, is the creator of the Cambridge crime series, featuring likeable male police lead DC Gary Goodhew, who first appeared in *Cambridge Blue* (2008). Although she chose a male lead for this series, Bruce says there are elements of herself in Goodhew.

'He loves maths, he is detached, he susses people out in his mind and he owns the jukebox,' she said. 'I wish I had. He is the character I wanted to read about that I hadn't found in other people's books. There were plenty of detectives at the other end of their career, three marriages down the line, a bit depressed, a bit alcoholic. Goodhew is working on his first murder investigation. He is a young man who had wanted to be in the police since he was eleven. He is sort of idealising what he thinks a detective is going to be. He was a guy I wanted to root for.'

Alison's first book came out of a deeply unpleasant relationship that went 'horribly wrong'. When it was over and she came to terms with the fact that she had been a victim, she mulled over the possibility that it could have been a great deal worse. I ended up in this situation that, in my head, included a dead body,' she said. 'And it was a way of murdering people that I hadn't read in anybody else's book. And I thought, this is interesting.'

Bruce did not set out to write a police procedural. 'Initially the book centres round a woman who has been in this abusive relationship,' she said. 'When the relationship breaks down, she takes control of her life by stalking her abuser so that she knows where he is. Then she realises that, wherever she finds him, there is a pattern tying his locations to a series of murders happening in the town. The woman phones the police anonymously and says if this man is stopped, the murders will stop. And I needed a policeman to answer that call. So, I wrote this policeman, just totally on the fly.'

Bruce believes there are advantages to having a male protagonist. 'When you write crime, much of the time the person in peril is female,' she said. 'If it's a woman or child, the odds are higher. Also, I've got three brothers and have always been a tomboy, so I found it easier. Writing a male lead was the natural thing to do, although the strong characters in all my books are women. They may be in danger, but they are at a crisis point and need determination to make hard decisions. All of them are determined. My women in my books are strong in the face of adversity.'

Two features of Alison Bruce's novels stand out. One is her detailed and memorable depiction of Cambridge, the other is the way she sets Detective Constable Goodhew, with his affection and respect for women, against Detective Sergeant Kincaid's misogyny.

Tana French does for Dublin what Alison Bruce does for Cambridge. French, born in Burlington, Vermont, is an American-Irish writer and theatrical actress and a longstanding resident of Ireland. She has been called the First Lady of Irish Crime. Her 2007 debut novel, *In The Woods*, expertly walks the line between psychological thriller and police procedural.

In *The Secret Place* (2014) and *The Trespasser* (2016), the Dublin Murder Squad's abrasive detective is Antoinette Conway who has a huge working-class chip on her shoulder and is disliked by her senior officers (and curiously also by her squad mates) for the very qualities that make her an excellent detective: cynicism, tenacity, outspokenness. Conway believes they are waiting for her to fail and she is determined to prove them wrong.

Alice Vinten has written a memoir called *Girl on the Line:*

Life – and Death – in the Metropolitan Police (2018), based on her own ten-year police career, from rookie constable to experienced officer. The book not only has the tension and excitement of crime fiction but exceeds it because it is real. This gritty and gripping account follows PC Alice Hearn through ten years in the Metropolitan Police, from rookie to constable. Her life is lived amidst petty crime, violent criminals, heart-breaking domestic situations – and the realisation of how different and how much more frightening her life is compared to the lives of her fellow male officers.

Crime writer Jane Casey, who has described Vinten's memoir as 'deeply moving and inspiring', has a similar protagonist in her series featuring Detective Sergeant Maeve Kerrigan. Kerrigan's attitude to her investigations is different from the hard-drinking, hardboiled stereotype of the typical male detective. 'Maeve has more in common with the victims than with anybody else in the room,' Casey said. 'They'll be looking at the body of a young woman, but she *is* the young woman. I think that gives her a different take on it. Maeve feels, that could be me lying there, while the other officers are thinking this person made mistakes that have put them in this position. As if it's their fault they've ended up dead.'

Kerrigan is an outsider. Like her creator, she is an Irish woman living in London, finding it hard to fit in. 'I think for crime writers, and for their characters, the best thing is to be a bit of an outsider,' Casey said. 'Maeve was the only woman on the team in the first books; she was on her own completely in every respect. She had to justify her place and work harder than everyone else. If you talk to actual police officers, they will say it's still a lads' club. And the women who do well in it are the ones who can engage with that kind of sense of humour and deal with it or ignore it completely and pretend it's not happening.'

It is important to Casey that her detective doesn't become

hard as a response. 'One of the things about her is that she's a sensitive person and quite attuned to other people,' she said. 'And it's about her finding ways to make people accommodate how she is, as much as it is about her working out how to cope with various things.'

On a day-to-day level, Kerrigan has to deal with her immediate boss Detective Inspector Josh Derwent, a difficult colleague who is unspeakably macho on the surface but with a much-hidden golden heart. The couple are constantly sparring. 'I brought him in to be a very difficult person for her to deal with,' Casey said. 'Somebody who was overtly sexist and abrasive. He put her in difficult situations constantly in that she was trying to juggle doing her job and not losing her temper with a senior officer who was actually all the time trying to get at her.

'But if you spend the amount of time that police officers do together, with the intensity of a murder investigation, I think you become very dependent on the people who are having the same experiences as you, and who see the same things as you. Maeve has the potential to be a bit of a goody two-shoes. She's very particular and perfectionist and she wants to do everything brilliantly. And he's a good balance because he's really quite reckless and she pulls him back. And he also pulls her back from trying to do the right thing always.'

In the later books, Kerrigan does have other women on the team: Liv, a 'very elegant and lovely' lesbian, and Georgia, who competes with her. 'Georgia is the younger of the two and she wants to step into her shoes, if necessary by pushing her out of them,' Casey said. 'And I think that's an interesting relationship. That Maeve doesn't want to be her mentor, but also doesn't want to be her victim. They're always angling around one another. And seeing Georgia do things differently is quite interesting. She is very pretty and trying to flirt with people and Maeve is saying, hold back from that, even though she could probably do that if she wanted to.

'I think women always have choices: is there room for me and you? Is there space for both of us in this very masculine environment? Do we have to pick between the two of us?'

Casey's novels are a taut mixture of police procedural and psychological thriller. There are issues Casey wishes to highlight throughout her police books, but she is wary of starting a novel with a central issue. 'I don't want to get into the polemical zone,' she said. 'Also, because I write in the first person, I have to be careful about putting my opinions in characters' mouths and taking away from who they are.'

In what ways do women writers think the police force in real life in Britain has changed in relation to women? 'I think they have tried to be more welcoming and more considerate and more aware of career progression,' Casey said. 'Although in this country there are some not good things happening with the police. Things like direct-entry superintendents. They are recruiting people who have no experience of police work, bringing them in as superintendents, because basically they are managers. I think that is difficult in an organisation based on trust and teams and on respecting authority. It is very difficult to say you must accord this person the same respect, even though they have no experience and they've never done the actual job of policing.'

Casey, like many contemporary crime writers, has in some ways made her central character stereotypical; she is white, fairly young, able-bodied and heterosexual. 'I do realise that I didn't think of making her older, or black, gay or disabled,' she said. 'But I have to say that some of these seeming advantages I have given her are, at the start, disadvantages. Being female, attractive and young also means not being taken seriously by men in the force. She has to make decisions about what she's going to do with her life, which a male detective doesn't have to do. Is she ever going to have children? Is she going to do something more desk-based? There are lots of things that are challenges for her despite the fact that she is a very privileged person. Some of those privileges are part of the challenges.

'I think I'm on the fence about this,' she added. 'Because I am a white woman and I don't necessarily want to write the story of what it's like to be a black detective in the Metropolitan Police. I want someone to write that story and do it brilliantly and I want to facilitate that, but I don't want to be the person who says, I know what this is like.'

Casey said she has tried not to have everyone in her novels heterosexual. Aside from her lesbian Liv, she has also featured a trans character. 'I thought about it and thought about it. It's the one thing I keep coming back to,' she said. 'Did I do a good enough job when writing this character? I wrote it four or five years ago, before there was so much about being trans. I did my best. I researched it. I was as sympathetic as I think I could be, given that it is not my story. I think I was fair to the characters, but I'm not sure that somebody who is trans would read it and think, this makes me feel seen or understood.'

In her 2013 novel *Dying to Know*, Alison Joseph's lead character Detective Inspector Berenice Killick is also the only woman in a police department run by men. Like Casey's Kerrigan, Yorkshire-born Killick is an outsider and has to struggle to get her voice heard. 'I tried to make a big change to my lead character's fictional entry into the police force by making her mixed race, and a stranger; a foreigner in a conventional police force,' Joseph said. 'I also tried to make my novel a very unconventional police procedural. In most police procedurals, you can't make your policewoman a lone hero because it is all about teamwork and team spirit. That is admirable, but for me it is not the fun stuff of crime writing. I wanted Berenice, my copper, to be slightly on the edge.'

Former bookseller Sarah Hilary has won a heap of writing awards including the Cheshire Prize for Literature (2012) and the Theakstons Old Peculier Crime Novel of the Year award for her debut novel *Someone Else's Skin* (2014), which was also a Richard and Judy pick and was selected as a title for UK's World Book Night. In the US, it won a Silver Falchion. This was followed a year later by her second novel *No Other Darkness* (2015) which was shortlisted for a Barry Award. There is nothing standard about the personal history and background of Hilary's protagonist, Detective Inspector Marnie Rome, nor her sidekick Detective Sergeant Noah Jake. The single-minded and often prickly Rome is one of the genre's most troubled detectives. Her parents were both murdered by her foster brother, who is in prison. Jake is both gay and multi-race and has family troubles of his own to contend with.

In the first book, the pair have to deal with the fallout after a domestic violence shelter is attacked. Marnie, who is tough in the competitive world of policing, finds she needs also to show the compassionate and intelligent, caring side of her nature. The plots in all of Hilary's novels are pacy yet sensitive and her prose is effortless and spins along.

Fellow writer Leigh Russell also takes a typical fictional police situation and lifts it out of the ordinary. She has female Detective Inspector Geraldine Steel partnered with the solid and reliable Detective Sergeant Ian Peterson, an enterprising duo in a genre that is overcrowded with similar detective partnerships. Russell is to be congratulated for making her Detective Inspector stand out in the crowd as both go-ahead and likeable.

The other feature that stands out about Russell is that, unlike most of the female writers I spoke to, she isn't especially critical of the police and she doesn't see herself as political. 'According to my sources, in London anyway, more than half of the top jobs in the force are now held by women and there is very little institutionalised sexism,' she said. 'It used to be rife, but things have changed.' Although Home Office figures show that, in March 2020, there were a little over 40,000 female officers working in England and Wales, only 31 per cent of the total, Russell said: 'I'm not 100 per cent certain about this gender divide. I think at heart we are all people, even if I don't know how men think. We all have the same fears and hopes and anxieties. Even if we are trained differently as we grow up. I don't think there should be organisations for women crime writers or men crime writers. We are just all crime writers. All people. We focus too much on differences, on colour of skin, on age, on gender. In my books I am even-handed. I have male killers and female killers, men who are abused, men who are stalked. And I have women the same. I am passionate about justice, that is what matters.'

Two high-flying, brilliant authors are Kate Atkinson and Susan Hill, who won the Somerset Maugham Award for *I'm The King of the Castle* (1970), the Whitbread Novel Award and a Booker Prize shortlisting for *The Bird of Night* (1972), the John Llewellyn Rhys Prize for her short story collection *The Albatross and Other Stories* (1971), the Nestle Smarties Book Prize for her picture book *Can It Be True? A Christmas Story* and a DBE for Services to Literature in 2020. Both writers have included in their repertoire two crime series that deal with a range of difficult and traumatic incidents: suicide, dementia, child abuse, sex trafficking, road rage and arson among them. As I have mentioned earlier, Atkinson has to date written five novels featuring the emotionally troubled but sympathetic private investigator Jackson Brodie. Hill has created the detached yet exceptional Detective Chief Inspector Simon Serrailler who works in the idyllic, fictional English cathedral town of Lafferton. Although their plots are skilful and engaging, what distinguishes Atkinson and Hill from many of the other writers I have read is their intricate hold on characterisation, the in-depth and insightful way they handle each character – not only their major protagonists – and their imaginative philosophical world view. In terms of writing literary, literate and dramatic fiction, they are unrivalled. Several crime writers I spoke to said they fear their own books were ephemeral and might not last. Patently Kate Atkinson and Susan Hill need not fear that.

Mari Hannah is another successful writer of unusual police procedural thrillers: the DCI Kate Daniels series. Having won a series of prizes for her early crime writing, she is now firmly established as an award-winning author whose major protagonist Daniels is a forthright lesbian, but one who conceals her sexuality within the police force. 'Kate, my protagonist, was loosely based on my partner of 30 years, who chose to hide her sexuality within the police for the same reason Kate did in the first novel,' Hannah said. 'She felt if she was open, it would hamper her chances of breaking through and getting a higher rank.'

Today there are moves within the police force to make it possible for women to be 'out' without overt recriminations. 'True,' Hannah said. 'But it is still a punitive institution. I have friends who left the police because of remarks by other officers. They felt they were vilified for life.'

The fictional Kate Daniels is not a stereotypical-looking woman. 'She doesn't wear five-inch heels,' Hannah said. 'She can run. Also, she is very clever and is seen to be clever.' She is noticeably clever in the novel *Without a Trace* (2020), where a plane en route from London to New York suddenly disappears, with Daniels' lover on board. She is not allowed to investigate the disappearance without authority but is unable to let it rest and puts herself in great danger trying to discover the truth.

Hannah believes police attitudes to women are changing, although imperceptibly. 'There will always be a label the police can hang on you,' she said. 'They have made many inroads. People can go on training courses and learn not to be homophobic. But whatever they say out loud is different from what they might be thinking.'

In spite of this, Hannah finds writing crime empowering. 'I feel through crime writing I can tackle big issues, both political and financial,' she said. 'The best crime writing can hold up a mirror to society.'

Another idiosyncratic idea comes from the feisty, fiery Martina Cole, whose protagonist DI Kate Burrows has a male partner, Patrick Kelly, a well-known criminal gangster. Kate Burrows is interesting because, in order to invent her, Cole broke her usual pattern of writing from the perspective of the criminal to write from the viewpoint of the police. Cole said she was determined to cross over to the other side of the law. When Burrows was first created in *The Ladykiller* (1993), Cole knew she had to be a very strong woman character to confront the fiercely competitive male police world. She made Burrows straitlaced to test whether a woman with high principles and a moral outlook could fall in love with such a notorious and powerful gangster. The developing interaction between Burrows and Kelly over the four books is even more fascinating than the compulsive, complex plots.

Cole, who has fans all over the world and has been called the Queen of British Crime Writing, is – after JK Rowling – Britain's most successful woman novelist. By the time she was 61 years old, she had written more than 22 crime novels, most of which explore London's gangster underworld. She has sold more than nine million books, over a dozen titles have been bestsellers and her work has been translated into 28 languages. Her hardbacks each sell an estimated 300,000 copies. Yet when you meet her, it is easy to think she is still just a blonde Essex-girl-made-good – honest, forthright and unbelievably talkative in a gravelly voice tinged with East London vowels. She comes from the brutal society of the London underworld. She knows to her bones whereof she writes, whether it is riotous girl gangs or male or female serial killers. She famously said that men are frightened of her, either because she has too much money or because she might axe them in the night. Her books are charismatic – they sweep you along – and when you meet her, she is just the same.

Advocate of good white wine, writer of good red books, if ever a series of crime novels matched their creator it is Cole's. They are sharp, edgy, always funny, sometimes violent, but as incisive and smart as is she. Her storytelling is immaculate and addictive.

I felt positive about her books before I met her and then I felt positive about her after I had. People who know her say she is warm, loving and kind and 'won't take shit from anyone'. She might be Britain's most independent woman, but there is one fact that continues to rile her. She is still marginalised by the literary community and rarely gets lengthy – or even any – reviews in the quality press. The snobbishness of journalists and critics does her and her writing a deep injustice.

Ann Cleeves is the outstanding British creator of three wonderful fictional police characters: Northumberland's Detective Chief Inspector Vera Stanhope; the dogged and determined Detective Inspector Jimmy Perez, who investigates crime in Shetland's close knit island community; and – in a new *Two Rivers* series set in north Devon – the diffident and angry gay detective Matthew Venn. Venn first appeared in *The Long Call* (2019) and the screen rights have been optioned by Silverprint Pictures, the company that produced the television series *Vera* for ITV and *Shetland* for the BBC.

Cleeves is unique in the way she describes and characterises Vera Stanhope. This detective stands out amongst all fictional women detectives by riding against stereotype and yet still being hugely popular. (Cleeves continues to be non-stereotypical by giving her newest Detective Inspector, Matthew Venn, a husband. No other mainstream, bestselling British crime writer has been that bold in coming out in such a positive direction on the male gay front.) Stanhope is proud of being on the wrong side of middle age, wears dreadful clothes and is plain and overweight. She is also highly competent, brainy, sensitive, witty and much loved by readers and viewers alike.

I have read remarkably few female crime protagonists who are in any way like Vera, except for Elly Griffiths' Ruth Galloway, a much younger woman who shares several key features with Vera. Galloway, who is in her late 30s, is awkward and ungirly and, like Cleeves' heroine, elicits a similarly loyal and affectionate response from readers. Galloway is not a member of the police force, but a forensic archaeologist who works closely with Detective Chief Inspector Harry Nelson, with whom she embarks on several mysteries and murder hunts.

Here is the first appearance of Galloway in the first of Griffiths' series, *The Crossing Places* (2009). She is in the shower. 'Ruth rubs herself vigorously with a towel and stares unseeingly into the steamy mirror. She knows what she will see. Shoulder-length brown hair, blue eyes, pale skin – and however she stands on the scales, which are at present banished to the broom cupboard – she weighs twelve and a half stone. She sighs (I am not defined by my weight, fat is a state of mind) and squeezes toothpaste onto her brush. She has a very beautiful smile.'[22]

Our first glimpse of Cleeves' Vera Stanhope in *The Crow Trap* (1999) is equally untypical. 'She was a large woman – big bones, amply covered, a bulbous nose, man-sized feet. Her legs were bare, and she wore leather sandals. Her square toes were covered in mud. Her face was blotched and pitted, so Rachael thought she must suffer from some skin complaint or allergy. Over her clothes she wore a transparent plastic mac and she stood there, the rain dripping from it on to the floor, grey hair sleeked dark to her forehead, like a middle-aged tripper caught in a sudden storm on Blackpool prom. She dismissed the policewoman. "Tea please, love". Then she held out a hand like a shovel. "Vera Stanhope," the woman said. "Inspector. You'll be seeing a lot of me".'[23]

We do see a lot of her. All of it funny, dashing, powerful and compelling. Cleeves told me she knew exactly what she was doing when she created Vera. 'I knew she was unlike every female protagonist I'd read,' she said. 'Those women with long hair and long legs. You think they wouldn't dress like that if they were real investigators. I loved Sara Paretsky's book but even VI, she can run, can't she? She can get a bloke, but I wanted someone different. I wanted Vera to be dowdy and overweight. But I wanted her to have authority and be confident.'

Cleeves says that when Vera makes her first appearance, she describes her as more of a bag lady than a detective. 'She came fully formed,' she said. 'Even with her name. She arrived scruffy, but smart. I want my characters to be credible. So, they don't all have to be middle-class. Vera certainly isn't. I want Vera to be a strong female character who will shake up people's preconceptions.'

Had her publishers acquiesced to such an unconventional protagonist? 'When *The Crow Trap* was published, I sold so few books nobody cared what I wrote,' Cleeves said. 'Until the first Shetland book came out in 2006, I was at the bottom of the heap and just managed to keep a publisher, because of public libraries really. It was really library readers who kept me going.'

Has being unacclaimed for so long affected how she feels about her enormous success today? 'Oh yes. I don't take anything for granted,' she said. 'I know how precarious this business is. And I know that I've been incredibly lucky. There are lots of brilliant, especially crime, writers out there who just haven't been picked up and haven't had the luck that I've had. If you are new and young, you can get seduced by the hype. You believe success comes because you are brilliant. Most sales come because you've got a very, very good marketing team behind you.'

Places are very important to Cleeves, for defining her characters. 'Community is very significant,' she said. 'We grow out of the people we live next door to. I believe the landscape we inhabit shapes us.' Vera's sidekick Joe Ashworth, like Vera herself, grows out of the Northumberland hills. 'Vera represents a certain part of the county,' Cleeves said. 'The country, the hills, the long horizons, the big skies. And Joe, I think, came out of the south east of the county, which used to have a lot of pits. He's a very principled part of the north east. So, it's about place again.

'I just tried to see them as how they would possibly work together,' she added. 'Because Joe starts off being quite gauche and scared of the educated middle classes. Vera doesn't give a damn. She'll go in and tell them how it is. And she's brought him on and made him more confident, I hope. She needs him just as much as he needs her. He is like her conscience, I think. And he doesn't want to break the rules. And again, that's kind of the other way around from most crime dramas and stories. That if you have a woman, she's the more caring, she's the more compliant. And I did want to swap that around a bit.'

Former police psychologist Emma Kavanagh is interesting for two reasons. First of all, she has written the first of what will be a three-book series featuring mentally and physically scarred DS Alice Parr as her lead along with an able woman detective partner called Polly. Secondly, she was a police and military psychologist when she was only 24 years old, providing training for police hostage negotiators. Her fascination with the workings of the criminal mind – and the people who operate on the extreme – began at university. 'Other students went into clinical psychology to see what happens when the brain goes wrong,' she said. 'I wanted to know what happens when it goes really right. When you put normal people into an extraordinary situation. How they cope and what it looks like in terms of brain function and performance. Kidnap and ransom to me, like a lot of the aspects of policing, is one of these extreme situations. As a negotiator, it's very much about keeping your cool, not allowing your emotions to take hold. The capacity to play somebody else, to manipulate someone else's emotions, it intrigued me.

'I'm interested in people operating on the extreme – in the hardest possible environment,' she added. 'And how they can do it successfully. A lot of what we do when somebody is recovering from a trauma is explain how they became traumatised. So, what I always wanted to do was to give them the knowledge beforehand in terms of how their brain was functioning when they went into a highly stressful situation, because that has a lot of behavioural influences in terms of decision-making, in terms of attention. And so, I always felt that there was a big difference we could make by putting that knowledge in and then incorporating it into their training.'

When she first started, it was terrifying. 'I was going up to these often big burly guys saying, I know something that could help you. And I was met with more than my fair share of scepticism. But I had made it my business to understand their world. I was familiar with guns. I was familiar with tactics. I could speak their language. I was very young, and it was terrifying, but I thought I could make a difference. I thought it could be of use to them if they would listen to me.'

Emma worked with NATO forces to prepare them for imminent death in Afghanistan. 'It all comes down to the same thing,' she said. 'It's about perceptual awareness, tension, memory and how all of those things function under stress. And it doesn't really matter what environment you're in. You can be talking about somebody having a panic attack in a supermarket, it's the same physiological response as somebody in a firefight in Afghanistan.'

Friends and colleagues had expected Kavanagh to write non-fiction about her experiences. 'But I knew I was a storyteller,' she said. 'I wanted to tell stories about people in extreme situations. And of course, crime is one of the most extreme situations you can find yourself in. And so, I wrote a story and my agent said, this is crime. And I'm like, okay, sure. And then it becomes about working it into the constraints of the genre. But I didn't set out to do that. I set out to tell stories. And I think even now, I write stories rather than I write crime.'

7

Women in the US Police

In America the facts and statistics relating to women's roles, representation and experiences within the police force are of great concern. To a lesser extent this is also true of Canada.

Today in the US, women only represent approximately a tenth of all law enforcement officers throughout the country. This is exceedingly low. More significantly, that figure has barely moved in the last 20 years. Women first entered the police force as prison matrons in the nineteenth century, charged with ensuring the welfare of female prisoners. In the early 1900s, some women became involved in moral reform movements, involving behaviours seen as vices, such as prostitution, alcoholism, gambling and public obscenity.

The first US policewomen were 37-year-old Alice Stebbin Wells, who was commissioned as an officer in Los Angeles city in 1910, and Lola Baldwin, who worked for the Portland police department in 1908, dealing with issues involving women and children. Also active were Marie Owens, who entered Chicago's police department in 1891, and Fanny Bixby, who worked in Long Beach city in California from 1908.

Policewomen who came after them were mainly middle or upper-class. Some had previously counselled criminals and some were energetic Christians; most of them were used for desk work, supervising criminals, dealing with runaway children, 'sexual delinquents' and prostitutes, and helping homeless women and girls. Women's roles, which also included dealing with shoplifters and petty thieves, reflected a focus on moral reform and this characterised how they were seen in law enforcement during the late 1800s and early 1900s.

In 1915, the International Association of Policewomen was formed to work for more opportunities for women. Sadly, the movement, which did see more women enter the police, gradually diminished and its role grew stale. From 1930 until the early 1960s, policewomen took on more secretarial and clerical duties. They also worked as parking meter attendants or despatchers or questioned female offenders or witnesses. Very few actively investigated crimes. It wasn't until working-class women began to train as police officers and, aided by the Civil Rights Act of 1964, agitated for diversity and power in their responsibilities, that women had more official and widespread roles at all levels.

When the second wave of feminism overtook America in the late 1970s and 1980s, and equal opportunity legislation was established, policies that limited opportunities for women to take leadership roles were changed and men could no longer openly discriminate against hiring women and minorities. The number of policewomen had crept up to 11.9 per cent by 2014, yet there was a definite brass ceiling and, within each police department, no one actively recruited female officers. The culture was entirely dominated by males. There were no family-friendly policies and most recruitments were heavily biased towards physical agility testing. The rates for female employment stagnated. Women who would not or could not join the 'boys' club' did not join the police. If women did pass the entry tests, they were more often given traffic jobs or administrative posts. Few went out on patrol. Recruitment today still favours candidates who have high upper body strength and military experience. The highest percentage of female officers today can be found in larger police departments in big cities, such as Los Angeles, New York and Chicago.

Contemporary American female crime writers face the reality

that, outside their novels, women dealing with law and order have struggled for decades to gain acceptance from male colleagues in the workplace. They suffer from a huge lack of representation and from stereotypes around women which continue to hold them back on every front. American policewomen still have very low rates of participation. They are often afraid to go for promotion over male colleagues because they fear they will be harassed and oppressed for so doing. In their everyday police life, they are left out of office events, are not part of squad bonding events and are often subjected to rude, sometimes obscene comments and sexual harassment. Because of this, they find it almost impossible to build trust or connections with their colleagues. This makes their work in the field more dangerous.

American crime novelist Kristen Lepionka has written a series of four novels featuring private investigator Roxane Weary. Weary made her first appearance in *The Last Place You Look* (2017), which was given a Shamus award for best first PI novel. Lepionka said she wrote from the perspective of a female private eye because, like other women crime writers, she wanted to take on what has historically been 'a bit of a boys' club'. 'A crime novel from the point of view of a female detective is much more than just a difference of chromosomes,' she said. 'Women obviously have a different experience to men of moving through the world – and law enforcement – which is necessarily reflected in these stories. Female detectives in fiction contend with rampant sexism, being underestimated, excluded, and harassed, in addition to battling the mysteries at the centre of their cases. They also bring a different sensibility to their work and solve crimes in ways that men never could.'[24]

American crime writer Katherine V Forrest, who created LAPD lesbian detective Kate Delafield, has a related but different take on some of the problems faced by women in the police, and by women writing about those issues. 'There is a real resentment of women in law enforcement,' she said. 'Even though women bring to it a very needed and necessary leavening of police work in general. Some significant fiction mirrors this.'

Forrest did think the US police had changed its attitude towards gay women in the last few years. 'Police organisations throughout America reflect our society in general,' she said. 'Life has always been a little easier for lesbians than for gay men. There seems to be an irrational – and it is irrational – hatred of gay men. And I have told my gay brothers, I've told them every chance I get; feminism is not *our* issue, it is *your* issue. Homophobia is really based, I profoundly believe, on contempt for women. And that's why I think male homosexuals are in so much more danger than women are.'

Forrest credited Sara Paretsky, not only for bringing issues of social justice into mystery fiction for the first time, but for giving the world the strong, assertive private investigator VI Warshawski, who was brave enough to stand up to the police. 'I think women have been hungry for ever to see these strong, assertive and powerful women in fiction,' Forrest said. She believes Kate Delafield, her own detective, brought a modicum of justice to the world when she first appeared in *Amateur City* in 1984. 'And it was a world that we lived in back then where there really wasn't much justice,' she said. 'So, those portraits, I think, were extremely important to us. Although frankly, this isn't anything I thought about at all when I was writing.'

Ironically, in some crime narratives, the policewomen protagonists are considerably more able to stand up to discrimination, sexism and verbal abuse from their male colleagues than their counterparts in real life are. According to writer and former physician Tess Gerritsen, police officers who read her books say that her narratives do not accurately reflect real life; that they greatly over-represent women police officers and are extremely optimistic about their treatment within the force. It was only in 1982 for instance, that women in Chicago were able to take the detective exam and serve with the regular police force. The situation was similar in Boston, where Tess Gerritsen lives and sets her novels.

'It was very difficult in the police force when I first started my research for the Rizzoli series,' she said. 'I interviewed detectives at the Boston homicide unit, where at the time there was one woman in a twelve-person unit. When I went back a few years later, that one woman had resigned, so it was back to being an all-male unit. It must be tough to be a woman in the police, certainly in Boston. That city does not have a good record for being kind to female cops.'

Gerritsen believes one of the problems for women is the fact that the police force attracts people who feel that men are dominant. A woman who wants to make it as a cop has to be tougher than the men. And sometimes – often unlike their fictional counterparts – they have to turn the other cheek. 'I talked to a couple of women who are Boston patrol officers,' Gerritsen said. 'They told me working with the men gives them problems, but they don't bother to complain anymore because nothing ever changes.'

In Gerritsen's novels, policewomen are more active and successful than they may be in similar real-life situations. In *The Silent Girl* (2011), investigating detective Jane Rizzoli has to work twice as hard as her male colleagues to solve the grisly murder of a young woman in Chinatown. She refuses to back off, even when her husband Gabriel becomes worried about her safety. Gerritsen chose to introduce a police detective rather than a private investigator in the first in the series, *The Surgeon* (2001), because the story was about a serial killer and the hunt for him would inevitably involve official police business. 'At that point, I knew little about the American police force,' she said. 'But touring the Boston police department helped, as did conversations with a retired Boston cop, who told me some hair-raising stories.'

Gerritsen believes women write police fiction in a different way from men. 'My main characters are female, so that in itself is different,' she said. 'I make a point of them having outside lives and personal struggles, such as finding love. Women crime writers seem to focus more on that. Maybe because we feel our biological clock ticking. We have to settle down early on if we want to have children. We have to struggle with such questions as, do I want children, or how do I combine that with a really demanding job?'

How does Gerritsen avoid the trap of falling into stereotypes when creating her female characters? Are the women police and other female protagonists in crime novels destined to be white, young and attractive? 'I avoided that trap with Rizzoli,' she said. 'I purposely said she was *not* attractive. I did not want her to be a good-looking woman. I wanted her to be somebody we would all identify with. Jane Rizzoli started by being the homely gal that men don't pay attention to, and I loved that about her. As the series has progressed, that seems to be the thing most readers like about her, that she is not attractive. She is Everywoman. And then when they made it into a TV show, she became gorgeous, of course. They changed everything.'

Gerritsen also avoided stereotypes when creating Rizzoli's fellow crime fighter, medical examiner Dr Maura Isles, who is first introduced in *The Apprentice* (2002), the second novel in the series. In *Body Double* (2004), the adopted Isles discovers her long-lost birth mother is a serial killer and her younger brother is a murderer. Gerritsen came up with this idea after reading a true crime story about a man who discovered both his father and his grandfather were serial killers. 'What a horrifying thing to discover,' she said. 'What does that make you? It makes you question yourself. Who am I, that I come down from such evil? That's really where that particular thread came from. The idea of being a child of monsters and being horrified by it. Does it make you wonder about your future?'

Gerritsen is aware that none of her police characters to date are elderly or gay, although she has been working on a story about a retired spy, a woman in her 60s. 'We do need more older women as heroines,' she said. 'Not only are they just as capable as a young person, they have the wisdom of experience. Here's the reality of it. When we write books, it seems that Hollywood only cares about stories that have young, glamorous characters in them. That's one part of the market we're always considering – is this saleable to movie rights? The other thing is that it seems the audience itself is much more interested in reading about attractive people. So, it's the readership we are thinking about. But I think that there's certainly a number of readers who are very happy to read about somebody very much like themselves.'

Maureen Jennings and Louise Penny, two of Canada's foremost crime writers, both have police investigators as their lead protagonists. The two women went to the same university, although at different times and they both started writing later in life. Both had their early work rejected. Louise Penny, a former radio journalist, was 46 years old when she published her debut novel *Still Life* in 2005. The book had been either rejected or ignored by 50 publishers, yet went on to win the CWA John Creasey Dagger, the New Blood Dagger Award, the Arthur Ellis Award, the Dilys Award, the 2007 Anthony Award and the Barry Award. Her *New York Times* bestselling mystery series has since won more than 30 awards and she has sold more than six million books worldwide. In 2014, she was awarded the Order of Canada for her contribution to Canadian culture.

Penny's lead protagonist is the thoughtful and deeply disciplined Armand Gamache, the chief inspector of Surete du Quebec, the provincial police force for Quebec. Gamache, a native French speaker who speaks English with a British accent picked up when he was an undergraduate at Christ's College, Cambridge, is kind, compassionate, philosophical and highly intelligent. He lives in the fictional village of Three Pines, where he investigates a series of horrific murders. Gamache's job means he has to dig below the idyllic surface of village life, to discover long-buried secrets. He is surrounded by a family and group of friends who appear in every novel.

The books are suffused with Canadian history and are intensely character-driven, with a focus on analysis of Gamache's own personality and life, and his relationships with his wife and friends. They are beautifully written literary novels that happen to contain a crime. Dan Bilefsky, writing in the *New York Times,* said Penny's books were 'more intricately wrought tone poems than procedurals' with Gamache at their moral centre.[25] Hillary Clinton, in her memoir, said Louise Penny's books brought her solace after her 2016 election defeat. The novels bear many of the trademarks of the classic British whodunnit genre and feature murders by unconventional means, red herrings, idyllic village settings and a large cast of suspects.

Fellow Canadian writer Maureen Jennings was 55 years old when her debut mystery novel, *Except the Dying* (1997), introduced her sympathetic and much-loved Victorian detective William Murdoch, a kind-hearted Catholic working in a Protestant city. Murdoch is ahead of his time, preferring to use science, including the then radical methods of fingerprinting, lie-detecting machines and trace evidence, rather than muscle or fists to get to the bottom of some of Toronto's most gruesome murders.

Except the Dying finds Murdoch grieving for his dead fiancée, while investigating the murder of a young housemaid. The book was shortlisted for Arthur Ellis and Anthony awards for best novel and received a Heritage Toronto Certificate of Commendation. Later Murdoch books have also received literary awards. As well as achieving global popularity, the novels have been adapted for the long-running, award-winning television series *Murdoch Mysteries,* which has been shown around the world.

Maureen was born in England, where she grew up without a father, who was killed in action during World War II. With her mother, she emigrated to Ontario in her late teens. Always a bookworm, she moved to Toronto in the 1960s to study for a Masters' degree in English Literature and went on to teach English at Ryerson University. On the faculty were a group of writers, including poet Gary Geddes, the late rapper, Californian Eric Lynn Wright, and the Canadian novelist Graeme Gibson, who was later Margaret Atwood's partner and father to their daughter Jess. Together that group inspired Jennings to consider writing as a career, although it was not until years later, after she had trained as a psychotherapist, that she would commit to the craft.

'I had started to write creative expression books to help women – it was mostly women – to find out what was lurking in their hearts,' she said. 'One day I thought, what am I doing? I am trying to release creativity in these women, but for myself I have just piddled around. I've done a little of this, a little of that. It is time to commit to writing. I was about 53 years old when I seriously said this is what I want to do. My first book was published when I was 55.'

It was easy for Jennings to choose crime as the category to write in. She had been addicted to the genre when younger. She decided to focus in her novels on the workings of the police in the late nineteenth century because the Victorians fascinated her. She has also written a series of four novels set in England during the Second World War, featuring detective Tom Tyler, and two novels about forensic profiler Christine Morris. Her 2019 novel *Heat Wave,* which is set in Toronto in 1936, introduces Charlotte Frayne, a junior associate in a two-person private investigation firm.

All of Jennings' stories subtly address important social and political issues, such as prejudice, injustice and inequality. 'I like writing about domestic and social issues, especially in wartime,' she said. 'And the problems of those who were coping at home. And I can never reconcile myself to the inequality in finances, between social classes and between women and men. Not just here but everywhere.'

Although two of Jennings' lead protagonists are men, women play big roles in her books. She worries about the challenges for women in all classes and in all occupations, including the police. In *Heat Wave,* Charlotte Frayne has to go undercover into a sweatshop because the employer thinks the women there are going to go on strike and he wants to discover the identity of the 'Commie' agitator.

Writing first-person female characters has been both a change and a challenge. 'I've always liked having a male protagonist because they become like the idealised man,' she said. 'They know what they are doing. They save the situation. I love Sara Paretsky and Sue Grafton and I love their female protagonists, but there is something about this fatherly figure that has always satisfied me. What I like is that, at the end of each book, the detective has figured it out and has re-established order. That is very satisfying.

'At the same time, I really tried to make the male characters believable, but you can't. Not really. I don't think you can – unless you're a guy writing about a guy – capture all those internal things.'

Jennings acknowledges her training as a psychotherapist – her understanding of how the human mind works – has been invaluable to her writing. 'Certainly, as a therapist, it is not unlike a mystery,' she said. 'People come presenting certain problems. You have to find out what they are. When I am writing, I always try to do a detailed background, even if it is not obvious. That person should have a reason, even if they are the killer. Why are they doing it? I try every time to bring that in. I try to make the characters have dimensions, not only for the convenience of my plot. That comes from working in therapy, from knowing how much depth there is in everybody.'

Former Deputy District Attorney Alafair Burke, who continued to teach criminal law in New York while writing her first five crime books, has Portland prosecutor Samantha

Kincaid as the lead protagonist in her first three novels. The series brought her instant acclaim and praise for her idiomatic prose, offbeat style and great pace. Her second series featured NYPD detective Ellie Hatcher. 'It wasn't hard to shift to a detective novel because, as a prosecutor, I'd spent two years as a liaison to the police and worked out of a police precinct,' Burke said. 'I went out regularly with patrol officers.' Burke says that misogyny in the American police force varies from city to city. 'There are departments that are very good about handling the culture that includes not only women but also people of colour,' she said. 'Then there are those that are not so good about it. I think New York as a diverse city is fairly good, yet I think some people would be surprised at how old-school the NYPD can be.'

To date, Burke is the internationally bestselling author of 20 crime titles. Her standalone novels have earned her a reputation for being a genius at plot. Her two series are prized for their authenticity. She has also written a third series, 'Under Suspicion', with bestselling suspense writer Mary Higgins Clark, who died in 2020, aged 92. These five novels feature another female protagonist, Laurie Moran, the producer of a television show that re-examines high-profile cold cases by examining the people closest to the crimes: the victims, suspects and witnesses.

Burke was born in Fort Lauderdale, Florida but grew up in Wichita, Kansas. Her lifelong fascination with crime and its consequences can be traced back to her childhood, and a series of murders in Wichita. Over a 17-year period between 1974 and 1991, Dennis Lynn Rader murdered 10 people. He was not caught and arrested until 2005 and Burke grew up knowing the killer could be anyone in her hometown and that he could strike anywhere, at any time.

'We had just moved to Wichita,' Burke said. 'This guy would knock on a family's door in the middle of the day and kill the entire family. It was terrifying, I was eight years old. Wichita is a fairly small city of around 300,000 people and everybody who grew up there, grew up with this ritual. You would immediately lock the door when you got home. People kept locks on their basement doors and would always check the phone line as soon as they got home, as he would cut the phone lines. You'd always check to see if the phone line was working.'

Safety for women is a central issue in Burke's novels. 'In my recent books I explore a different kind of danger,' she said. 'The danger you don't know to look out for. You don't realise how dangerous the people closest to you can be. Statistically that is unique to women. We now know that women are more likely to be victimised by the people they love, the people they are trying to take care of.'

Detective Ellie Hatcher and her first outing in *Dead Connection* (2007) came directly through Burke's own experience with an online dating service, through which she met her husband. 'Whenever I opened one of those emails, I wondered about how and why we decide it is safe to trust a stranger,' she said. In that first Hatcher novel, two New York women are killed after arranging dates via an online service. Hatcher has only been in the police force a year when she is moved to the homicide task force to help track down the killer. Hatcher's father is believed to have committed suicide after failing in his hunt to find a Wichita serial killer. One legacy her beloved father left her was the belief that if you can discover the motive, this will lead you to the killer. This is at the root of Hatcher's scalpel curiosity about human motives.

'I think this is quite typical of fictional detectives,' Burke said. 'Arguably, Harry Bosch is always trying to solve his mother's murder. Dave Robicheaux is always trying to save his mother. If you have the investigator have a reason for chasing these alleys of darkness, it's more compelling.' Dave Robicheaux is the recovering alcoholic Cajun detective created by masterly crime writer James Lee Burke, who is also Alafair Burke's father. In the Robicheaux novels, the elder Burke gave his fictional detective an exotic adopted daughter, also called Alafair. Harry Bosch is a veteran police detective with the Los Angeles Police Department, a lead character invented by fellow crime writer Michael Connelly, whom Burke much admires.

Burke's characters are always positive advocates for people on the margins, something which shows in her first Samantha Kincaid novel, *Judgement Calls* (2003). The young female prosecutor is prepared to take up a case where a young girl prostitute gets attacked. 'Kincaid is willing to fight for that case in a way the more seasoned male attorneys are not,' Burke said. 'She's willing to go out on a limb for what she really thinks is right. And I think Ellie Hatcher shares that attribute. That they're really willing to stick their necks out, a real sense of right and wrong.'

Meg Gardiner, who was born in Oklahoma, is 12 years older than Burke but, unlike her fellow writer, did not come from a literary background. She has native American Chickasaw heritage and still has voting rights as a Chickasaw citizen. Her background is academic rather than literary. Her father was an English professor and, after graduating from high school in Santa Barbara, she went to Stanford University where she attained a Bachelors' degree in economics. 'I think I knew then I wanted to become a professional writer, but my father suggested I stay cautious,' Gardiner said. 'He said I could either try to become a novelist and end up waiting on tables in a deadbeat café while writing the Great American Novel or I could become a lawyer who writes novels after work.'

She took his advice and became a trial lawyer. In California she practised law professionally and was a travel writer. Today she lives in Austin, one of America's loveliest and most exciting cities. She did however spend a considerable time in the UK, moving with her family to Surrey in England in the 1990s, where she stayed until 2013, and this is where her writing flourished. 'It was hard for me to practise law or even teach law in England,' she said. 'As all my children were at least going to pre-school, and I had more time, I joined a Women's Group, the American Women of Surrey, which was fabulous. I found out they had a writers' group. I joined that and they became my little community of inspiration, motivation, deadlines... They really kept my feet to the fire.'

Gardiner's first novel, *China Lake*, was published in 2002 and featured spirited and quick-witted Californian freelance journalist Evan Delaney. Four further Delaney novels followed over the next four years, but Gardiner's big break didn't come until 2007, after writer Stephen King picked up a copy of *China Lake* by chance at an airport and wrote a column for *Entertainment Weekly* saying how great he thought the book – and Gardiner's writing – was. *China Lake* won the Edgar Award for Best Paperback Original in 2009.

Gardiner followed the Delaney series with four novels featuring rock-climbing forensic psychiatrist Jo Beckett, whose job is to analyse the dead for the police by examining their possessions, obsessions, habits and rituals. *The Dirty Secrets Club* (2008) was chosen as one of the top ten thrillers by Amazon. It also won the Romantic Times Award for Best Procedural of the Year. Her fourth Beckett book *The Nightmare Thief* (2011) won the Audie Award for Thriller/Suspense audiobook of the year.

The third series revolves around the life and work of fictional former police detective Caitlin Hendrix, now a rookie FBI profiler. The first of these, *Unsub* (2017), is based on the true story of the Zodiac Killer, who was never caught, a case that terrified her as a child, lingered in her mind for years, and heavily influenced her writing. The second, *Into the Black Nowhere* (2018), is inspired by the Ted Bundy killings. The third, *The Dark Corners of the Night* (2020), draws on the case of the LA Night Stalker, who terrorised families in Los Angeles in the 1980s.

'I am interested in what makes people tick and what is going on in their psyche,' Gardiner said. 'Crime narratives are about people facing extreme dangers. Taking terrible risks. It is also about confronting evil, which you don't do in many aspects of your life. I think crime writing gets to the very heart of the human condition.'

In all of her books, Gardiner is driven by the idea of justice, and the fine line between morality and crime and what has to be done to get the right results. This is due partly to her legal background and partly to her own fierce views on morality. In all of her writing, she tries to explore the boundary between morality and wrongdoing. No subject should be taboo. 'If it scares me, it will scare a reader,' she said. 'And then I know it is suitable.'

In the *Unsub* series, Gardiner may have been writing about three evil serial killers, but she wanted specifically to explore the mind and the motivations of her investigator Hendrix and her family. 'I wanted to write about a cop,' she said. 'I wanted to write about someone who gets in over her head with a case that has both public and personal resonance.'

Gardiner's books also explore those all-important family relationships: Hendrix and her broken father, Evan Delaney and her ex-sister-in-law, who has joined a dangerous and fanatical religious cult. 'I love writing about family relations,' she said. 'As an author, what makes any story more resonant is the connections between the characters; their tangled histories, the bond of family and how they're estranged. That's one reason why I've used family so much in a lot of the books. We're all part of families, whether we like it or not.'

The United States and Canada have such a large number of female crime writers who focus on police mysteries that it is impossible to do justice to them all. But it is important to mention some of the finest: Linda Castillo, Karin Slaughter, Martha Grimes, Deborah Crombie and Elizabeth George, the last three of whom, idiosyncratically and highly successfully, have set their police books in England.

Linda Castillo is the *New York Times* bestselling author of the Kate Burkholder series, which is set in Amish country in the sleepy rural town of Painters Mill, Ohio. Amish and English residents have lived peacefully side by side in the town for two centuries until a series of brutal murders by someone called The Slaughterhouse Killer shatters the community. Burkholder was a young Amish girl who survived its terrors but decided she no longer belonged with the Amish and left town. Many years later she is asked to return as Chief of Police. It is an intriguing narrative and makes me think of Melanie McGrath's similar eccentric but compelling Arctic mystery series involving Inuit hunter and guide Edie Kiglatuk.

Karin Slaughter, who was born in Georgia but lives in Atlanta, is one of the world's most popular and acclaimed storytellers. Published in 120 countries with more than 35 million copies of her work sold across the globe, her 19 novels include the Will Trent books and the Grant County series, featuring Chief of Police Jeffrey Tolliver and the woman he married twice, paediatrician and coroner Sara Linton.

The level and nature of violence in Karin Slaughter's work has been criticised. Certainly, the narrative around Sara Linton is brutal. After working her shift as paediatric resident at Atlanta's Grady Hospital, Linton is savagely attacked in the restroom, raped and left for dead. The rape results in an ectopic pregnancy and partial hysterectomy, meaning she will never be able to have children. Linton moves back to Grant County, where she remarries her former husband Jeffrey Tolliver. The couple apply to adopt a child and eventually receive word they will become parents to a nine-month-old boy. Only minutes later, Tolliver is killed in an explosion.

Slaughter's second police series features Special Agent Will Trent, who works for the Criminal Apprehension team of the Georgia Bureau of Investigation where he teams up with Faith Mitchell, a homicide detective with the Atlanta police department. Sara Linton also features alongside Trent and Mitchell, having moved back to Atlanta after Tolliver's death. Together, the trio investigate a series of brutal and bloody murders. The plots are tense and cleverly twisted, the gruesome descriptions include women's mutilated bodies left in pools of their own blood, a teenage girl found dead by her mother as a man with a bloody knife looms over the body and a torture chamber hidden outside a hospital where female patients have been victims of a sick and sadistic killer.

As well as the two police series, Slaughter has written the Edgar-nominated and *New York Times* bestseller *Cop Town*, her first standalone novel, which is set in 1974 Atlanta and is in development for film and television. It is an epic tale of a city in the midst of seismic terror, as a serial killer targets cops at the male-dominated police department.

'The point about writing thrillers is to hold a mirror up to society,' Slaughter said. 'And society in the 1970s was rigidly restrictive to women. They couldn't do most things like getting a mortgage, even getting contraception without a man's permission, or a man co-signing the documents. I have invented two new women protagonists in *Cop Town* who both face huge misogyny from their police colleagues.'

American writer Martha Grimes is known best for her Scotland Yard Detective Inspector, Richard Jury, one of whose patches is Long Piddleton, an idyllic British rural town very different from Slaughter's Atlanta. Piddleton was first introduced to enthusiastic American readers in *The Man with a Load of Mischief* (1981).

Grimes' fiction, like many writers of classic English mystery, is highly literary. There are regular allusions to Shakespeare, Browning, Rimbaud, Henry James, Marlowe, Coleridge and Trollope. A pertinent example of Grimes cleverly using her literary knowledge is how, in *The Man with a Load of Mischief*, one murder is made possible by the way in which a specific scene from *Othello* is staged. Grimes' two detectives are reminiscent of classic English upper-class policemen. Her two central characters are Richard Jury and his collaborator Melrose Plant, who was formerly the twelfth Viscount Ardry and Eighth Earl of Caverness.

Jury is handsome, tall, formidable yet reflective. Although absolutely professional, he resembles the classic literate and cultured amateur detective, such as P D James' Adam Dalgliesh and Ngaio Marsh's DCI Roderick Alleyn. Melrose Plant is wealthy and a little precious, an aristocrat who takes some elements from Dorothy L Sayers' Lord Peter Wimsey and some from Margery Allingham's Albert Campion. Plant even has a gentleman's gentleman to look after him. Grimes, though in some ways thoroughly American, manages to reproduce British idiosyncratic lingo perfectly and her books have a comic sparkle, which is a relief, coming as it does amongst so many heavy and grim crime novels.

Deborah Crombie, who was born in Dallas and grew up in Richardson, Texas, has also set her 18 novels in the UK. She has always had a passion for Britain, a connection cemented when she took a post-university trip there. Later she immigrated to the UK with her first husband Peter Crombie, living initially in her husband's home country Scotland, and later in Chester, England.

A trip to Yorkshire inspired her first Gemma James/Duncan Kincaid novel, *A Share in Death* (1993), which was shortlisted for Agatha and Macavity awards for Best First Novel. Her skilful plotting and compassionate understanding of her characters contributed to her winning other prizes, including a *New York Times* Notable award for her fifth novel *Dreaming of the Bones* (1997). This title, also named by the Independent Mystery Booksellers as one of the 100 Best Crime Novels of the Century, was an Edgar nominee for Best Novel and won the Macavity Award for Best Novel.

Crombie's Detective Inspector Gemma James is one of the most sympathetic and engaging fictional police officers I have come across. James' colleague and husband, Scotland Yard Detective Superintendent Duncan Kincaid, is also emotionally textured and richly realised, as a human being as well as a police officer. In her first book, Crombie translates the English country-house puzzle for contemporary times. Several American critics have suggested that her combination of British whodunnit with an intense psychological examination of her characters is reminiscent of P D James. Although she travels to England frequently, Crombie now lives in a Texas Craftsman bungalow with her second husband Rick Wilson and several cats and dogs.

Sometimes called the Crime Queen of the Anglophiles, American Elizabeth George has reaped enormous critical acclaim and huge popular success with her series of mysteries set in England. Both the original novels and the addictive television adaptations feature charismatic CID Detective Inspector Thomas Lynley, who is also Eighth Earl of Asherton, has an Eton and Oxford background and is as classically British as any of the Golden Age detectives. When he is described in *A Great Deliverance* (1988) as a 'tall man who managed to look as if somehow he'd been born wearing morning dress', it is hard not to recall Lord Peter Wimsey.[26]

Lynley's movements are in keeping with his appearance, being graceful, fluid and cat-like. Powerfully adept at his job and universally liked, he is also rich, lives in Belgravia, owns an ancestral home in Cornwall and has a Bentley to deliver him from one house to the other. It is hardly surprising that, in that first book, Detective Sergeant Barbara Havers initially loathes him. She is confrontationally working class, lives initially with her parents in Acton, north London, wears ill-fitting, badly designed clothes and is chubby, awkward, plain, honest and rude. Although she admits Lynley is 'the golden boy in more ways than one' and acknowledges he is 'the handsomest man' she has ever seen, on first sight she cannot stand him.

She has been assigned to work with him as his sergeant and becomes, over the books that follow, his permanent and eventually much liked and admired partner. So far in her police career, the huge chip on her shoulder rendered her incapable of getting along with a single detective inspector. She has been cautioned, warned, advised and even demoted, but nothing stops her angry outbursts and what her superiors see as 'insolent' behaviour. She has been given one last chance, to work with Lynley, who is seen as a man of infinite patience, rare understanding, and impeccably good manners. This partnership is a witty feast for readers in a very long series of fascinating books. Eventually the partnership pays off for both Lynley and Havers, who may never become equals but will learn to respect one another, to understand their divergent qualities and finally become friends.

A Great Deliverance opens up the characters of the two initially embattled protagonists and has many twists and turns that mirror Barbara Havers' sad and unruly life, which is cleverly detailed. Her parents are unsettled and unsettling; her mother is edging towards dementia, her father is addicted to snuff and to betting, habits which severely strain the family finances. Visually, their house is intimidating, as there is a huge shrine in the living room devoted to Havers' brother, who died when he was ten years old. Havers has placed the shrine there to make sure her parents feel guilty for not visiting their son when he was sick, and because of her own guilt for not being with him when he died.

Elizabeth George expertly matches pieces of the plot with Havers' home life. In their first outing together, Lynley and his sergeant are sent out to a Yorkshire dale village to investigate the murder of a Yorkshire farmer, who had built a shrine to his wife, who had mysteriously disappeared. The elder of two daughters, who was found next to her father's body, initially confessed to the crime before reverting to a long silence and a coma-like stupor. Lynley and Havers are unable to find a motive or a murder weapon or track down the younger daughter. Ultimately, they discover the father had been a religious obsessive who had systematically sexually abused his one remaining daughter. When Lynley and Havers witness the two girls' reunion, their ensuing outbursts about the abuse have such a terrifying effect on Havers that she is violently sick in the rest room before being overcome by weeping, for her own guilt and misery and sadness. Lynley follows her and, without speaking, takes her in his arms and comforts her. This triggers the first big change in their relationship. Havers now realises he is not a loathsome, superficial womaniser and he now understands her pain. And he appreciates her honesty and her ability as a policewoman. He is also self-aware enough to realise that Havers' anger against him, although misdirected, is not entirely off its mark for he does have failings and, in the past, has behaved badly. Together the detectives are able to stumble through the case and discover that it is the younger daughter who murdered her father.

This first book is important because it shows that both protagonists are highly serious and moral people who, every time in every novel, are determined to find the truth. It is this moral severity and deep conscience which makes Elizabeth George's novels markedly different from those of the Golden Age. Earlier aristocratic detectives, like Wimsey and Albert Campion, are flimsy and light-hearted. Lynley is not. Elizabeth George's novels are entertaining to read but they have a moral purpose, as all profound crime fiction should. Lynley is a decent, principled and moral character who is not designed purely for readers' entertainment. More police fiction with such thoughtful and serious moral purpose would be welcome.

8

Lesbian Protagonists Appear

Today there are more than 1,000 lesbian mystery titles and more than 250 authors writing lesbian mysteries, around 95 per cent of whom are still living and writing crime. In spite of these highly encouraging figures, most readers will have seen very few of these titles in bookshops or online, largely because only a small cluster of prominent lesbian authors are being published by mainstream publishers.

Crime fiction featuring a lesbian protagonist was initially limited to small specialist publishers, such as Seal Press and Naiad Press. It wasn't until the early 1990s that mainstream publishers dipped their hands in the water. Even then, they restricted their venture in the US to already well-known writers, such as Katherine V Forrest, Ellen Hart and Sandra Scoppettone, who were liberal feminist rather than radical feminist and seen as less likely to rock any boats. Shamefully, this was more than ten years after the boom in female private investigators in the 1980s.

Readers in Britain may now be familiar with the American and Canadian writers, who include Forrest, Hart and Scoppettone along with Joan Drury, Sarah Dreher and, of course, Patricia Highsmith. Americans and Canadians may now be able to find in their own bookstores a variety of English and Scottish lesbian authors, including Val McDermid, Mari Hannah, Manda Scott, Stella Duffy, Natasha Cooper and Nicola Upson.

Publishers on both sides of the water are still inclined to stick to traditional definitions of a lesbian mystery for their intake. Two features must hold steady. First of all, the main character must be a lesbian or bisexual woman in a same sex relationship. Secondly, the main character must investigate a crime or solve a mystery or puzzle central to the novel's narrative. Protagonists can be private investigators, law enforcement officers or amateur sleuths of any profession.

British writer Claire Macquet set her first novel *Looking for Ammu* (1992) in South Africa and London. The descriptions are unusual and excellent; seamy surroundings, menacing criminals and even explicit sex, a contrast to the clean and pleasing Harriet Weston, the book's lead protagonist. Macquet has also written a book of distinctive short stories, *The Flying Hart* (1991).

Writer Peta Fox offers a series featuring advertising copywriter Jen Madden, whose sideline is solving sex-related murder cases, several of which curiously take place in funeral homes. The deaths are violent, but the writing is jaunty.

Former self-defence tutor and band singer Nicola Griffith has won three science fiction awards and five Lambdas for her stories, which are set in Norway and the US and feature detective Aud Torvingen, a wealthy security consultant who also seems to be a powerful robotic killing machine. The series charts the evolution of Torvingen from that strange creature into a human being. These are curious novels. When Torvingen spends time with other humans, she considers ways in which she could kill or be killed by them. They remind me of the television programme *Killing Eve*, though without its stylish panache. Although there is something addictive about them, they are not for the weak or sentimental.

Cari Hunter is a full-time paramedic, enjoys muddy walks in the Peak District and writes fiction in her spare time. The Peaks provide an exciting setting for her intriguing crime thrillers featuring Detective Sanne Jensen and her friend and occasional lover Dr Meg Fielding.

Vicki Clifford, who was born in Edinburgh and until recently taught religious studies at the University of Stirling, has an unusual career background. She is a freelance hairdresser with a PhD in psychoanalysis from the University of Edinburgh. She had her first book, *Freud's Converts*, published in 2007. Her investigator Viv Fraser also has a PhD and is a hairdresser – a stylist to the Edinburgh establishment – although a far from ordinary one. She leads a double life as an investigative journalist and becomes involved in a series of fast-paced mysteries. These books have wit and style and are a good read.

In *Dirty Work* (1990) Vivien Kelly's investigator Jo Summers is an office manager for a hostel for the disadvantaged. When one of her residents, a young lesbian, is found dead of an overdose, Summers is the only person who suspects foul play and is forced to investigate on her own. Kelly's *Two Red Shoes* (2002) is a very different kind of novel and follows the expertly told story of Nicholas – who was four years old when his mother took him away from his father, his brother and his Ukrainian home and brought him to Britain – and his only friend, the effervescent Faye.

Award-winning author Elizabeth Woodcraft has been practising as a barrister since 1980. She has represented striking miners, the Greenham Common women, animal rights protesters and victims of sexual and domestic abuse. Her detective Frankie Richmond is also a barrister. Woodcraft has been shortlisted for the CWA John Creasey Memorial Dagger for *Good Bad Woman* (2000) and was co-winner of the Best Lesbian Mystery Lambda Award for *Babyface* (2001). All of her books are urban noir thrillers. She says she wanted her novels to reflect what happens to people when they go to court, and how the judicial process affects them. In spite of the serious nature of the material, Woodcraft's books are very funny.

As we have seen, Nicola Upson's series of expert mysteries feature a fictional version of the real author and playwright Josephine Tey. Upson was born in Suffolk in England, educated at Downing College, Cambridge, and has worked in the theatre and as a freelance journalist. She has to date written nine Josephine Tey novels, the seventh of which, *Nine Lessons* (2017), was shortlisted for the CWA Historical Dagger award. Nicola has written two non-fiction works and the recently published biographical novel *Stanley and Elsie*, which covers five years in the life of Sir Stanley Spencer and his wife Hilda and is narrated by Elsie Munday, the woman hired as their housekeeper. Upson lives and works in Cambridge and Cornwall with her partner, who is also a novelist. The first Josephine Tey mystery, *An Expert in Murder* (2008) is unusual in that, at the start of the book, the fictional Tey has yet to come to terms with her sexuality. Readers know she had a male lover who was killed in the First World War and it is only gradually through the series that Tey, along with her readers, begins to understand that her preference is for female love and companionship.

Nicola's style is leisurely, with lengthy, beautifully constructed sentences, and the reader is made to feel the author is slowly getting to know her lead character. These novels are not quick reads, nor are they for hasty mystery readers who are keen on convoluted plots. These are books it takes time to assimilate, yet they are worth the trouble and will remain in the mind and the imagination. Nicola's work is highly literary and amply repays the time a reader will need to spend on it.

English writer Natasha Cooper is 69 years old and a voracious crime reader whose dyslexia held her back from embarking on a writing career earlier in her life. Instead she became a publisher before writing historical novels under a pseudonym and then turning to crime with a second series featuring fictional barrister Trish Maguire. In the Maguire series, the earnest, enthusiastic barrister heroine becomes involved in investigating vicious murders, corporate scandals, and cases of injustice. Cooper's other main protagonist is lesbian police officer DCI Caro Lyalt, who is Maguire's best friend. Cooper has written a third series centred on forensic psychologist Karen Taylor. The fourth Taylor book, *Vengeance in Mind* (2012), was shortlisted for a CWA Gold Dagger Award. Natasha Cooper reviews books for *The Times* and the *Times Literary Supplement*. She writes a column for the website *Crime Time* in which she reviews new books. Cooper has held the prestigious position of Chair of the Crime Writers' Association and has done a great deal to support and publicise the crime fiction genre in the UK and in the US. She is a very generous reviewer and has been known to say she won't review a book she has read and dislikes.

Today, Val McDermid is so well-established and respected for her crime writing that in Scotland, her birthplace, she is almost considered a national treasure alongside Drue Heinz, Nicola Sturgeon, Ali Smith, AL Kennedy and Annie Lennox. McDermid has sold 16 million books and her work has been translated into 40 languages. She has also written several outstanding fiction and non-fiction standalone books, as well as short stories and books for children. The bulk of her novels fall into four main series. The first of these includes six books featuring cynical, feminist/socialist journalist Lindsay Gordon, who is a lesbian. Readers met Gordon for the first time more than 30 years ago in *Report for Murder* (1987), in which she investigates the murder of the star attraction at a fund-raising gala at a girls' public school, who is found garrotted with her own cello strings. In this first book, Gordon openly displays her sexuality.

Val McDermid was warned at the time that writing a novel with a lesbian theme would be commercial suicide. She wrote it anyway for The Women's Press, which was then a small feminist publishing house whose books went largely unreviewed by the mainstream press and were ignored by major booksellers. These books helped to bring lesbian detective fiction to popular attention in a way perhaps matched by only one other female crime writer, Stella Duffy. McDermid has stated openly that, at the time of writing this series, her decision to feature a lesbian as her amateur detective protagonist was part of a wider project to introduce an openly homosexual character into mainstream fiction and help normalise lesbian and gay sexuality. Some critics say Gordon's lesbianism is secondary to her socialism and that her novels, in spite of their feminist agenda, are all concerned with aspects of contemporary British society and politics rather than the specific politics of gender. In the years in which Val McDermid was writing this first series of novels, the association of deviant sexuality and gender transgression with criminality was very much prevalent and McDermid did much to oppose this idea.

Lindsay Gordon was soon followed by a growing number of lesbian detectives. In the years following Gordon's first appearance, the number of professional lesbian detectives in the literary marketplace more than tripled, from 14 in 1986 to 43 in 1995. While literary novels were engaged with debates around sexuality and feminism during the 1980s, the lesbian sleuth became central to crime novels.

Val McDermid admits that her protagonist is very like herself. In the 1980s, she did not have the confidence to move far away from her own experience. As a consequence, Gordon shares many of McDermid's own characteristics. She is a Scottish journalist with a working-class background and an Oxford education, who is broadly left in politics. Nevertheless, McDermid says their personalities are very different. Gordon is more foolhardy than she is, as well as being braver, more stubborn and more fun. McDermid grew up with no lesbian role models and therefore wanted to make her heroine a kind of 'everydyke'. She made Gordon a lesbian because she wanted her to be part of the wider world, not a small lesbian community.

Subsequently, the lead investigators in the remainder of McDermid's novels were either straight women or men. The second series of six books features Manchester-based private investigator Kate Brannigan. The third series of eleven books revolves around clinical psychologist Dr Tony Hill and DCI

Carole Jordan. The fourth series of five psychological thrillers centres on the life and work of DCI Karen Pirie, who works out of Fife, Scotland.

It is interesting to look at the trajectory of McDermid's publishing houses and note that all of the early Lindsay Gordon books were published by the Women's Press. Once she dropped her lesbian protagonist, all the publishers are large mainstream ones. Today, in a less homophobic climate in which her books have thrived and obtained huge international commercial success, McDermid feels free to sprinkle her gay characters casually and occasionally into her novels when they fit her narratives, though none of them are ever lead characters as Lindsay Gordon was. Those early books broke through a frightening homophobic barrier. McDermid's courage, at a time when making lesbianism visible was a bold stroke, has inspired many younger lesbian crime writers. The Lindsay Gordon novels are still in print and never out of fashion.

Scottish former veterinary surgeon Manda Scott is the author of more than a dozen novels, including several contemporary crime thrillers, the four Boudica novels – which explore the world of the legendary war-leader – and a series based on Imperial Rome. Now she has turned to espionage, recently winning the McIlvanney Crime Novel of the Year Award for her thriller *A Treachery of Spies* (2018). This book moves between the present day and Nazi-occupied France during World War II, dissecting the scars left by the legacy of the Resistance and revealing the frightening lengths people will go to keep old secrets buried. In this novel, the rebellious assassin and spy Sophie Destivelle harks back a little to the heroine Lee Adams in Scott's first novel. 'They are both small, slight with dark hair,' Scott said. 'Sophie Destivelle is modelled on women I know who are transformative. I was trying to explore the question, what does it take to get women to kill? That has been a theme in all my books.'

When Scott began writing, almost ten years after McDermid's

unique and risky entry into lesbian fiction, there was still very little lesbian fiction in mainstream literature on either side of the water. Scott credits McDermid for writing lesbian fiction that was not anguished but where lesbianism was merely part of who her protagonist was. She decided to write her Kellen Stewart three-book series on the similar premise that the heroine's sexuality was not a matter to become stressed about. Kellen Stewart is a lesbian therapist involved in plots that revolve around genetic engineering and veterinary science. The debut book in this series *Hen's Teeth* (1996) was shortlisted for the Orange Prize. That novel was also hailed by Fay Weldon as a 'new voice for a new world'. Scott's standalone novel *No Good Deed* (2001) was nominated for the 2003 Edgar Award.

Today it is worrying that there are not enough 'out' lesbian crime investigators, tackling cases in the way Kellen Stewart did. Scott wanted her heroine to be happy about her sexuality. 'I didn't want to write another angst-ridden dyke book,' she said. 'The whole point of those books was that the sexuality was just there, like red hair. But making her a lesbian did feel like a political statement. The only person writing at that point and being published in the UK was Val McDermid. And I thought, there's more of us than that. And also, there are other things to say than Val was saying. My writing has always been some kind of political statement. And in the early days, sexuality was one of the political statements I wanted to make. It's really, in the scale of things, not relevant anymore. But then it felt like it was really important.'

Stella Duffy created lesbian detective Saz Martin for her first novel *Calendar Girl* in 1994. Martin was so popular that four further books followed, between 1996 and 2005. 'I made Saz Martin a private eye because I know nothing about police and procedurals,' she said. 'That's why everyone says the Martin novels are whydunnits not whodunnits. But I really wanted to write a book with lesbians in it who didn't hate men, didn't bang on about lesbian politics all the time, weren't traumatised and felt it wasn't hard being a dyke. I wanted a whole novel about what it's like being gay.'

Darley Anderson, who was Martina Cole's agent, telephoned Duffy after reading the first novel. He told her he wouldn't be able to sell it with a lesbian protagonist and asked her if she could make Martin heterosexual. 'I told him, no,' Duffy said. 'Not because I was politically correct, but because I was proud of having written a lesbian protagonist, something I hadn't seen before. Also, I didn't know how to change it. It was my first novel. I would not have known how to handle the plot points that relied on them being two women if they'd been a woman and a man.'

The Women's Press also rejected the book, because the publishers didn't feel comfortable with the idea of a lesbian villain. 'So, we had the straight world telling us they can't sell us,' Duffy said. 'And, on the other side, is the lesbian bullshit feminists who believed only men are bad and only women are wonderful which, frankly, if you're a dyke you know better than that.'

'Have you seen *Killing Eve*?' she added. 'It's so frustrating for us. It takes a bloke – Luke Jennings – to write a book in which a sexy, bisexual woman is doing amoral things for people to go, oh yeah, we could put that on the telly.' Peter Ayrton of Serpent's Tail, a small, fully independent firm, eventually bought Duffy's first book. 'I was paid £1500 for my first novel in 1993,' she said. 'I still think that's quite good money considering I am a literary novelist. Also, I learned how to write novels with Peter.'

Duffy has continued to have lesbian protagonists in her novels, although they are not crime novels. 'I know we are still not allowed to write happy lesbian characters, unless they are in costume,' she said. 'So, Sarah Waters has been able to write those books. Costumed lesbians are far more palatable. Historical lesbians, like Anne Lister, are on telly now. Dead modern lesbians are okay. Historical lesbians are palatable. A single fucked-up unhappy lesbian is palatable. But the characters that interest me, who are grounded and not just white, middle-class women and have a whole different range of stuff going on; they're not often given permission to exist.'

Mari Hannah is a fine lesbian writer who is going against the grain and is doing very well, but it certainly wasn't easy for her to get her first DCI Kate Daniels book *The Murder Wall* (2012) published. 'I wanted to make her a strong and clever detective,' Hannah said. 'A woman in charge of a large team in a service that is largely dominated by men. I was sick of seeing on TV, and reading in books, lesbian characters who were merely add-ons. And my Kate Daniels was too good a character not to play the central role. She would be the one in charge. There are too many lesbians in real life in fantastic jobs who are never properly recognised, and I wanted to write someone with whom I identified.' It had never occurred to her that she would encounter any problems getting *The Murder Wall* into print. Yet it was incredibly difficult to get it published. Hannah said: 'Most publishers said some version of this comment: "We absolutely adore this woman's writing, but we are going to pass. We don't think middle England is ready for this." Time and again I was praised, then passed. They call them passes but they are downright rejections, and they still hurt.'

Hannah was finally published in Germany. Her second book *Settled Blood* (2012) won the Northern Writers' Award while the first book was still sitting on editors' desks. After that it became easier. *The Murder Wall* won the Polari First Book Prize and she was later shortlisted for the Dagger in the Library award for a full body of work. Hannah is now Reader in Residence for Harrogate's International Crime Writing Festival. The seventh Kate Daniels book, *Without a Trace*, was released in 2020.

In her debut novel, Hannah does not reveal that Kate is gay until a third of the way through the story. 'I wanted people to love her for the job that she did, for being the clever detective she is,' Hannah said. 'I did not want her defined by her sexuality from the start.' Hannah, whose lead character was inspired by her partner Mo, who was a Northumbria police officer for 30 years, and a murder detective for much of her career, says her lesbian Detective Chief Inspector Daniels isn't 'out' in her early books because she probably would have lost her job in the police force at that point if she had been.

Once the series became successful, Hannah's publishers wanted to market the books as crime and did not put the Daniels novels in any category that identified her as gay. 'I thought they were wrong,' Hannah said. 'I said to them, haven't you heard of the pink pound? I had had so many letters from readers who identified with Kate Daniels. Finally, I changed publishers and the new one put the books in the gay categories and the books have gone bananas. If you look on those shelves, you will see they are frequently in the top twenty, sometimes in the top ten.' The television rights for the DCI Kate Daniels series have been optioned by Gina Carter and Stephen Fry for Sprout pictures.

In the US and Canada, there are and have been many interesting lesbian crime writers worth reading. One that will already be familiar to many is Patricia Highsmith, whose novel *Carol*, first published as *The Price of Salt* in 1952, was made into a British-American film in 2015. Highsmith remains the archetype of the psychological crime fiction author who has an extraordinary ability to convey high levels of anxiety and apprehension, not only in the minds of her edgy, tense and agitated characters, but also into the minds of her readers. *Gone Girl* author Gillian Flynn has said that her favourite book is Patricia Highsmith's *Deep Water* (1957). 'She has a strange ability to make completely unreasonable emotions and actions seem reasonable, where you find yourself completely empathising with a sociopath and murderer,' Flynn said. 'There's something incredibly chilling about that, looking up from a book and finding that you've been rooting for an average person's murder.'[27]

During her life, Highsmith, who died in 1995, was an

energetic and committed lesbian who had insightfully mined her own life and sexual adventures for *The Price of Salt*, although she decided to publish the novel under the pseudonym Claire Morgan to avoid being labelled a 'lesbian writer'. In the story, the lonely young Therese Belivet, who works in a Manhattan department story, falls in love with and becomes obsessed by a wealthy and beautiful customer, the older Carol Aird. Early in her own career, Patricia Highsmith also took a temporary job in the toy section at Bloomingdales in New York and Therese's obsession, and the way in which she stalks Carol – even taking a train to New Jersey to spy on her – is a replica of Highsmith's real-life obsessional attraction to one of her own clients. When Highsmith described her own experience, she added in the notion that she had fantasised about putting her hand round the older woman's neck and strangling her to death. In the novel nothing so pathological occurs. Although she is a married woman, fighting her estranged husband for custody of their child, Carol also falls for Therese.

In 1990, Highsmith was finally persuaded by Bloomsbury to bring out the book, retitled *Carol*, under her own name. The paperback edition of *Carol* went on to sell almost a million copies. In my view, *Carol* is the most brilliant of all Highsmith's 22 novels. It is significant in gay literature because it was the first to have a happy ending for female lover-protagonists. Unlike many of Highsmith's novels, which deal with strange, abnormal situations and evoke feelings of dread, disquiet, unease and bleakness, this story is about love. And it remains resolutely positive with some emotionally beautiful scenes. A British radio adaptation of the novel was broadcast in 2014. The 2015 film adaptation, starring Cate Blanchett as Carol, received six Academy Award nominations and nine British Academy Film Award nominations.

Carol is a rarity in Highsmith's oeuvre. It is a domestic story, yet a lot of the action happens on a road trip taken by Therese and Carol. It is loving. It is hopeful. It takes women as its centre and at its heart. There is no crime committed within the confines of that book. The women fight the only man of consequence in the book, Carol's husband Harge, and although they do not get an undisputed win, Carol achieves partial custody of her child and the two women are able to remain together. It is without doubt one of Highsmith's most brilliant novels, yet she refused to publicly acknowledge it for 38 years.

Other striking American lesbian novels can be found. I use the word 'found' to indicate that a search may be necessary because not all of them are widely available. In my own search, I was struck by the work of Abigail Padgett – particularly her first series featuring San Diego child protection investigator Bo Bradley – and Iza Moreau, who writes for young adult lesbians and has won several awards for her novels. When she is not writing, Moreau rides dressage and shoots target archery in her spare time.

Among the Canadian novels I enjoyed reading, were those written by Gina L Dartt, who was born and raised in Nova Scotia, where she set her 'Unexpected' series. In the debut novel, *Unexpected Sparks* (2002), the lead protagonists, bookstore owner Kate Shannon and police despatcher Nikki Harris, are brought together when a male insurance agent is found dead.

I would like also to draw attention to Californian Mabel Maney – who is the author of the Nancy Clue series, a lesbian parody of the Nancy Drew, Cherry Ames and Hardy Boys series – and Robin Brandeis, whose novel *She Scoops to Conquer* (2003) is as much a romantic comedy as a crime narrative. Also well worth mentioning are Jaye Maiman, whose protagonist Robin Miller is a lesbian travel writer and romance novelist, Rose Beecham (the mystery pen name of romance author Jennifer Knight) and Kate Allen, who lives in Denver, Colorado and has created the lesbian cop Alison Kaine.

Penny Mickelbury is important because she created both a black female police detective and an amateur sleuth. However, she is also known for her lesbian mysteries. One of the most moving is her *novel Two Wings to Fly Away* (2019) which paints a powerful picture of a divided nation hurtling towards Civil War and is set against a backdrop of courage, community, and the ways in which love can redeem the horrors of life.

Ellen Hart, who was born in Maine and was a professional chef for 14 years, has written a series of 27 Jane Lawless novels, 5 of which have won LAMBDA awards. Lawless is a lesbian restaurateur who shares the lead with her smart-mouthed best friend Cordelia Thorn. Her novels deal with LGBT issues. She has also created the Sophie Greenway culinary mystery series. Hart calls her own books maximal suspense and minimal gore. She has been called the 'Lesbian Answer to Agatha Christie'. In 2005, she was inducted into the Saints and Sinners Hall of Fame. In 2010, she was given the coveted Trailblazer Award from the Golden Crown Literary Society and, in 2017, was the first openly LGBT writer to be named Grand Master by the Mystery Writers of America.

Sarah Dreher, who was born in Pennsylvania and died in Amherst in 2012, was a clinical psychologist as well as a playwright and novelist. She was best known for her amateur sleuth Stoner McTavish. The themes in her novels include the anguish of lesbian relationships beginning, ending or mending. Her highly contemporary protagonists are all in some kind of search for identity or integrity. When she was 17 years old, Dreher was threatened with expulsion from Wellesley College for 'being too fond of girls' – although she wasn't 'out' at the time – and admitted she had considered committing suicide. Sarah's play *Alumnae News* parallels this experience in her life. As in her novels, the poignancy and exuberant energy are lightened by humour, and by the author's empathy with her characters. Her captivating protagonist Stoner McTavish is a lesbian travel agent who turns into a reluctant amateur detective.

Joan Drury is the former publisher of Spinsters Ink, the

highly esteemed feminist press. She owns the independent bookstore Drury Lane Books in Minnesota. Her sassy sleuth is Tyler Jones, a San Francisco newspaper columnist and feminist lesbian activist who is devoted to women's issues and helping victims of abuse.

Deborah Powell was born and grew up in Sunflower, Mississippi before relocating to Houston, Texas where her novels, which feature crime reporter Hollis Carpenter, are set. Carpenter, who quits her job at the beginning of the series and never returns to journalism, turns out to be a first-class investigator. These 1930s mysteries parody the classic male hardboiled style and the appearance of Carpenter herself is somewhat of a caricature; she is a large imposing woman who wears saddle shoes and slacks and faces off men who try to harass her with a very sharp tongue. There is something of Ann Cleeves' indomitable and hugely likeable protagonist Vera Stanhope about her. Carpenter is strong, funny and indefatigable. There is not a hint of a stereotype in her character.

Born in Long Beach, California, Barbara Wilson writes novels that are generally concerned with progressive and feminist social issues. Her background is in feminist publishing and the Women's Movement. Her first three books – *Murder in the Collective* (1984), *Sisters of the Road* (1986) and *The Dog Collar Murders* (1989) – all feature the reluctant investigator Pam Nilsen, who is part-owner of a printing press and active in left wing and lesbian circles in Seattle.

Sandra Scoppettone was born in New Jersey and is the holder of Shamus and LAMBDA awards for her work, which spans almost 60 years. She writes adult fiction and books for young adults. The most popular of her novels are the Lauren Laurano series, featuring a Greenwich Village private investigator, and three freestanding novels she wrote under the pen name Jack Early. She is also famed for her Suzuki Beane series, which has become a cult classic. Scoppettone did not come out as a lesbian until the 1970s. Her book *Happy Endings Are All Alike* (1978) was one of the earliest young adult books to depict a lesbian relationship. In the 1980s, she was one of the eight women mystery writers who started the organisation Sisters in Crime, which was led by Sara Paretsky, to confront the growing use of sadism against women in mystery fiction and the lack of review space given to women mystery writers.

Scoppettone wrote a number of young adult novels before moving into the crime genre. The books were not well reviewed. Suspecting this was because she was a woman, Scoppettone then wrote three crime books under the pseudonym Jack Early, including one featuring Soho-based private eye Fortune Fanelli. The Jack Early novels received generally good reviews and Scoppettone remains convinced this is because reviewers assumed a man had written them.

She later put out five Lauren Laurano books under her own name and believes this may have been the first time a lesbian character was portrayed in a novel as a 'normal' person. She has also written two further books about young private eye Faye Quick and continues in her work to address the social and political issues that trouble her, including homosexuality, alcoholism and rape. Scoppettone has said that her work is partly motivated by the fact that she is a recovering alcoholic and a lesbian.[28]

Katherine V Forrest was born in Canada but has lived and worked in the US, and considers herself an American writer. For ten years, she held tenure as the fiction editor of Naiad Press and has received a great many awards for her writing, including a LAMBDA Literary Foundation's Pioneer Award. In 2008, she received the Bill Whitehead Award from The Publishing Triangle and the Trailblazing Award from the Golden Crown Literary Society. She is also a recipient of The Alice B Readers Award medal. Today she is the supervising editor at Spinsters Ink publishing house.

Forrest's ex-marine homicide detective Kate Delafield was the first lesbian police professional to emerge in the whole of American literature. 'I happened to catch a particular movement at a particular time,' Forrest said. 'Women police in the US had just won all the court cases and we were only just emerging into the higher echelons of police work. Before that women had been confined to juvenile and jail where we were matrons and things like that. That is why I decided to make my investigating detective a woman.'

Originally Katherine had thought of making her protagonist an amateur detective, but when she decided she was going to have a lesbian investigator, she saw Kate walk on to the page. 'I thought, yes,' Forrest said. 'Here is a woman who presents the absolute best case for being in the closet. She was in a paramilitary organisation with the most hostile environment there could possibly be, plus she was in a high visible, high pressure, high stress position. This character, I thought, is going to be interesting to write about. Of course, she dovetailed right into my own great passion as a writer, which is the closet. Because I profoundly believe that the closet kills, spiritually and sometimes physically. I don't know how visible this is to my readers over nine books, but Kate's development as a character reflects the damage that has been done to her. She has been in the closet even when she didn't need to be, and it damaged her and damaged her relationship with her partner and damaged any relationship she might have had with her police colleagues. Kate Delafield also chose to walk her own path, not to rely on her community, or share anything and that led to isolation and alcoholism.'

Forrest said many of Kate's fears had been her own. She had been a victim in a hostile world. 'When I came of age, we were seen as criminals,' she said. 'We were thrown out of our jobs, out of our churches, out of our families. We were not allowed in the military, we were institutionalised. I don't judge. It sounds as if

I am judging Kate Delafield, but I am not. The novel just reflects the damage that was done to us all.'

Forrest said that it was 'unbearably hard' to get lesbian protagonist books published in the early 1980s. 'What made anything possible was the rise of our independent book stores, our small lesbian feminist book stores and also our small presses,' she said. 'The mainstream would *not* publish us. A lot of printers came into being, including Naiad Press, who published me early on and also published a lot of my fellow writers. Suddenly these small presses flourished. Then finally, the mainstream press discovered our sales figures.'

Forrest did publish four of her books mainstream with Putnam (Berkley), a decision she says was a political one. She believed that she and other lesbian writers were integral to the American literary scene, and that they needed to be published in hard cover and get reviews. The small independent presses only used soft covers and were not often reviewed.

Forrest is also known as the author of the ground-breaking romantic novel *Curious Wine* (1983) which is considered a classic lesbian romance and a classic of American literature, although at the time of its publication, it was dismissed as being 'light'.

'I think it's as political as hell,' Forrest said. 'Here were two women who had a lot of choices in life, a lot of options, and out of all of those options they chose the hardest one, which was to love each other.' The novel is now credited as the one to break through many misconceptions about lesbians and lesbian relationships.

Having talked to many crime writers, both gay and straight, I was left with the question, why are there still so few women writers penning novels which have gay female protagonists? Crime writer Frances Fyfield said she doesn't write gay characters because she would be tentative about going into areas she doesn't properly understand. 'One is coming from one's own standpoint,' she said. 'I would want to do them justice.

And I can't, without considerable research. A way to get more interesting protagonists is to get more interesting writers.'

Leigh Russell agreed: 'We write about the world we know or the world we grew up in, don't we?' she said. 'Today I have a mixed race granddaughter and my son-in-law is black, so it is not that I don't know any people who are not white, but white and straight is who I am. And white and straight is the world I grew up in.' Russell has however introduced a gay woman sergeant into her London scene. 'I don't make an issue of it,' she said. 'She just is. She has a girlfriend. Nobody remarks on it. It is just accepted, as indeed it should be. But that was a recent, conscious decision because I thought, yes, everyone has been heterosexual. I ought to do something about that. It took me many books to notice.'

Sarah Hilary has created a Jamaican male gay character – Detective Sergeant Noah Jake – in her DC Marnie Rome series. 'I wanted the fact that he was Jamaican and gay not to be the point of Noah Jake,' Hilary said. 'I didn't want to write a series in which he is constantly running up against racism and homophobia. But actually, writing the sixth book, given he and Rome are working in London, it is impossible to ignore the new feelings of hostility, the incipient racism that's now not incipient anymore but is actually at the forefront of a lot of problems people are having. I think I'd probably naively imagined life would get easier for someone like Noah six years down the line, whereas in actual fact, with one thing and another, it's now harder. It became increasingly difficult to write Noah as a very, very comfortable, happy-go-lucky character. The world generally is much more hostile than it was six years ago. We shouldn't be saying that. We should be saying that the world is becoming *more* civilised as time goes by. But I think we're definitely living in a new, dark age. It's really frightening.'

Nicola Upson said she didn't know or understand why straight writers avoid lesbian protagonists. 'Most of my audiences at festivals and literary events have been comfortable with Josephine Tey being a lesbian,' she said. 'I only had one reader in an audience who was horrified, and she said, how could you do that? How could you make her a lesbian when she was somebody's auntie?'

One esteemed American novelist, who is white and straight, has taken the chance to create a lesbian protagonist, with enormous success. She is Laurie R King, who was married until his death to historian Noel Quinton King, and has written 27 novels. She is probably best known for creating the fictional partnership of Mary Russell and the retired Sherlock Holmes. Before that however, she wrote a series of six crime novels featuring lesbian homicide detective Kate Martinelli, who works out of San Francisco police department. Martinelli's work partner is Al Hawkin, her life partner is female psychiatrist Lee Cooper. The first Martinelli novel, *A Grave Talent*, came out in 1993. *Beginnings*, the most recent in the series, came out in 2019. During that time, the Martinelli books have won the Edgar, Creasey and Lambda awards and been nominated for the Edgar, Macavity, Anthony and Orange awards.

In a question and answer discussion on the website *Goodreads* in 2012, King said: 'The spectrum of human sexuality means that few of us write precisely the place we inhabit, no more than we limit ourselves to writing (for example) white women in their 50s with a graduate degree, living in a liberal community on the Pacific coast.

'We as writers explore constantly, trying on different faces and backgrounds in an attempt to find common ground with those inhabiting our stories. I wrote Kate as a lesbian because I couldn't imagine her otherwise, and I was fortunate that the LGBT community welcomed me in. I'd have been sad if they found the stories intrusive.'[29]

9

Black, Disabled, Visible

Some able-bodied female crime writers prefer to create able-bodied protagonists, on the grounds that they write better about what they know. However, several have enjoyed breaking new ground.

Kathy Reichs is widely known for her hugely popular forensic scientist Temperance Brennan who, like Reichs herself, is hazel-eyed, has a ponytail, is five foot five inches tall, weighs 120 pounds and is, above all, able-bodied. But the forensic anthropologist and academic has created another distinctive character, the tough-talking wild card Sunday Night – or Sunnie for short – who is badly disfigured and has one eye. Night, who is former military and an ex-police officer, is scarred both physically and psychologically and has spent years running away from her nightmarish past.

In spite of the physical differences between Brennan and Night, Reichs says the two characters do share characteristics. They are both competent, confident, independent, self-sufficient, resourceful and witty. And they are both driven by compassion and the desire for justice, for the victims of crime and their families. But where Brennan is cerebral, logical and disciplined, Night is fiery, bad-tempered and unsociable, and skilled with firearms. Reichs did not find Sunny Night hard to write and saw it as a positive change from writing about Brennan, who recently featured in her nineteenth book, *A Conspiracy of Bones* (2020).

When readers meet Sunday Night in the standalone novel *Two Nights* (2017), she is in self-imposed exile on the lonely and secluded Goat Island, which is situated off the South Carolina coast. 'I wanted her to be a really unique character,' Reichs said. 'She has so much baggage going on, both emotionally and physically. And she is more your old-style Raymond Chandler type. She is like a gun-toting, hardboiled private eye.'

Stella Duffy has been writing a new book which has a disabled woman as a lead. 'The setting is the 1950s,' Duffy said. 'This woman, as a teenager and a 20-something, was tall and statuesque and Jane Russell-shaped, with all the admiration that comes with it. But in her 70s and 80s, she is disabled. This is naturally both shocking and a shock.' Duffy, who had her first cancer aged 36 and her second at 50, added: 'I have some knowledge of what it feels like to have a disability. I believe being disabled for some time and looking at our mortality is a good thing.'

I have looked at a range of thrillers and mysteries and have been struck by how many different disabilities writers have used, how authentic the descriptions are, and how upbeat the tone.

A writer of more than 30 psychological thrillers might be assumed to choose as a disabled protagonist someone with a mental health disturbance, but Jane A Adams took a different approach. Adams, a British crime writer and Royal Literary Fund Fellow who teaches creative writing at De Montfort University, has written a series of novels in which her lead protagonist, ex-policewoman Naomi Blake, is blind.

Adams, whose first book *The Greenway* (1995) featured male Detective Inspector Mike Croft, was nominated for the John Creasey Award and received an Authors Club Best First Novel Award. Her Naomi Blake novels – there are 12 in the series – are set in the Midlands in England. Blake has been forced to retire from the police after being blinded in an accident. In the first in the series, *Mourning the Little Dead* (2002), she turns private eye when new evidence appears to shed light on a 23-year-old case, the disappearance of her childhood best friend Helen Jones. With the help of her guide dog Napoleon and her lover, Detective Inspector Alec Friedman, the visually impaired Blake is driven to finally solve the mystery of her missing friend. In all the novels, blindness, although an obvious disability, does not hamper the determined heroine.

Elizabeth Cosin is a New Yorker who worked as a journalist and sports writer in Virginia and as a feature writer in Washington DC and Los Angeles. Her series features the tough and unconventional private investigator Zenaria Moses, a former sports journalist who lives in Santa Monica, California and who has lost a lung to cancer. The independent and resourceful Moses quaffs micro-brew, smokes cigars, rides a mountain bike and never lets being a cancer survivor hold her back. The novels feel fresh and lively and the characters alert and invigorating. Cosin, who writes from her home in Los Angeles and also lost a lung to cancer, received an Honours On Line Mystery Award for the first novel in the series, *Zen and the Art of Murder* (1998). Two further books followed: *Zen and the City of Angels* (1999) and *Zen Justice* (2001).

Amy Myers is a British mystery writer whose investigative *Marsh and Daughter* series features the ebullient wheelchair-bound ex-cop Peter Marsh, who was injured in a shooting incident, and his daughter Georgia. The pair work together to solve murders in Kent, England. Often these are old crimes that nevertheless take them into frightening territory in the present. Georgia Marsh has escaped from a disastrous early marriage to a conman and is now married, curiously and somewhat usefully, to Luke Frost, the publisher of the books 'Peter and Georgia' that have been written about their cases. The spirited, sometimes astringent relationship between Peter and Georgia Marsh is a spur to their resurrecting forgotten or unsolved crimes to establish justice. Amy Myers is excellent on twists and convoluted plotting, which neatly complement her genial understanding of a pair of engaging characters.

Another wheelchair crime novel – *Murder on Wheels* (2000) – is written by British crime writer Mary Scott. The protagonist Bryan Greyshott, who was paralysed in a hang-gliding accident, now lives a half-life in a North London suburb. Greyshott becomes a murder suspect when he is discovered holding a crutch next to a dead body and he is left to try and find the perpetrator.

In Gail Bowen's Joanne Kilbourn series, her academic heroine marries a paraplegic lawyer, Zach Shreve. Bowen does not shy away from the reality of how perilous being paraplegic can be. 'All of these organs in our body were not intended to be trapped into a place that isn't functioning,' she said. 'There's no small disease, no small illness for paraplegics. So, Joanne goes through all this with Zach.' Bowen learned about the physical and health challenges from a former colleague. 'He had to be so careful with his skin,' she said. 'Even if a sore appeared, it could turn into an ulcer that could kill him.'

She is delighted with the warm reception readers have given Zach. 'It has pleased readers to see that a man with that particular level of physical limitation lives his life fully,' she said. 'He and Joanne have a really great life together. They have a great sex life and a really good relationship. They change each other and I think that's the really wonderful thing. His doctor tells Joanne that Zach never figured he'd live past maybe 30. And here he is. So, he just lived alone, what the hell. And then he meets Joanne and all of a sudden, he sees another possibility.'

The American writer Penny Warner devised a string of seven novels, featuring newspaper publisher Connor Westphal. On the surface, Westphal looks and sounds like any other female publisher, but something is radically different. When she was four years old, she had a serious bout of meningitis and became profoundly deaf. In the first book in the series, *Dead Body*

Language (1997), the independent and intuitive Westphal is a reporter living in Flat Skunk in Gold Country, California. In spite of her severe disability, Westphal has two aids to help her: her hearing-ear dog Casper and her TTY telephone. This is a special electronic appliance, similar to a teleprinter, which allows deaf people, or those who are hard of hearing or speech impaired, to use the telephone to communicate. Westphal also has an extraordinary third support, an ability to see what other people can only hear. This novel manages to be both inventive and authentic. It went on to win a Macavity Award for Best First Mystery and earn a nomination for an Agatha and an Anthony Award.

American crime writer Abigail Padgett is a former court investigator for the county of San Diego who now works as an advocate for the mentally ill. She broke new ground in the 1990s with her series about Bo Bradley, a child abuse investigator for Child Protective Services in San Diego County. Bradley also happens to suffer from bipolar disorder. Padgett's debut novel, *Child of Silence* (1993), was the first to feature an investigator living with manic depression. Padgett has said two key events were the inspiration for the series. The first of these was the suicide of a woman who had worked for years to advance the cause of reproductive health, a woman Padgett had long respected. In her suicide note, the woman asked that her mental illness not be disclosed, since she feared it would be taken up by opponents of her cause to discredit her good works. The second spur was the Thomas Harris novel *The Silence of the Lambs* (1988).

'I loved that book. He's a great writer,' Padgett said. 'But there is one scene in which Hannibal Lecter is describing one of his prison mates, and he says you can tell he's schizophrenic because of "the smell of the goat". That is such a terrible, stigmatising thing to say, and it is just wrong.' Padgett decided to write to Harris and put him right. She did so and suggested Harris should be more careful. She also told Harris that she intended to write a novel in which the hero would have a mental illness. 'He wrote me a lovely, elegant letter back, and apologised and said he wouldn't do it again. He was a gentleman. He said I should go ahead and write that story.'[30]

Padgett did more than that. She sent her first Bo Bradley manuscript to St Martin's Press, Harris' publisher, telling them Harris had encouraged her to write her book. Her scheme worked. Padgett was immediately referred to long time editor Ruth Cavin and, although St Martin's Press did not end up publishing the novel, Time Warner did through Mysterious Press.

Newspaper reporters are often warned not to become the story, but merely to report it. Mystery writers should be warned of the same possibility. Certainly, crime writer Anne Perry is very much aware of it. London-born Perry, best known for her two separate historical detective series featuring Thomas Pitt and William Monk, was convicted of murder in 1954 – when she was 15 years old. Perry, who was living in New Zealand at the time and called Juliet Hulme, helped to bludgeon to death the mother of her closest friend, Pauline Parker. Hulme, who had been in hospital with TB for months before the incident and was said to be traumatised by her parents' impending divorce and the prospect of being sent alone to South Africa to live with an aunt, helped Parker kill her own mother Honorah Rieper, because they thought she stood in the way of them going to South Africa together. Hulme served five years in a women's prison in Auckland. The grisly story was the subject of a New Zealand psychological thriller movie *Heavenly Creatures* (1994) directed by Peter Jackson and starring Kate Winslet as Hulme.

After her release, Hulme changed her name and eventually moved to Scotland. Her first book, *The Cater Street Hangman*, was published in 1979 and featured Victorian policeman Thomas Pitt and his wife Charlotte. Another 31 books followed in that series, making it arguably the longest sustained crime series by a living writer. In 2017, Perry started a new series featuring the Pitts' son Daniel.

Perry has been extraordinarily prolific. Her second series, about Victorian private investigator William Monk, has so far yielded 24 titles, the most recent of which, *Dark Tide Rising*, was released in 2018. Monk, the working-class son of a fisherman, is ambitious and clever but has suffered from amnesia since being involved in a coaching accident. In the first novel, *The Face of a Stranger* (1990), Monk tries to keep his disability secret in case he loses his police job. In his second outing, *A Dangerous Mourning* (1991), he is fired from the force for insubordination and becomes a private investigator, solving crimes alongside nurse Hester Latterly and aristocratic barrister Sir Oliver Rathbone. The books are clever and tinged with ruthlessness, and they deal effectively with the stigma attached to disability in the Victorian era.

A further series of six books, published between 2003 and 2007, is set against the backdrop of the First World War and features former Cambridge don, Captain Joseph Reavley. The first novel in the series, *No Graves as Yet* (2003), is set in Cambridge just before the onset of war and went on to top the *New York Times* bestseller list. In an interview with *Guardian* journalist Angela Neustatter after the book was released, Perry said: 'It is vital for me to go on exploring moral matters. I wanted to explore what people will do when faced with experiences and inner conflicts that test them to the limit.'[31]

J K Rowling is one of Britain's most distinguished, witty, imaginative and kind authors, screenwriters, producers and philanthropists. She is also one of the world's most successful writers. After the amazing *Harry Potter* series, she decided to turn to writing crime using the pen name Robert Galbraith. Her aim was to write a contemporary whodunnit with a credible backstory. She has succeeded beyond even her own wizardry. The first four books in her new Cormoran Strike series – *The*

Cuckoo's Calling (2013), *The Silkworm* (2014), *Career of Evil* (2015) and *Lethal White* (2018) – all topped the national and international bestseller lists. They have also been adapted for television by the BBC and HBO. The fifth book, *Troubled Blood*, was published in 2020.

Rowling is such a good storyteller. The novels are arresting, compelling and original, with rich, skilled and dramatic plots, vivid detail and a charismatic and sometimes annoying central character, Cormoran Strike, who is disabled. Strike, formerly attached to the Royal Military Police Special Investigation Branch and now a London-based private investigator, is a war veteran who lost the lower half of his right leg to a land mine in an attack in Afghanistan. He has severe emotional scars matching his terrible physical injuries. Making Strike the illegitimate son of the famous rock star Jonny Rokeby gives Rowling the opportunity to inject an element of glamour and celebrity.

The novels have been awarded rave reviews. The books offer a kind of humorous riff on contemporary private eyes, while being carefully structured around a sharp, biting whodunnit. There is also ongoing romantic tension between Strike and his assistant Robin Ellacott, who later becomes his professional partner. The first book is elegant, smart, surprising and funny and the decision to make Strike an amputee war veteran was very well thought out. Strike's enormous pain, his difficulty with running, his limp, his constant problem with his prosthesis and his dislike of it, are all skilfully and at first cautiously woven into the plots of each novel. When he felt the terrible pain of his missing leg, both physically and psychologically, so did I.

Rowling herself has said on her website: 'Making him an amputee added another dimension, allowing me to show the day-to-day reality of living with a disability, which many war veterans are having to face these days.'[32]

Disabilities are clearly close to Rowling's heart. Her own mother Anne died from multiple sclerosis in 1990, seven years before Rowling's first novel *Harry Potter and the Philosopher's Stone* (1997) was published. Since then, Rowling has become a keen philanthropist and has donated millions of pounds to disability charities around the world, including multiple sclerosis.

The disability community and press have heralded her venture into this world with deep pleasure and admiration. Statistics show that one in ten people live with a disability, and an estimated one in four will be affected by mental health issues at some point in their lives. These are the challenging realities that people around the world are living with every day.

The fact that the Galbraith books are the first series of bestselling novels to follow an openly disabled character and his regular trials during his everyday life is hugely significant. A lead protagonist who is openly physically disabled, and almost certainly struggling mentally, is particularly relevant for our time. The key word here for the novels is 'bestselling'. Rowling's determination to create a disabled hero reminds me forcibly of Ann Cleeves' triumph in creating her anti-stereotypical heroine in the bestselling *Vera* novels. They are each writing against the popular grain. They each have a well-earned literary victory as a result.

Representation of disability is something writers must get right. I think the enormity of this literary task may be what has put off several crime writers from trying to imagine and create a disabled character. Some crime writers have told me that to write about the experience of impairment felt either beyond them or off limits. But good writing is fundamentally about having a fine and free imagination. This is something J K Rowling has in goblin bowls.

I am impressed at the slow yet steady way the writer brings in Strike's disability in the first novel, *The Cuckoo's Calling* (2013). Like the reader, Ellacott, who is at this point Strike's new secretary from the agency Temporary Solutions, has no idea that her new boss has a prosthetic lower limb. This is the clever and subtle way Rowling lets us into Strike's disability. Early in the story, he 'limped to the bar' in a pub. Later on, he reflects on his inadequacies: 'There was his recent weight gain; a full stone and a half, so that he not only felt fat and unfit, but was putting unnecessary additional strain on the prosthetic lower leg... Strike was developing the shadow of a limp purely because the additional load was causing some chafing.' Later, while working on a new case, he recalls with distress his recent break-up from his beautiful, rich and duplicitous girlfriend Charlotte. Having left her flat for good, Strike is now sleeping on a camp bed in his shabby office. 'By the neon glow of the street lamp outside, Strike undid the straps of his prosthetic, easing it from the aching stump, removing the gel liner that had become an inadequate cushion against pain. He laid the false leg beside his recharging mobile phone, manoeuvred himself into his sleeping bag and lay with his hands behind his head... He could still feel the missing foot, ripped from his leg two and a half years before. It was there, under the sleeping bag; he could flex the vanished toes if he wanted to.' This treatment is delicate and absorbing. By the time we get to a full display of Strike less privately putting on and taking off his leg, we, the readers, are ready for it. Though Robin, who has not had our careful preparation, has to face it less prepared.

Throughout the series, every mention of Strike's disability is authentic. There is a meticulous regard for detail, no matter how graphic or horrifying those details might initially appear. In *Career of Evil* (2015) Rowling also has a sub-plot around transableism –the condition in which non-disabled people either seek to become disabled themselves or become devotees of those with a disability.

I found this intriguing, as this body integrity and identity disorder was new to me. Yet Rowling's treatment of it in this novel had its critics. In a speech about the representation of disability in literature, researcher Katharine Quarmby picked out a section from the book in which one protagonist, Hazel, is describing another:

'I'll tell you what she wanted,' she burst out. 'To be in a wheelchair – pushed around like a baby and to be pampered and the centre of attention. That's what it was all about. I found a diary, must have been a year or so ago. The things she'd written, what she liked to imagine, what she fantasised about. Ridiculous... Such as having her leg cut off and being in a wheelchair and being pushed to the edge of the stage and watching One Direction and having them come and make a big fuss of her afterwards because she was disabled... Imagine that. It's disgusting. There are people who are really disabled, and they never wanted it. I'm a nurse. I know. I see them. Well,' she said, with a glance at Strike's lower legs. 'You don't need telling.'[33]

Quarmby finds the way Rowling writes about transableism unsuccessful, partly because she thinks the plot is overloaded with social issues and this is merely another one. She thinks if you lifted out that small piece, the plot would still work.[34] I disagree. Keeping it in shows up the character of Hazel as hugely insensitive and distasteful and adds another level to Strike's own feelings about what it means to have had a limb chopped off.

The Cormoran Strike novels work for me on two levels. One is the clear, unsentimental insight into the physical and mental problems faced by a disabled character. The other is the creation of a unique and compelling detective in a series of books that are bewitchingly written.

Black crime writers

Until fairly recently in America, the presence in crime fiction of black women writers, especially those who were African-American or Asian-American, has been rare. Black female authors wrote in many other genres but tended to stay away from mystery or crime.

In the wider world, black female police officers were – and still are – pretty scarce. There were few real-life models therefore to encourage women writers to create police procedurals featuring black female leads. It was little better in the area of private investigators. There were so few black female private eyes in thriving American cities, that black writers would be unlikely to portray one in a starring role.

Having turned away from depicting black police officers or black private investigators, black female crime writers focused instead on investing their energies in a series of amateur detectives. Amateur sleuths had already dominated the early years of the detective novel; think Hercule Poirot, Miss Marple, Kate Fansler, Ellery Queen, Paul Temple, Perry Mason, Lord Peter Wimsey and Albert Campion. However, they were all white. And almost all male.

For black female writers, it has been a hard transition from writing to getting published, and then to being read. Black authors tell me that sometimes it has even been difficult to write books about black women, even when they represented their own race. Danny Gardner is the male author of *A Negro and an Ofay* (2017) which was nominated for three best first novel awards. 'The face of crime in America is a face of colour, the face of crime fiction is kept white – aggressively so,' he said. 'Folks have bills to pay. Why waste time on a genre that wants us to stay away?'[35]

His fellow writer of colour, Naomi Hirahara, the Edgar award-winning author of two mystery series based in Los Angeles, said: 'Writers of colour, until maybe several years ago, were writing more literary fiction than genre, specifically crime. The large publishing houses connect with mystery readers through conventions and other activities that skew older and white. That's made it difficult to mobilise younger and more diverse readers – and writers.'

Rachel Howzell Hall, who created the acclaimed series of

mysteries featuring the black detective Elouise (Lou) Norton, believes novelists who are prepared to face danger and honestly depict the failures of the criminal justice system or put the experiences of black protagonists centre stage can face severe career challenges. 'It's difficult to find an audience in a genre where older white women are the biggest consumers,' she said. 'Some readers are unwilling to see past colour and are willing to believe that a writer of colour has nothing relevant for their life experience.'[36]

In an interview with Reuters in 2011, Asian-American writer Tess Gerritsen said: 'You know, I have hidden my race for 22 books. I have hidden behind my married name, which is very Caucasian, because I didn't feel safe coming out with it. I didn't feel that the market would really accept me. I think I felt it's time to start bringing in an Asian-American point of view.'[37] In *The Silent Girl* (2011) Gerritsen wove into her story Chinese lore, a female wushu grandmaster, a myth of The Monkey King and a male translator, Jonny Tam, an ambitious Chinese American who works with investigating duo Rizzoli and Isles to solve a murder in Boston's Chinatown.

What special challenges are there for black writers and their black protagonists within the three worlds of homicide detectives, private investigators and amateur sleuths?

Police procedurals which feature homicide detectives all emphasise investigative procedures, unlike the other genres which focus on the work of a private eye or amateur sleuth. These police protagonists have the full force of law on their side. They work within a department, may have very heavy caseloads and have to juggle cases. They are usually paired with a partner, with whom they share the workload and details of the investigation. Police officers are required to play by the rules, including how they handle witnesses and how they deal with evidence to ensure it is admissible in court. Fictional homicide detectives are likely to find themselves in dangerous situations.

Thus, the tone of these novels is usually bleak and the content often violent.

There are few examples of authors who have created black female police detectives in crime fiction but those that do exist are interesting. They include the late Eleanor Bland, a former cost accountant who died in 2010 at the age of 65 and whose 1992 novel *Dead Time* was the first in a 14-book police procedural series set in the small fictional town of Lincoln Prairie, near Chicago. The books revolve around the life and work of Marti MacAlister, who was the first African-American female homicide detective to have her own series. A widow and mother of two, MacAlister is a smart, passionate and dignified professional, and her character challenges negative stereotypes of black women in crime fiction. Community is a powerful element in these books and both MacAlister and her young partner Matthew 'Vik' Jessenovik have family lives that are central to both character and plot.

Many black writers are creating detectives who have children and a family life that is as central to their lives as their police work. Bland herself once said: 'The most significant contribution that we have made, collectively, to mystery fiction is the development of the extended family; the permanence of spouses and significant others, most of whom don't die in the first three chapters; children who are complex, wanted and loved, and even pets.'[38]

Judith Smith-Levin was born in Chicago and, at various times in her life, had been a disc jockey, a model, a news reporter, a secretary, a television line producer and a bookstore owner. She made history in 1974 when she became the first uniformed female patrol officer in Worcester, MA. Smith-Levin's main protagonist is the African-American homicide detective Lieutenant Starletta Duvall, a mettlesome veteran officer who has been in the police force for 15 years. With the confidence of being a cop's daughter, the tough and beautiful Duvall solves crimes in Massachusetts through a series of four novels. Smith-Levin, who died in 2009, claimed she wrote the novels to help her get through the crises and challenges of police work.

Penny Mickelbury worked in print and television media for ten years before she decided to focus on writing fiction. Her work includes two crime series, the first of which introduced African-American Mimi Patterson, an investigative reporter who first appears in Mickelbury's 1994 debut novel *Keeping Secrets*. The second series features African-American criminal defence attorney Carole Ann Gibson, who becomes an amateur sleuth after her husband is killed.

Rachel Howzell Hall

Howzell Hall was born in Los Angeles, where she currently lives with her husband and daughter. She is the author of eight novels, including four in the critically-acclaimed series featuring black police detective Elouise 'Lou' Norton. *Trail of Echoes* (2016), the third novel in the series, received a Kirkus Star and was one of Kirkus Reviews' 'Books That Kept Us Up All Night'. *Land of Shadows* (2014) and *Skies of Ash* (2015) were included on the *Los Angeles Times*' 'Books to Read This Summer'. Howzell Hall also co-authored with James Patterson *The Good Sister*, one of the three novellas contained in his 2017 book *The Family Lawyer*. A featured writer on NPR's acclaimed 'Crime in the City' series, Rachel has also served as a mentor in AWP's Writer to Writer Program and is currently on the board of directors of the Mystery Writers of America.

Howzell Hall's Elouise 'Lou' Norton is a black woman homicide detective working in a squad of white men in South Central Los Angeles. Lou's childhood ended early when her older sister disappeared, and she chose to make the police her career, partly to make sense of what had happened. Norton, who works with her police partner Colin Taggert, is a tough and determined investigator with a smart, snappy and witty voice. The *New York Times* described her as 'a formidable fighter – someone you want on your side'.

Before she wrote the Norton series, Howzell Hall wrote commercial fiction and self-published two mysteries. Her first book, *A Quiet Storm,* was published with Scribner in 2002. Yet afterwards, she found herself unable to secure another book deal. She believes this was due to the fact she was writing in the time of 'urban lit'. 'It was all those gritty types of literature,' she said. 'Editors didn't see my work as black enough. Or as urban enough, which was insulting because I am black, and I grew up in the Crenshaw area of Los Angeles. I couldn't understand it.'

Speaking during the round table discussion *'It's Up to Us'*, Howzell Hall said she was initially 'terrified' of writing a police procedural mystery because she didn't know anything about the police process. When pregnant with her daughter Maya, she was diagnosed with breast cancer. Three years later she had another cancer scare. 'I figured I am not guaranteed to be here, and I need to figure out what I want to do before tumours take me,' she said.

'I decided that I wanted to write a procedural with a character who's like me, like the women I went to school with, a black woman in contemporary black Los Angeles, doing things and solving crime and all the rest of it. So, 'Lou' came out of my need to one, normalise my life, and two, kind of reckon with my mortality. And I grew up reading Chandler and Stephen King and all these cool people who wrote about cool places, and I love Los Angeles and I thought it was a cool place, so I wanted to write something about my part of LA.

'While in the past it had been scary and frustrating, now I'm here and this is my voice and I'm glad I've written a character who resonates with a lot of people.'

Many black writers with white editors have to make changes in the character's language, but Howzell Hall's editor let her keep Lou's dialect. 'White folks get to say things that none of us understand, but they keep going,' she said. 'My editor lets me say what I have to say and let Lou be who she is and that way you bring the reader along. My character Colin is white, so I get him to be the clueless white guy Lou has to explain to. That's my out for explaining random black things to a white audience.'[39]

Private eyes

Although private investigators *were* paid for their work, they investigated without the aid of an institution. The appeal of private eyes to both writers and readers is the way they are able to challenge authority, triumph over the seemingly impossible and right society's wrongs. Among the most well-known authors of the PI genre are, as we saw earlier in this study, Sir Arthur Conan Doyle, Dashiell Hammett, Raymond Chandler, Sue Grafton, Sara Paretsky, James Lee Burke, Marcia Muller, and Alafair Burke.

Private investigators usually have some training, many useful skills and a licence they can lose if they cross the police too often. The dialogue is usually witty, the tone is dark and gloomy. They act like medieval knights or Western heroes and, very often, have had a traumatic childhood or past. They also have a very sincere, personal moral code and are always on the side of truth and justice, often taking justice into their own hands. This makes them very appealing to readers.

A private eye series will often forefront social issues. Sara Paretsky, for instance, assimilates feminist issues with social, cultural, political and environmental concerns. Jacqueline Winspear, the writer of the Maisie Dobbs novels, addresses issues related to First World War veterans.

The first known black female author to write a novel featuring any kind of black 'investigator' was Dolores Komo who, in *Clio Browne: Private Investigator* from 1988, introduced her eponymous protagonist. Browne is the daughter of the first black private detective in St Louis and the novel, while sticking firmly to the traditional private eye formula, has a semi-humorous tone.

There are very few examples of contemporary black PIs. The most well-known is Tamara Hayle, who was created by Valerie Wilson Wesley. Wilson Wesley, a former executive editor of *Essence* Magazine, grew up in Ashford Connecticut, graduated from Harvard University, received her Masters' from Columbia Graduate School of Journalism, then settled down to write. She has written for children, teenagers, young adults, and adult readers of non-crime fiction, but she is best known for her private eye Tamara Hayle, who inhabited a series of eight novels. A brilliant, independent and persistent former cop and a single mum, Hayle is important as she is the first female black private eye to be published by a mainstream publisher. She has a vibrant personality and is known for her wisecracks.

Amateur detectives

Unlike private eyes, amateur sleuths are not paid for their work. They are not licensed to work a case. Nor are they employed by any police force. They are more often the heroines of cozies and mysteries than of thrillers. In books that feature these sleuths, the characters are often quirky, the dialogue is frequently amusing, and the tone is generally upbeat. This however is not always so. Some amateur sleuths have a darker profile. These include Ellen Hart's Jane Lawless, Nevada Barr's Anna Pigeon, and Kate White's Bailey Weggins, whose novels have a tone and atmosphere that is gritty, highly tense and full of suspense. Amateur sleuths hold down a variety of different jobs. Jane K Cleland's Josie Prescott is an antiques dealer and Donna Andrews' Meg Langslow is a decorative blacksmith.

Attica Locke, a former Los Angeles screenwriter, has written several award-winning books set in her native Texas. Her three sleuths are Jay Porter, a black lawyer and former civil rights worker in Houston, black Texas Ranger Darren Matthews, who investigates crime in a small east coast town, and Caren Gray, a young African-American woman who manages an estate that used to be a plantation.

Pamela Thomas-Graham, a Harvard educated entrepreneur and the first black woman partner at a New York consulting firm, developed the Ivy League Mystery series, featuring amateur sleuth Nikki Chase, a black economics professor. Terris McMahan Grimes is responsible for the award-winning Theresa Galloway mystery series. Her sleuth is a personnel officer for a state agency in Sacramento, as well as a 38-year-old wife and mother of two and is unusual among the amateur sleuths I have so far encountered in being largely oblivious of race, racial identity and racism.

New Jersey-born Kellye Garrett worked as a staff writer on the CBS crime drama Cold Case before writing her first novel *Hollywood Homicide* (2017), which was named one of BookBub's Top 100 Crime Novels of All Time before going on to win the Agatha, Anthony, Lefty and Independent Publisher IPPY awards for best first novel. This story introduces the amateur sleuth Dayna Anderson, an out-of-work actress who answers an advertisement for a private investigator. She is a complicated heroine and the plot is whimsical and witty. Both in the book and in her own discussions around it, Garrett focuses more on her protagonist's personality than her colour. *Hollywood Ending* (2018), the second 'Detective by Day' novel, was chosen as best mystery of 2018 by *Suspense* magazine, Book Riot, and CrimeReads. Today Garrett is a member of Mystery Writers of America and International Thriller Writers, and is on the board of directors at Sisters in Crime. In 2018, with award-winning authors Walter Mosley and Gigi Pandian, she co-founded the mixed-sex black crime organisation Crime Writers of Color, which now has 170 members. Her vision for Crime Writers of Color is to provide a space to highlight crime and mystery writers from traditionally under-represented racial, cultural and ethnic backgrounds and to enable them to support one another when dealing with the unique issues that come with being a person of colour who writes crime fiction.

'Publishing hasn't always been kind to its writers from marginalised backgrounds,' Garrett said. 'You see something like Frankie's List that shares the appallingly low number of marginalised writers who are crime fiction writers. What that list doesn't share are how many of those listed are still being published today. That number is even lower.' This isn't due to lack of talent, she says, but because black writers have not been offered the opportunities their white counterparts are afforded. 'I'm so happy because it seems like publishing is finally fully embracing diverse voices in almost all subgenres in crime fiction,' she added. 'But I want to make sure our stories become status quo and not just a trend like it has in the past.'[40]

Barbara Neely has created dark-skinned African-American amateur sleuth Blanche White, a 40-year-old mother and domestic worker. Ironically, her name means 'white white'. White has big bones, big hips, big breasts and big arms, and a very big spirit. She works in North Carolina for a white woman and, over a series of four novels, has to juggle her job, her child-care duties and the crimes she solves. Neely's novel *Blanche on the Lam* (1992) is one of the most successful first crime novels ever written. It received the Agatha award for Best First Mystery Novel and the Macavity and Anthony awards for Best First Novel.

In *Blanche on the Lam*, White's first encounter with crime is a thirty-day jail sentence, handed down because four of her employers left town without paying her and, as a result, one of her cheques bounced. The feisty White goes on the run and is able to hide out with a wealthy family, who only take her on because they mistake her for a previous employee, apparently not noticing that she is a different woman. Readers are made to see that, to white people, blacks are invisible – they all look alike – and black domestic servants are doubly invisible. The strong racial theme in this novel is as arresting as the mystery and crime theme. Over the series, the political narrative grows firmer, although the original and memorable White remains a highly independent and proud figure.

I asked several white crime writers whether they felt they would – or could – successfully create black characters for their novels.

Alison Bruce is currently writing a book with a black character called Celia. 'She's a Windrush baby who has had a career in journalism and now writes puffy pieces for glossy magazines, but she can't help being dragged back,' Bruce said. 'I like the character very much, but I worry about not representing somebody well enough. Obviously, I am a white woman and I am writing about a black woman and I don't want to write a stereotype. I want to write somebody who seems authentic. If you care about what you are writing, it can be daunting to think, what if I don't get this right? I don't know. I can't see that I haven't got it right. So, I am hoping that I nail the character.'

Anna Mazzola says she feels 'slightly nervous' writing her first black character. 'I don't want to be accused of stealing people's stories,' she said. 'It's a former slave I am writing about and I'm doing my own research. I do think it is important to tell these stories. It is easy in a way, because I am dealing with eighteenth-century Paris and there were a number of black slaves. He is not a main character.

'I did have an idea for a modern novel set in the 1950s, where one of the protagonists would have been black, but I talked to several writers about it and lots of them felt uncomfortable about me having a main character who was black when I myself was not. They said people would criticise me for that. They thought it would be difficult for me to get published. I think it is partly to do with the writers, but it is also partly to do with the publishers and what they are willing to publish.'

Ann Cleeves believes progress is being made. 'I think we are getting there, there is a lot more diversity,' she said. 'But there needs to be more. I was one of the judges with Abir Mukherjee for the inaugural Harvill Secker/Bloody Scotland competition to find BAME writers who maybe did not have the confidence to submit work. He and I agreed that class is actually more important than colour and race in lots of ways. It is so hard if you don't have contacts within the publishing world. Or if you don't live in London. We need to encourage people from working backgrounds, and those who are not white, not artistic, not well educated, because they have so much to say, and know a lot more about crime than we do. We feel those voices ought to be heard.'

Sara Paretsky said the big sea change in publishing – the conglomeratisation of the industry and the way writers' incomes have plummeted – is largely responsible for the lack of representation. 'Writers of colour, who were doing crime fiction, were the first to be moved out of the market,' she said. 'You have someone like Valerie Wilson Wesley, whom I think is enormously talented, featuring a middle-class African-American woman... beautifully written, really interesting. But there just wasn't room for her. And in the publishers' minds, there wasn't a market for her.

'Similarly, several years ago I mentored an African-American woman who had created, long before that, a policewoman who spoke like a middle-class person – and publishers wanted ghetto talk. They didn't want a normal African-American person. We never could get through. We worked and worked and worked, and wrote and rewrote, and no one would ever give her the time of day. It was infuriating and heartbreaking.'

Paretsky said that she would not consider writing a main

character who was African-American. 'Here in the US, issues of race are such that it would feel to me like cultural appropriation, or misappropriation, for me to try to create a main character who was African-American. When I first imagined VI Warshawski, I knew Chicago was such a place where everyone's racial and ethnic identity matters enormously. I knew she couldn't be African-American or Latino. Instead I have several smaller characters who are African-American and who come and go.

'Man, I can tell you, when Warshawski had an affair with a black police officer, I was startled by the hate mail I received. Unregenerate racist! And my two characters broke up. Not because of the black/white thing, but because they were a private eye and a policeman.'

10

Women in Forensic Science

Soon after forensic fiction entered the crime writing world it became the most popular genre in that field, both on the printed page and on the television screen. The explosion of women's writing in this arena was huge.

What is it about forensic science that is both so complex and so gripping that it takes hold of the imagination of several superb women crime writers and many thousands of women readers?

The human body holds many secrets. After death, it is left to a range of forensic scientists to analyse the physical evidence for clues about a crime scene and its victim, and help find the killer. There are differences between the work and the skills of a forensic pathologist and those of a forensic anthropologist. The former will perform autopsies to try to establish the manner and cause of death, with a general focus on analysing blood, soft tissue, organs and bodily fluids. The latter analyse the bones and human skeletal remains.

Crime writers who use forensic science as the backdrop to their novels, or give their protagonists jobs as forensic scientists, need either to have the expertise at hand and already be scientists, or do a great deal of research.

Foremost among the many exciting forensic thrillers are those by Elly Griffiths, whose heroine Ruth Galloway is a forensic anthropologist, and those by former physician Tess Gerritsen, who created the remarkable duo of homicide detective Jane Rizzoli and medical examiner Maura Isles.

Elly Griffiths was a former publisher who initially wrote a series of novels about Italy under her real name Domenica de Rosa. The plot of her debut crime novel, *The Crossing Places* (2009), came to her fully formed one day during a trip to Titchwell Marsh in Norfolk with her husband, who had just given up his city job to train as an archaeologist. Griffiths has described seeing Ruth Galloway – the forensic archaeologist who would become her lead character – walking towards her through the mist. Her agent suggested the switch to writing crime meant she needed to think of a pen name, more suitable for the genre, and Elly Griffiths was born. Since the publication of that first book, Galloway has featured in 13 further novels to date, the most recent of which is *The Night Hawks* (2021).

Tess Gerritsen studied anthropology at Stanford University and went on to study medicine at the University of California in San Francisco before working as a physician in Hawaii. She initially wrote romantic thrillers and didn't bring her first-hand knowledge of the human body and the medical world to her novels until 1996 when she published *Harvest*, a chilling and suspenseful story about the black market in human organ trafficking. *The Surgeon*, her first Rizzoli and Isles thriller, was published in 2001 and succeeded in bridging the gap between medical thrillers and crime fiction. Homicide detective Jane Rizzoli was initially only a secondary character, and medical examiner Maura Isles did not feature until the second in the series, *The Apprentice*, which came out the following year.

Gerritsen's novels are not for the squeamish or highly sensitive reader, although much of the violence takes place off stage. Gerritsen says her medical background not only provided her with material, but also the education and wherewithal to tell the story from the point of view of the medical characters involved; specifically, her medical examiner Isles. 'As I went into crime fiction, my knowledge and experience gave me a comfort with the autopsy room,' she said. 'And a comfort with cause of death and manner of death, all those little forensic details that I didn't have to research as hard.'

Gerritsen admits that Isles is in many ways based on herself, although she was also only introduced as a minor player in the second story. 'As soon as I put her on the page and started to describe her as being aloof and mysterious, I wanted to know more and more about her,' she said. 'And I guess I grafted my own character on to her character.'

Having trained as an anthropologist as well as a scientist and a physician has elevated Gerritsen's status as a crime writer. But when she wrote her first medical thriller, her agent didn't even know that she was a doctor. 'I didn't tell her before because it wasn't relevant,' she said. 'Then I wrote *Harvest* and I had to tell her. Her response was, why the hell haven't you written a medical thriller before?'

Also topping the forensic crime charts are two exceptional writers: Patricia Cornwell, who has brought to life the famous and hugely popular fictional forensic pathologist Kay Scarpetta, and Kathy Reichs, who created world-class forensic anthropologist Temperance Brennan.

Kathy Reichs, who was born in Chicago, is now one of America's two most critically, creatively and commercially important crime writers. Her first novel *Déjà Dead* (1997) introduced to the world her first-person narrator Temperance Brennan, Director of Anthropology for the province of Quebec, today the most famous forensic expert in the world of crime fiction. Against all Reichs' expectations, that debut novel won the 1997 Ellis Award for Best First Book and became a *New York Times* bestseller. After many more chartbusters in the series, Reichs became a producer on the long-running Fox TV series *Bones,* which is based on the novels and on Temperance Brennan's work and life.

Like her much-loved character, Reichs is also a leading

forensic anthropologist, one of only a hundred to have been certified by the American Board of Forensic Anthropology, where she has served on the board of directors. She has also been a vice president of both the American Academy of Forensic Sciences and the American Board of Forensic Anthropology and is currently a member of the Canadian National Police Services Advisory Council. For many years she acted as a consultant to the Office of the Chief Medical Examiner in North Carolina. She also consults for the Laboratoire de Sciences et de Médecine Légale for Quebec province. As a teacher and mentor, she shows FBI agents how to recover and dissect human remains. Her practical work has included helping exhume a mass grave in Guatemala and journeying to Rwanda to testify at the UN Tribunal on Genocide. She carried out forensic work at Ground Zero in New York and has aided in the identification of the dead from the Second World War, Korea and South East Asia.

Unlike Patricia Cornwell, who is first and foremost a writer, Kathy Reichs needs to do very little research. From the start of her writing career, she has used her work experience to authenticate her dramatic thrillers, giving her readers not only an engaging and suspenseful plot, but a fascinating glimpse into the world of crime and forensics. When bones are found and answers are needed, the authorities call Brennan. And she takes every case to heart.

'In the early days, when nobody knew who Temperance Brennan was, when we were doing marketing and promotion, I know they (the publishers) pitched the fact that I was still engaged in forensics,' Reichs said. 'Perhaps that was a successful marketing ploy. It definitely gave the books a certain authenticity.

'The labs in which I worked for 20 years were the full set, from crime and medical legal labs. I was regularly interacting with all the different forensic specialities, whether it was ballistics or arson, or pathology or dentistry. I was constantly interacting and being actively involved in cases. I saw how it worked. I was also involved with the investigating officers. If there was a criminal situation, I did not have to go out and telephone people or visit labs or research it. I had every scrap of it and what it meant right there with me. I do think that gave my books an authenticity that other authors might not have had.'

She admits that, in spite of her knowledge, expertise and experience, she remains fanatical about getting the science right in her novels. At the same time, she and her fellow forensic science writers have to tread a fine line between accuracy and authenticity, and making sure the story is pacy, entertaining and accessible. 'You can lose readers,' she said. 'If you put in too much jargon, too much detailed scientific information.'

The success of her books and the companion television series *Bones* – and the huge popularity of forensic crime novels and television shows in general – has surprised Reichs. People have always been interested in crime and mystery, but since the 1990s, readers and viewers seem to have been increasingly drawn to the science-driven stories. Reichs' books are more intriguing because the stories are based on her own real experiences in the field and, although loosely, on real cases she has worked. Her debut novel *Déjà Dead* was inspired by a serial murder case, one that involved dismemberment. *Grave Secrets* (2002) was based on her experiences exhuming mass graves in Guatemala.

Although the novels, by necessity, include graphic descriptions of victims' bodies and human remains, Reichs tries hard not to be gratuitous or sensational. 'You try not to put any grisly scenes in unless they advance the plot,' she said. 'I don't want to put gratuitous gore in my books. I'll never do that. I do want to be realistic. I'll put it in there if it's realistic, if there's a point to it. It's hard to do that. It's a balancing act to do that and not be offensive. You have to be sensitive about it. You are dealing with violent death. You really have to walk this tightrope to get it right.'

In her novels, Reichs often undercuts or interrupts the more shocking and gruesome scenes with humour, something else that reflects her own real experiences of working in the field. 'There is what we call gallows humour, or black humour, which goes on in the autopsy room,' she said. 'It is a tension breaker. Or a stress reliever. Cops make jokes. Sometimes the pathologist or dentist, or whoever happens to be working on the autopsy, will do it. The only situation where it never takes place is when it is a child. Then there is absolute total silence. But I wanted humour in the books because I enjoy that. I'm told that when Tempe says something – she's kind of a smart-ass – my friends say they can hear me saying that.'

As well as making the stories authentic, the more gruesome scenes and details emphasise a very powerful desire to obtain justice for the innocent victims of crime. Through her plots, and through her lead protagonist, Reichs tries to bring to her stories the emotions she herself has felt in the course of her work. And that's what makes the character of the cool, professional and hyper-focused Temperance Brennan such an appealing and relatable one. Reichs believes some of the lead characters in forensic science fiction can come across as cold and unapproachable.

She admits that Temperance Brennan does share many of her own characteristics, at least in terms of her career and her appearance. 'I wanted to have a strong female protagonist who worked in the world of forensic science,' she said. 'It just seemed easier to base her on me, professionally, not personally. She's got her own thing going.'

In all of the books, Brennan handles any sexism from her male colleagues or police contacts with firm, yet friendly spirit. 'I think that's the way I handle it as well,' Reichs said. 'She's not prickly, she's not overly defensive, but she's strong in her views. I think she probably adheres to the old, "you get more flies with honey than with vinegar" idea if she wants to turn these guys around.' Reichs acknowledges that there is relatively little sexism and discrimination in the real forensic anthropologist world, partly because it is academic-based and partly because the ratio of men to women is around three-to-one, much lower than in other disciplines. Yet she has encountered situations where men have been resistant to working with a female, especially one who might be in a position of authority, or more knowledgeable than they are.

Reichs did not want her brilliant, empathetic heroine to be perfect, so she gave her some very human vulnerabilities and flaws, in her personal life at least. As well as being a smart, hard-working and intuitive professional, Brennan is a divorcee and a recovering alcoholic. 'I just wanted her to have something that she might struggle with,' she said. 'Something people could identify with. Even if you don't understand alcoholism, you understand the idea of having that kind of character flaw.'

A positive feature central to all the novels is the importance of women's friendships. Before Brennan's closest friend Gabby dies, this is made very explicit. 'I feel very strongly how critical friendships are to women,' Reichs said. 'They are very different from male friendships. With some exceptions obviously, females form networks that I don't think males do. Maybe they are doing so a little more now than in the past. My husband still has a few good men friends from the Marine Corps who connect regularly, but they don't do it like women do. They gather. They talk about sport. Not the kind of emotional things women do.' These friendships are possibly more important because, in Reichs' books, they occur within a dangerous, deadly and often frightening circle of events.

Although Reichs often uses real cases and experiences as inspiration for her stories, and Brennan does share some of the writer's own traits, she has always been reluctant to reveal too much of her own personal life in her work. In her 2020 novel *A Conspiracy of Bones* however, she puts her lead character through the same medical condition that she herself suffered. Reichs gives Brennan an unruptured cerebral aneurysm as well as the subsequent surgery. This means she has to discover the identity of a faceless corpse and its connection to a ten-year-old missing child case without the facilities usually available to her through the medical examiner's office or forensic lab. Instead she is forced to rely on her own trusted colleagues and on her own resources. Brennan finds it hard, having to work the case as an outsider, especially from a psychological point of view.

Among the most rewarding aspects of Reichs' writing work are the people who have gone on to train as forensic anthropologists as a direct result of reading her novels. 'I've had people come up to me at signings and readings and tell me that Temperance Brennan inspired them to enter the field,' she said. 'I love hearing that; that Brennan might have inspired a whole new generation of scientists, especially when they are women.'

Reviewers and critics frequently contrast and compare Reichs' fictional work, and the ideas at its foundations, with those of fellow forensic crime writer Patricia Cornwell.

Miami-born Cornwell is now the biggest-selling crime writer in the world. Over the past 30 years, she has sold more than 100 million books. Her novels are a perfect fit between the standard police procedural and forensic science stories in which much of the investigation is based on painstaking rigorous posthumous evidence.

A former crime journalist, who also worked for six years at the Office of the Chief Medical Examiner, Cornwell burst onto the mystery scene in 1990 with *Postmortem*, the first book in her Kay Scarpetta series. The story was inspired by a series of murders in Richmond, Virginia where most of the series is set. That debut pioneered the forensic scientific crime novel and won the Macavity, the Edgar, the Anthony and the John Creasey Awards for Best First Novel, as well as the French Prix du Roman d'Aventures, a ground-breaking march of success that not only points to the novel's original and innovative qualities but also to the fact that American women writers were now clearly visible to juries and award-giving panels – unlike their British women counterparts who had been visible over the water for the previous 60 years.

Once *Postmortem* was published, dozens of different awards were picked up by American women. Nancy Pickard walked away with prizes for *IOU* in 1991. A year later, Barbara Neely took awards for *Blanche on the Lam*. In 1993, prizes were given to Nevada Barr for *Track of the Cat* and, three years later, Terris McMahan Grimes walked away with awards for *Somebody Else's Child*. At roughly the same time, private eye novels featuring lesbian protagonists sprang up, mainly from small presses, and were seen everywhere. Suddenly, powerful women writers became prominent in every crime writing sub-genre.

Cornwell's debut novel did not have an auspicious start, however. She wrote three novels before *Postmortem*, all of which were rejected. At the book's launch, not one buyer turned up, only a single stray shopper who wanted directions to the store's cookery department. On its release, the story attracted a degree of controversy, owing to its similarities to the real-life case of Timothy Spencer, a serial killer who raped and murdered four women in Virginia in 1987. Cornwell had been working as a computer analyst at the Office of the Chief Medical Examiner in Richmond when the killings took place. Yet her terrifying and thrilling story – and her intriguing and compelling lead character Kay Scarpetta – very quickly caught the imagination of the reading public.

An interesting point about Kay Scarpetta – and her character arc – is that while she has an official status as a medical examiner, she operates much of the time like a private eye, partly because of the way she is drawn into each investigation, both professionally and personally. In the first book, the villain is a sadistic serial killer who, it later transpires, is after Scarpetta herself and even manages to break into her house. This novel is high on tension and mounting suspense. The sense of threat throughout is terrifying and the violence is graphic and gruesome. The autopsy scenes are equally detailed and macabre.

Scarpetta, the Chief Medical Examiner of Virginia, is fascinatingly rendered by Cornwell. Like Reichs' Temperance Brennan, she shares a resemblance with her creator. Born in Miami, she is described as blonde and blue-eyed and is tall and striking with a strong Southern accent. She has no problem confronting and doing battle with her chauvinist colleagues. Cornwell's perspective is not radical in any way; it is that of a strong liberal feminist. She ensures Scarpetta is seen as a highly competent, high-ranking professional career woman who stands as an equal to the males in her work life. This does not prevent her male boss from breaking into Scarpetta's computer to alter crucial data in order to undermine her career. Nor does it stop the machinations of the male attorney whom we assume would be on Scarpetta's side. The Virginia attorney who ought to support Scarpetta is finally unmasked as a rapist with designs on the medical examiner herself. What Scarpetta needs is kind, compassionate, supportive backup from her team with whom she has to work very closely. Yet Pete Marino, the police sergeant assigned to the case, is seen in this book as a sexist redneck. Marino will go on to become one of Scarpetta's closest friends, whose loyalty to her is never in doubt. In *Postmortem*, it is Marino who shoots the rapist at close quarters and saves Scarpetta's life.

Two features of this first novel make it seem like a throwback to an earlier, more conservative age, in spite of the fact it uses the most modern forensic evidence to empower its plot line. Its ethos is very black and white, very good and evil, very absolute. And in these unambiguous scenarios, the shooting (by one of the good guys) of a rapist and murderer (the bad guy) who is armed only with a knife is seen not only as just, but essential and intensely desirable. The reader, who has shared in the terror and suspense for 16 gripping chapters, goes along with this. The killer is portrayed not as a psychopath who is nevertheless a human being with a past and with challenges and motivations of his own, but as a monster. He is given a non-human smell, a sickening body odour caused by a rare and strange metabolic disorder. Readers are asked to accept that he behaves like a monster because he *is* a monster.

The finest parts of the novel involve Cornwell's authentic use of the most recent technological advances in forensic science alongside the more traditional mix of police procedural and private investigative work. This provides the blueprint for her subsequent work and there are several key themes. The behaviour of the male rivals who sabotage her work. The killer who will come to target Scarpetta herself. In these stories, it is the forensic science, the autopsy techniques and the high-tech computer know-how, along with the tenacity and determination of the key characters, which eventually bring down a string of sadistic serial killers. As in many crime novels written by women, females are both victims and heroines or – as is the case with Scarpetta – both of these at the same time.

When Scarpetta was created, she lived in a relatively low-tech world. Society was only just waking up to DNA. In her first outing, Scarpetta has to fight for DNA evidence to be analysed. Cornwell wanted to do more research into this new discipline called forensic science, yet technology progressed at such a pace that the new research was always a few steps ahead of her. She was – and is – constantly trying to catch up and keep up with the latest forensic innovations, to remain authentic and stay on the cutting edge so that the books continue to sell. Her research has always been wide-ranging, far-reaching, meticulous and obsessive. Over the last 30 years, she has spent millions of dollars on it. She now has a team of consultants, who are experts in every aspect of crime, and owns her own extensive collection of weaponry and lab equipment. Much of her research, however, is not done in a lab, but out in the field. She works with people at the forefront of the very latest technology, with ideas and innovations that have yet to reach the average laboratory.

Yet her dark obsession with crime – and with the bleakest elements of the human mind and character – began much earlier in her life. To Cornwell, the world has never seemed a safe place and she carried fear and insecurity with her from an early age. She grew up in a world that was unstable, unsettling and often frightening. Her father, one of the leading appellate lawyers in the US, left the family home when she was five years old, walking out on Christmas Day, 1961. A lonely child, she spent much of the next few months wandering the streets, where she was molested by a local patrolman, whom she later discovered was a convicted paedophile. She was saved only by an extraordinary coincidence; her elder brother happened to cycle past and scared the man away. This traumatic incident meant she was forced to testify against her molester in front of a Grand Jury, a terrifying experience for such a young child.

Her mother Marilyn fell into a severe depressive illness that left her unable to hold the family together. In 1961 she moved with them to Montreat, North Carolina, the rural hometown of the evangelist Billy Graham, whose teachings she had discovered and come to admire. After several psychotic episodes, she was detained in a psychiatric hospital. Billy Graham's wife, Ruth Bell Graham, took in Cornwell and her brothers and arranged for them to be raised by foster parents, Leonore and Manfred Saunders. Under their 'care', Cornwell was bullied, abused and intimidated.

It was Ruth Bell Graham – who would eventually become a second mother to Cornwell – who recognised the young woman's writing talent, as well as her nerve and resilience. Under the older woman's guidance, she attended King College, in Bristol, Tennessee then moved to Davidson College on a tennis scholarship. From there she graduated with a BA in English in 1979 before securing a job as a reporter for *The*

Charlotte Observer. She later went on to work in the Chief Medical Examiner's office, as a technical writer and a computer analyst.

There have been plenty of other dark times since then. Her success and the consequent wealth did not buy her peace or happiness. In 1996, she was betrayed by so-called friends and very publicly 'outed' as a lesbian. She was so scared and humiliated that she did not leave her house for a month. She has been treated for anorexia, bulimia and bi-polar disorder and has crashed a car while drunk. In 2007, she had to go to court to seek an injunction against a cyber-stalker. Two years after that, she discovered that a 40-million-dollar chunk of her massive fortune had gone missing. Her obsession with Jack the Ripper and her exhaustive efforts to prove that he was British artist Walter Sickert have been dismissed and ridiculed by experts and the general public alike. Cornwell now travels everywhere with bodyguards, lives in a series of high security houses and keeps an arsenal of guns.

Her work as a crime reporter and the six years she spent in the Chief Medical Examiner's Office, along with her painstaking and extensive research, may have provided endless inspiration and ideas for her work and account for its authenticity. Yet it is the difficult periods in her life, and the fear she has carried around with her for so long, that give the books such resonance and go some way to explaining the great sympathy she shows for the fictional victims of violent crime, and Scarpetta's determination to give the dead a voice.

Cornwell believes her terrible early experiences helped her use her creativity in a very powerful way. It was a way of escaping a place she was trapped in, when she was in foster care and not allowed to leave the house, when she was not able to do the things her brothers could do. Her vivid imagination enabled her to transport herself into a different world, one that was more satisfying and just.

Like Reichs' Temperance Brennan, Kay Scarpetta bears a

resemblance to her creator that goes beyond her appearance. She is a divorcee with no children and she also lost her father young, although to leukaemia, not wilful abandonment. Scarpetta is a hard-working perfectionist immersed in her work. She is brave and resilient and has learned to take care of herself because she doesn't trust anyone else to do it for her. She has a strong and powerful sense of justice, and vengeance. The author herself however claims she has more in common with her lead protagonist's niece, the fiery and brilliant Lucy, who is gay and was created at a point when there were very few lesbians in mainstream fiction. Lucy is so daring and so successful a character that, although she doesn't actually throw flames, readers believe she could if she fancied.

Some up-front lesbian crime writers feel that Cornwell was still so afraid of public reaction to homosexuality that she did not make Scarpetta openly gay and had her hide behind her niece. Other contemporary female crime writers feel that Cornwell wanted the largest possible audience for Scarpetta, so that she could highlight the difficult position her heroine was in, simply by being a woman in a sexist scientific and criminal world.

Cornwell has also suggested that the character of Scarpetta, along with many other women protagonists written by women authors, can show readers how to be fully functioning human beings, and have more individuality and independence, and lead more complete lives. Today she lives with great happiness and some measure of calmness – and certainly with more emotional security – with her wife Staci Gruber, a Harvard neuroscientist who has helped Patricia come to terms with her lesbian sexuality and be more open about it.

In an interview with magazine editor and talk show host Tina Brown, Cornwell said: 'I think American feminists – American women – need to get a whole lot tougher. We need to be more supportive of each other. I am competitive. But I don't believe in doing so at the expense of another person. We should help each other. If I can help you be number one, then maybe you can help me be number one and we help everybody be number one. Let us do it for each other.'

Cornwell was speaking at a summit aimed at bringing together leading women activists and political change-makers from around the world to share their stories and experiences and to offer solutions to building a better life for women and girls. She said: 'I think that if women feel they are not empowered at all and don't even know what it is to be empowered, they don't even know they are *not* empowered, and they let things stay the same. Men should enjoy us a little more if we are an equal partner and not just a piece of property or something that is to be controlled.'

One thing does damage both Scarpetta's character and that of her niece Lucy in the novels. By overdoing the emotional charge that she gives to ordinary people and ordinary occurrences, Cornwell is in danger of distorting the characters. It is not only the villains who are changed into monsters, but in a lesser way so too are the heroines enlarged, often beyond credibility. Lucy, described as a genius intellectually, is also subject to depressions, bouts of out-of-control drinking, and extreme emotional instability. The average reader might wonder how she was ever accepted into such a hardcore, dangerous FBI unit in the first place.

Scarpetta herself is so determined to pursue a maximum impact in every book in the series that she sometimes seems implausible rather than the independent feminist protagonist for which Cornwell is aiming. Scarpetta certainly does suffer male supremacist sabotage in the later books, such as *Cause of Death* (1996) but Cornwell needs to be wary of not expanding this into the realms of paranoid suspicions merely to increase the suspense and terror she is facing. The novels are so high on tension and stress and mounting suspense that not only does it tax the readers' belief and credibility but for Cornwell it makes writing each subsequent book harder and harder. I am tempted to ask, with a great deal of admiration for Cornwell as a writer and as a person prepared to make changes sexually, politically, and creatively, how many dragons does she have to slay?

The explicit, and sometimes exploitative violence and the graphic crime and autopsy scenes which, while clinical, are often sadistically violent in themselves have sometimes made Cornwell's work controversial. She denies her books are gratuitous, insisting that authenticity demands the overt use of explicit medical details.

Cornwell does acknowledge how much the things she has witnessed – as a young child, a young woman and as a hugely successful, high-profile adult – have changed her. 'If it doesn't change you, there's something wrong with you,' she said. 'I've seen, I guess, thousands of autopsies by now, hundreds of crime scenes, going all the way back to 1985. And it is not made up, it is real, and it is right there on the table in front of you. I am touched by all the things I have seen that I will keep with me for ever, and I always change and alter what I do because of it. Hopefully it has made me care about what other people go through.'

Cornwell added that people should never underestimate the ability of people to do very savage things. The root of all evil is the abuse of power, a theme that runs through the Scarpetta series. 'If we realise that we are capable of abusing power ourselves, then maybe we don't give ourselves such a quick pass,' she said. 'You have to have constant vigilance; not only to not be a prey to bad people, but to not become a bad person.'[41]

Yet in her books, there is always a counterbalance to the hideous evil and depravity, always something to emphasise the strength, resilience and decency of the characters who keep on fighting to overcome the darkness. The deeply nurturing aspect of Scarpetta's character – she loves food and cooking and is fiercely protective of her family and friends and the victims – makes her intensely human. She is loyal, brave and steadfast in her fight against evil, cruelty and abuse of power and has a deep and unshakeable desire for justice.

The moral purpose behind Cornwell's books, and the critical social conscience, remind me forcibly of Elizabeth George's similar stance. As in the first book in George's Lynley/Havers series, this aspect of Scarpetta's character is important. The novels show the protagonists to be ethical and serious, not merely entertaining and powerfully addictive. Because the violence is so grisly and its effect on readers so spine-chilling it is easy, for both readers and critics, to overlook the ethical significance and honourable intent behind these novels.

11

Killer Women, Domestic Noir, Violence Against Women

Killer Women, a recently formed collective of 19 British crime and mystery writers, is one of the most enterprising, enthusiastic and efficient crime writing groups. The group, set up in 2015 by Melanie McGrath and Louise Millar, includes Paula Hawkins, Emma Kavanagh, Kate Rhodes, Alex Marwood, Jane Casey, Erin Kelly, Colette McBeth, Sarah Hilary, Amanda Jennings, Alison Joseph, Tammy Cohen, Kate Medina, Laura Wilson, Sharon Bolton, Elly Griffiths, Rachel Abbott and Julia Crouch.

These women work together to put on innovative crime fiction events for readers around the country and to bring crime writers – male and female – together. In 2016, they produced their first *Killer Women: Crime Club Anthology* of short stories. A second collection followed a year later. Their 2018 Killer Women Crime Festival in London's Covent Garden was sold out. Among the writers and experts at the event were Sophie Hannah, who talked about adapting Agatha Christie's work for a new series of novels, the independent blogger the Secret Barrister, who provided an insight into the criminal justice system, and criminal psychologist Jennifer Rees who talked about the psychology of a psychopath, and how to spot one. In 2019, the group launched a mentoring scheme to support talented new writers in some very under-represented groups, such as BAME writers, or those from poorer backgrounds.

Members are keen to stress that the organisation aims to

support all crime writers, including men. 'The group did not want it to be an all-woman show,' Jane Casey said. 'We did not want it to say, this is our world and you are not invited. We wanted it to be inclusive of a big selection of good crime writers of both genders.'

Sarah Hilary added: 'We include men in our festivals; some are great friends, and some are writing heroes as well, and that to me is equality. The best of us, I hope, are fighting for the same things in the same way. And we always support each other.'

This makes the group markedly different from the earlier women's collective Sisters in Crime, which was set up in America in 1986 by Sara Paretsky. In spite of the common goals to support fellow women writers, there is a noticeable difference in style and aims between the two. Sisters in Crime was a face-the-challenges organisation, whilst Killer Women is a feel-good group with a focus on camaraderie and practical support.

Casey admits Killer Women is not hard-line feminist in the same way as Sisters in Crime. She has discovered that speaking out and challenging political issues – being overtly feminist – can sometimes have a negative effect on a writer's career. 'I'm very soft spoken and very gentle in real life and, you know, very polite in the way I talk to people,' she said. 'But online, I might say something that's a little bit more abrasive or challenging, and some people don't like it. You can lose as much as you gain by standing up and shouting about these things. Sometimes it's soft diplomacy that works. Sometimes though, you have to speak out.'

There was always room for an organisation for women writers, not as an overtly political feminist group, but as a help and support one. Encouraging and promoting one another's work is not difficult for the Killer Women. Almost all of them have been journalists or have worked in the media or publishing world before becoming crime novelists. Seven were journalists, one ran a press office, one was a television documentary maker, two worked for the BBC, another two had been literary or media relations consultants, and two had been in publishing. All this makes it easier for them to raise one another's profiles and attract positive attention for their books.

Sarah Hilary said the original members were all London-based. 'There was a heavy contingent of former media people in that area who were prepared to say, we are not getting the exposure that we should, but if there is a critical mass of us, we have the contacts to make that happen.' Kate Rhodes pointed to one chief difference between Killer Women and Sisters in Crime. 'We don't really have a manifesto,' she said. 'We are instead a group of women who got together as professional friends. The sort of unwritten word is that we exist to help each other and be supportive, but also to help other writers.' Rhodes said the organisation's mentoring scheme for under-represented groups of writers has had a huge take-up. 'It is representative of something we all believe in,' she said. 'Which is that writing should be thrown open to the widest possible range of participants. Currently it is not.'

Rhodes feels strongly that Killer Women does not currently have enough working-class writers, black writers, gay writers or disabled writers. 'I think all writing, not only crime writing, remains a difficult profession to enter,' she said. 'It is a very narrow door. If you are in a smaller category, it is even harder. At our conferences we don't just talk about gender, we talk about issues of interest to us all, such as what is going on in crime right now. We all want to explore political and emotional issues that crime writing raises, for other people as well.'

Killer Women will be aware that some of the problems Paretsky and her fellow writers tried to resolve are still unresolved today and that little has improved. At least two significant challenges remain. One is the need to persuade mainstream reviewers to give as much review space to women's books as is given to those written by men. The other is the desire to change people's perceptions of the invisible line between so-called 'literary fiction' and so-called 'genre fiction'. One side of that line is accorded high status and the other side is not.

Many of the Killer Women write novels that fall into the recent hugely popular and significant crime writing category of domestic noir. The term was coined by British novelist Julia Crouch in 2013 as a reaction to what she saw as the limitations of the label 'psychological thriller' that was being attached to many crime books, including her own.

According to Crouch, the locations of domestic noir novels are primarily homes and workplaces and the ideology of the stories is based on the broadly feminist view that the domestic sphere can be a difficult and often dangerous place for women. The novels concern themselves largely, though not exclusively, with the female experience based around relationships inside these locations.

Crouch said she felt her own novels were more an 'unravelling', rather than the high-octane rollercoaster suggested by the term 'psychological thriller'. British contemporaries of Crouch who subsequently defined themselves as writing domestic noir include Erin Kelly, Paula Hawkins, Elizabeth Haynes, Paula Daly, Louise Millar, Natalie Young, Clare Mackintosh, Sabine Durrant and Araminta Hall.

Louise Doughty, Lionel Shriver and Julie Myerson, whose major output is referred to by publishers as 'literary fiction', have nevertheless written enormously successful novels that fall readily into the sub-genre of domestic noir. This category, which is large and flexible, is a form of realistic writing that encompasses such disparate ideas and ideals as the myths and reality of mental illness, women's rights in the home as well as in the workplace, liberal and radical feminism, religion, family, motherhood and domestic violence. These novels subvert the idea that the home is a sanctuary. For many women, home is the reverse. It is a cage. A place of emotional and psychological tyranny. A place where they cannot grow, sometimes a place where they cannot even breathe.

Television, cinema, and even videogames, have gradually become saturated with domestic noir over the last decade, prompted by the publication and enormous success of Gillian Flynn's 2012 bestseller *Gone Girl* and Louise Doughty's *Apple Tree Yard* (2013). *Gone Girl* was adapted for film by Twentieth Century Fox in 2014 and went on to make a profit of almost 130 million dollars worldwide, making it one of the year's most lucrative films. *Apple Tree Yard*, which sold in 26 countries, was shortlisted for the CWA Steel Dagger and the National Book Awards Thriller of the Year and was a Richard and Judy Book Club choice. It was also made into a four-part prime-time BBC television series.

Gone Girl cleverly nailed the idea that you can never truly know the person you are closest to, nor the terrible things they might be capable of when pushed to the limit. *Apple Tree Yard* is the story of an intelligent and seemingly happily married woman whose affair with a stranger has dire consequences and a dark, unexpected twist.

This literary explosion did not start with Flynn's *Gone Girl*, however. Nor with that other phenomenally successful domestic noir bestseller, Paula Hawkins' 2015 novel *The Girl on the Train*, which is a devastating portrayal of a woman – a troubled and lonely alcoholic – caught up in a complex missing persons case involving her ex-husband. In fact, it started many years earlier in the novels known as marriage thrillers, including those written by Charlotte Armstrong, Margaret Millar and Patricia Highsmith.

Other writers often cited as predating modern domestic noir are Vera Caspary, Dorothy B Hughes, Minette Walters, Barbara Vine (Ruth Rendell's pen name for psychological thrillers) and Daphne du Maurier, whose bestselling 1938 novel, *Rebecca*, tells the story of a young woman who marries a wealthy widower, only to discover he is haunted by his ex-wife and may have murdered her.

Marriage thrillers were almost all written around the time of the Second World War, a period characterised by loss and death, during which many men returned from frontline combat suffering from shellshock, now known as Post Traumatic Stress Disorder. The consequent personality changes and mental illness, including anxiety and paranoia, along with the stress of having to adjust to life at home, put an enormous strain on domestic relationships.

Marriage thrillers ultimately questioned the centrality of the heterosexual relationship, often finding it alien rather than natural. Spouses who were soul mates became strangers; marriages that had been warm turned hostile and unpredictable. Homes that were once seen as shelters turned into prisons from which women could see no way of escape.

Contemporary British domestic thrillers are largely concerned with sexual rather than national politics, whereas America's Charlotte Armstrong made a significant contribution to national politics as well as to American mystery literature. As the threat of Communism and the fear of punishment and reprisals for those accused – whether innocent or guilty – swept the country, Armstrong made several of her novels decisively anti-McCarthy. One of the most exciting was *Mischief* (1950).

Armstrong also created some of the first anti-heroines, who predate the brink of today's feminist movement. All her novels challenge the status quo of women of her period and *Mischief* is a particularly interesting psychological study of social status and mental breakdown. Set in New York City, it is the story of a couple who find themselves having to leave their nine-year-old daughter in the care of an unreliable and unstable babysitter, a choice which has devastating consequences. This has become a classic theme in domestic suspense; the trusted stranger, the one we willingly let through our front door, is the person who poses the greatest threat.

In this novel, Armstrong cleverly shifts points of view,

between the loving mother Ruth, the manipulative and unstable babysitter Nell, the disgruntled young man whose rejection by his girlfriend sets him up for Nell's enticements, and the hotel guests whose suspicions are aroused as the night wears on. *Mischief* is among several of Armstrong's books to explore the sexual dynamics of gender and is also a powerful emotional reading of a damaged woman.

Canadian Margaret Millar, who was born in Ontario and educated at Toronto University, was surrounded by mystery and thrills in her home life, as well as on her desk. Her husband Kenneth Millar, better known as the crime writer Ross Macdonald, is significant in crime literature for his series of hardboiled novels set in Southern California featuring private investigator Lew Archer. In his series, Macdonald initially imitated his fellow writers Dashiell Hammett and Raymond Chandler, but by his sixth or seventh book, he found his own voice. After they married, Margaret Millar moved with him to the US.

Her best-known novel, *Beast in View* (1955), was hailed at the time as one of the best psychological mysteries ever written, certainly one of the most sinister. It won the 1956 Mystery Writers of America Edgar Award for Best Novel and the 1957 Edgar Allan Poe Award. The frightening story revolves around a 30-year-old woman, Helen Clarvoe, who is the heiress of a small fortune, and resented by her mother. A series of disturbing and threatening telephone calls leads the woman into a dangerous world of extortion, pornography, vengeance and murder.

Some years later, the domestic noir writers would take up Armstrong and Millar's themes – domestic violence and mental illness among them – but concentrate more on traumas associated with gender power struggles during conflicts in the home.

Patricia Highsmith is an extremely unusual writer whose early novels fall into the domestic noir category. As an American novelist and short story writer, she was known mainly for her psychological crime thrillers which led to more than two dozen film adaptations. She wrote 22 books and a great many short stories and her five novels featuring the character Tom Ripley were among her most popular. She is even more important for the crucial influence she has had on contemporary domestic noir. Although her luminous lesbian novel *Carol* (1952) is, in my view, a much better book – more stylish, more powerful, more original – Highsmith considered her 1977 novel *Edith's Diary* to be her masterpiece.

Edith's Diary was initially rejected for publication as it was seen as a book which did not fit securely into the crime fiction category. Yet Highsmith was ahead of her time. *Edith's Diary* is classic domestic noir; a dark, sad and disturbing story about a woman's slow but steady descent into madness. Left wing, liberal and energetic housewife Edith Howland begins to unravel after she moves from New York to Pennsylvania with her husband and their young son, who has been having behavioural problems. Instead of the perfect new life she had envisaged, Edith becomes trapped in a life of domestic drudgery, her husband leaves her for his younger secretary and her son becomes increasingly disturbed. Yet Edith keeps a diary – a written fantasy – describing her life as one of domestic joy, the life it depicts a sharp contrast to reality. Her fantasy life is one of domestic joy, her husband does not leave her, but lives with her in blissful harmony, and her weird son marries a kind and gracious woman and has several fine children. Women have been saved by diaries before.

Both this story and the 1954 novel *The Blunderer* are expert examples of domestic noir. *The Blunderer* is a tale of obsession, jealousy, guilt and murder, and the lengths an ordinary person might go to when pushed to their limits. It is unusual in that it features a male protagonist, yet it is similar to subsequent domestic noir novels in the attention it gives to the domiciliary and conjugal hell society can inflict on individuals and married couples shackled in homes in the suburbs.

Writer Fiona Peters, a professor of crime fiction at Bath Spa University, sweeps away the fact that Highsmith has many more male protagonists than women by suggesting that she does not need her heroes to be biologically female in order to interweave the feminine as well as the domestic into what she calls Highsmith's 'profoundly disturbing perspective'. Peters, whose crime fiction research has been internationally recognised, does not believe that only female protagonists represent femininity. Highsmith is able to represent female experience by 'pathologising female agency'. Walter Stackhouse, the hero of *The Blunderer*, reacts to events in his life in the same way that Edith Howland does in hers.[42]

Having looked at several marriage thrillers from years gone by, we are left with three important questions. How different are the modern domestic noir novels from their antecedents? Are their themes similar? Could their characters come from any period?

Journalist and novelist Melanie McGrath has written a riveting and absorbing psychological thriller, *Give Me the Child* (2017). The novel's themes of lying, betrayal, infidelity, gaslighting and emotional and mental abuse place it securely in the domestic noir category. But its intelligence and spellbinding imagination raise it out of what is sometimes seen as a mundane, if skilful, genre. McGrath's empathetic and credible protagonist Dr Cat Lupo is a happily married mother-of one and a specialist in child personality disorders. Her orderly life falls apart after police turn up with her husband's 11-year-old love child Ruby, whose mother has just died. Dr Lupo agrees to welcome her into her household and tries to love her, but the child's behaviour is disturbing, and she begins to question the circumstances surrounding her mother's death.

The story is set against the explosive 2011 London riots. It is hard to stand aside from the turmoil into which McGrath draws readers as Dr Lupo tries to separate her own tendency to paranoia from the very real suspicion that something truly malevolent now lurks in their household. This book has insight and wisdom on every page and asks the question, can a child be evil? I am reminded forcibly of Doris Lessing's 1988 novel, *The Fifth Child*, which tracks the changes in the lives of a happily married couple after the birth of their fifth child, a son, who is strange, violent and dysfunctional, and threatens to tear the family apart. As in McGrath's novel, Lessing's story examines the theme of motherhood and the associated anger, agony and ambivalence women often feel.

Crime, as is apparent to McGrath and many of her fellow writers in the Killer Women collective, is a medium that lends itself easily to a mixture of violence and high ideals.

Clare Mackintosh is a British award-winning novelist who spent 12 years in the police, including time in the CID and as a police order commander. After leaving the force, she worked as a freelance journalist and social media consultant. She founded and directed the distinguished Chipping Norton Literary Festival before turning her hand to writing fiction. Her novels have already sold more than two million copies worldwide and are published in more than 35 languages. Her debut, *I Let You Go* (2015), was a Richard and Judy Book Club pick and won the Theakston's Old Peculier Crime Novel of the Year Award. The French translation won the Best International Novel at the Cognac Festival Prix du Polar Awards. Mackintosh's second novel, *I See You* (2016), was also a Richard and Judy Book Club pick, winning the readers' vote. It was number one in the *Sunday Times* bestselling charts of original fiction and shortlisted for the Crime and Thriller Book of the Year in the British Book Awards. Her third novel *Let Me Lie* (2018) was number one in the *Sunday Times* original fiction list and again a Richard and Judy choice. A year later, her fourth book *After the End* was published in hardback and became an instant *Sunday Times* bestseller.

This fourth book is very different from the previous three, which are all first-class noir psychological thrillers. It is based on a very personal tragedy: the life-or-death decision Mackintosh and her husband were forced to make 12 years earlier, after one of their young sons became terminally ill. The writer's fictional rendering of this heart-breaking dilemma charts the story of Pip and Max after their son Dylan falls ill with a cancer that will leave him severely brain-damaged, with no quality of life. Pip wants to let him die with dignity; Max wants to take him to a US clinic for controversial treatment. The book adopts a 'sliding doors' approach and follows the consequences of each traumatic decision and the effect on the couple's relationship. The dilemma is painfully and powerfully rendered, and I can only dimly imagine what it must have taken out of Mackintosh to write that story. I cannot recommend this novel highly enough.

Other stand-out domestic noir thrillers include Julia Crouch's 2017 novel *Her Husband's Lover*. This is a dark and disquieting story of two women: Louisa Williams – who loses her husband and her children in a car accident – and her husband's angry and unhinged, pregnant lover Sophie, who wants to take everything Louisa has left. Araminta Hall's 2018 offering *Our Kind of Cruelty* is another disturbing, twisted novel about obsession and desire. This frightening yet addictive story takes readers into the mind of a male sociopath and analyses the complex lines between truth and perception.

Louise Doughty's *Platform Seven* (2019) is a beautifully constructed book, a hybrid of psychological thriller and ghost story, and a moving meditation on love of all kinds, the loss of many, and what happens to the human spirit under terrible tension. In *Seven Lies* (2020), Elizabeth Kay tells the story of two women, who have been best friends since childhood, and the lies, obsession and jealousy – and the tragic consequences – that tear their friendship and their lives apart.

'Flawed female characters and unreliable narrators are very

much key to these new novels,' writer Rebecca Whitney said. 'But many of these newer protagonists are in control of their destiny, even if that destiny is not pleasant, and the novels deal with more than just the damaged relationship, exploring as well the notion of a sinister presence entering the heart of the home – the place to where we retreat, where we expect to feel most safe and loved – and setting off an emotional bomb. More often than not, the instigator of this event, if not the woman herself, is old junk from her past; secrets from which she has been hiding or attempting to control.'

Whitney's own clever and disturbing 2014 debut, *The Liar's Chair* is the story of a woman whose toxic marriage – and life – falls apart after she is involved in a hit- and-run. The novel, which has been described as startling, dark and audacious, takes an unflinching look at domestic abuse. Whitney says the novel came about partly as a study of why women are enticed into and stay in relationships that cause them such pain. 'We all know domestic abuse happens,' she said. 'But what we don't understand is why seemingly strong, independent and educated women end up in a place of such fear and subservience. How is it that they appear to tolerate and cover up the terrible things that happen to them, and why is it so hard for them to put a stop to the cycle?'

Whitney said the new generation of women novelists writing about domestic abuse may be vocalising a form of collective rage that not more is being done to understand and help women who suffer at the hands of an abuser. 'Literature can be entertaining, but it can also be informative,' she said. 'And these books work in some small part towards dissecting the shame and powerlessness, the psychological and often violent manipulation that abused women experience to keep them trapped in this most toxic of relationships, away from prying eyes, and in the environment we expect to be the most loving and nurturing.

'Through the unpacking of this more sinister side of some relationships and the empathy that that creates, perhaps we can cease to blame the victim, and concentrate on punishing the real perpetrator of the crime.'[43]

Domestic noir novels delve deeply into the perilous ground that can lurk at the foundation of the closest intimate relationship and examine issues of adultery and betrayal, and the fine line between physical and emotional abuse. That the fictional emotional abuse so often spirals into physical violence and death sadly reflects too many women's real-life experiences and how easy it is to get caught up in a cycle of emotional and physical cruelty and mistreatment from which it can seem impossible to escape. An average of two women are killed every week by their partner or an ex-partner, according to the UK charity Refuge, and one in four women will be a victim of domestic violence at some point in their lives. Domestic violence, called intimate partner violence or battering in the US, can be defined as a pattern of abusive behaviour in any relationship that is used by one partner to gain or maintain power and control over the other.

As I write this study in 2020, 90 countries are in lockdown in an attempt to slow the progression of Covid-19. The lockdown restrictions have seen four billion people sheltering at home to protect themselves and their more vulnerable friends and relatives from the virus. Domestic abuse calls to UK police during this period increased by 11 per cent compared to the same period in 2019. A study carried out by the London School of Economics showed police took an average of 380 more domestic violence calls per week. Many of these calls came from concerned friends and from neighbours, and not directly from the victims themselves, suggesting the actual number of cases is much higher, with women feeling unable to come forward because of the lockdown restrictions, or too ashamed or afraid that reporting their partners might exacerbate the abuse, and that no one will be able to protect them. Telephone calls to the UK's national domestic abuse helpline had risen by 66 per cent by the end of the second month in lockdown and visits to its website surged by 950 per cent. During the pandemic, police, helplines and shelters around the world saw a rise in the numbers of domestic violence reports and calls from women asking for help. In Argentina, Canada, France, Germany, Spain and the United States, government authorities and women's rights activists saw increasing numbers of domestic violence cases. The United Nations reported a horrifying global surge in cases.

But the violence is not something that has grown out of the pandemic. The lockdown restrictions, along with the financial and emotional toll, have merely highlighted and aggravated what is already a shocking picture across the world. In the United States, Canada and the UK, domestic abuse as a problem has been growing for a long time. In the UK, one in four women will experience domestic abuse and one in five will be the victim of sexual assault during their lifetime. Sadly, five out of every six victims – eighty-three per cent – do not report their experiences to the police. In the US, violence against women – which is taken to mean the use of domestic abuse, murder, sex-trafficking, rape and assault – has been recognised for some time as a public health concern. According to the National Center for Injury Prevention and Control, women experience about 4.8 million intimate partner-related physical assaults and rapes every year. The National Crime Victimization Survey, which includes crimes that were *not* reported to the police, reports that 232,960 women in the US were raped or sexually assaulted in 2006. That's more than 600 women every day. A significant number of crimes are never even reported. Again, as with the British figures, less than 20 per cent of battered women seek medical treatment following an injury.

In Canada, where every six days a woman is killed by her intimate partner, half of all women have experienced at least one incident of physical or sexual abuse since the age of sixteen. More than 6,000 women and children sleep in shelters on any given night because it isn't safe for them at home; 300 more are turned away because there isn't enough room for them.

Globally, the average number of women who will encounter physical or sexual abuse in their lifetime is estimated at one in three. Dr Margaret Chan, a former Director-General of the World Health Organization, said violence against women was a 'global health problem of epidemic proportion'.

As they recognise violence against women as a worldwide and pressing concern, female writers find themselves wondering how best to confront and write about the issue in their novels. A lot of them are using the crime and thriller genre to explore what real life is like for many women and telling honest and unflinching stories about what is going on, behind closed doors, in workplaces and on the streets – and the true aftermath of these traumas. Their work reveals a genuine and deep need to talk about violence, to write about it, to make some sort of sense of it and to represent in print their own real-life experiences – and those of their fellow women – as well as the long-term consequences.

Yet there has been a lot of controversy recently over the manner in which violence against women is depicted in fiction, especially in novels by female authors, and a growing unease about the increasingly brutal, even pornographic nature of these portrayals. In 2012, the Theakston's Old Peculier Crime Writing Festival in Harrogate held a debate headlined 'Deadlier than the Male', asking whether women were writing nastier and more violent crime novels than their male counterparts.

In January 2018, a new writing prize was launched to celebrate thrillers in which no woman is beaten, stalked, sexually exploited, raped or murdered. The Staunch Prize, established by Bridget Lawless, cited concerns that women in crime novels are depicted as the victims of extreme torture, rape and murder, graphically described, bloody, terrifying and prolonged, normalised and offered up as entertainment.

Organisers claimed the prize was not an attempt to censor

crime stories, but 'to offer an alternative narrative to stories based around violence to women'. Referring to a recent fall in rape convictions, they claimed that stereotypical representations of attackers and victims could influence juries in rape trials. The prize's website states: 'Fictional stereotypes of night stalkers, dark-alley attackers, serial killers and menacing strangers are dangerously misleading when 90 per cent of rapists are known to the victim and the majority of women murdered knew their killer. That this can so seriously affect justice for women is alarming, to say the least, and must be addressed. For these reasons, and because we love great writing, we invite thriller writers to bring us strong stories that don't resort to the same old clichés.'

Women writers have widely condemned the prize and described it as a backwards step, one that risks brushing important issues around violence against women under the carpet. However, Kate Rhodes believes there is a place for the Staunch Prize and that its aims at least are laudable. She chooses to never write about sexual violence in her novels. 'I'm just finishing my tenth crime novel now and I have never written about rape,' she said. 'I choose not to do that, because I fear it would be extremely difficult to do that without an element of gratuitous violence that I just don't want to go near. We all have our limits, I think, about what we are prepared to depict and rape for me isn't something I want to write about.'

Mari Hannah called the idea of calling for submissions from writers of books that do not include any violence towards women a 'curious' one. 'I am sorry, but you can't sweep violent behaviour towards women under the carpet hoping it will go away,' she said. 'It is unrealistic, and I think it is foolish.' Hannah acknowledges that there are violent scenes in her novels but says that she tries hard not to be gratuitous. The focus in her books is very much on the fall-out from crime and the ways in which the individual characters deal with it. 'I know writers who I think do overstep the mark, but I choose not to read those books,' she said. 'Those writers are females as well as males. The bloodier and more gruesome they can make it, the better. But likewise, if we are reflecting the society in which we live, we are reflecting all of it. I write books that are authentic, and I know that men are more at risk of assault than women are, but it's women in the main who are raped and killed in horrific ways and I'm damned if I'll cover it up.' American author Meg Gardiner agreed. 'You can certainly offer that prize,' she said. 'But my novels are unlikely to be nominated for it, because they mirror the real world, where women often become the victims of crime.'

Sophie Hannah, who told her publishers not to submit any of her own titles for the prize, dismissed it as 'very silly'. 'All the other crime fiction prizes, like the Gold Dagger, the Crime Thriller of the Year Award, the National Book Awards... all of those prizes take for granted what is being rewarded and approved of is simply the books,' she said. 'No one is approving of any crime. Nobody is saying, yay, murder is brilliant. Those prizes are being given to books that happen to be about murder. The Staunch Prize came along and said we are not considering any book for this prize in which violence happens to women. That would rule out *The Mirror Crack'd from Side to Side* by Agatha Christie and many other brilliant books.

'It sends a message that says we are not considering books in which violence happens to women. Now that is fine, as we all disapprove of violence against women, but that is also unconsciously saying we don't really mind violence against men. If you are going to take a stand against violence you have to take it about violence towards men as well. I smile when I think how silly that prize is. No self-respecting novelist should allow herself to be entered for it.'

Frances Fyfield was also amused. 'Jolly good. Jolly good show,' she said. 'I shall lend them one of mine. Because writing a book with no violence against women is not a reflection of life.

It is a strange piece of logic to say you can't write about violence towards women as if writing about violence towards women was going to encourage that violence. I think it is actually going to do the opposite. The perpetrators of violence against women are not going to be reading books. Not these books. I think it is really silly. Terrible things happen to women and it is your duty to the story to reflect that.

'I can't any longer write graphically about violence,' she added. 'Yet if violence is part of the story, you have to include it. But find a way to do it that you feel comfortable with.'

Emma Kavanagh thinks it is incumbent upon authors to represent what they see in the world. 'I have spent my entire adult life threat-assessing simply because, statistically, I am likely in more danger. I have to be aware of things males don't, generally. It is disingenuous to say we won't have violence against women in our books because then we are not representing society. This is a major issue.'

Anna Mazzola believes the intentions of the Staunch Prize are laudable but that it is misconceived. 'I've heard Bridget Lawless speak and talk about how her concern is about how violence against women is portrayed and how we should be thinking about that,' she said. 'And I absolutely agree with that. But I'm not sure you deal with the issue by saying, cut out the violence against women. I don't see how that helps. We do need to talk openly about violence against women and in particular sexual violence. And I don't think rewarding people for not talking about it is necessarily helpful.

'It's very important we continue to write about violence against women, domestic abuse, rape, and certainly I will be,' Mazzola added. 'I think, in that sense, it's a shame the prize chose to focus on a sort of absence of that. We need to think very carefully about *how* we write about victims of crime and survivors, and particularly how we write about violence against women. But it would have been better in a way if it was a prize about people who wrote about that well, rather than people who just didn't write about it.'

Alison Joseph agrees that the treatment of the issue within crime fiction is the prime concern. 'You know a lot of us are crime writers *because* of our concerns about the world we live in,' she said. 'And it's a brilliant way of addressing those concerns. How violence comes about is something that we need to think about. Even Agatha Christie; in her good books, there's an undercurrent of the danger faced by people. People's rage, it festers.

'I mean it is true that there have been moments when I'm reading a book and there's just something nasty... there's something that puts me in a position of supposedly finding it sort of appealing as a description of what's happening to a young woman. And at that point, I'll stop reading a book. I don't think it's an honest relationship with the reader to do that. To make me sort of implicit in something pornographic, I don't think it's right. But we need to hold this issue up to the light and say, this is what happens.'

Sarah Hilary says she sees it as her role as an author to write about things that are true, and that the Staunch Prize is a form of censorship. 'I think it denies the truth about what is happening,' she said. 'It creates an absolutely false premise. You give awards for content, don't you? Not absence of content. I've never heard of another prize given for the absence of something. And I can't see the point of it. I think it's misjudged. I mean, the idea that crime writers of any gender or any description are actually writing violence against women in order to celebrate it. Whatever way you cut it, it's a terrible idea. And it does a huge disservice to crime fiction, and to women as well.'

Jane Casey said the Staunch Prize was well intentioned and yet 'staggeringly ignorant'. 'I understand what they were trying to achieve, but they aimed at the wrong thing,' she said. 'I know male writers who are very wary of writing about violence against women, who feel uncomfortable about it and uneasy. And in some ways, it's much easier for me to write about a prostitute being murdered. I won't make the mistake of having the masculine gaze and having this kind of titillating aspect of it.'

Nicola Upson is genuinely upset at the notion that her books might in any way glorify violence or objectify women, but says that the prize itself horrifies her. Trying to sanitise the issue, she believes, is an insult to all the good women crime writers who talk about it thoughtfully, whether it is committed against men *or* women. 'It's not what you include, it's the way you include it,' she said. 'People are quite angry about that in the crime writing world and are quite rightly championing the thoughtful treatment of violence and its aftermath. I think that's something very important in my books. It's the effect that the murder has. It doesn't just end with the killer being brought to justice or not. It's the stain of crime.

'There is something inherently dodgy about writing death as entertainment,' she added. 'I think we'd all agree with that. It's very important you do it in a way which doesn't detract from the real violence that is going on every day.'

American writer Alafair Burke says the way any violence is represented in a work of fiction is key. She tries not to be prurient about violence on the page. 'I have friends who write much more violent scenes than I do,' she said. 'That's their prerogative. They want people to really feel it. The way I try to do that though, the violence tends to take place *off* the page. What I won't do is have some woman killed simply as a plot point. I'm always committed to showing the aftermath of violence, either on the victim if she's still living, or her family members if she was murdered. I don't really have the blood and guts on the page, but I have the human toll on the page.'

Tess Gerritsen agrees that violence doesn't have to be on the page. 'But if it's a crime novel, there is going to be violence,' she said. 'If one was to read my novels, they would find I have very little violence on the page. It is always the detectives walking in afterwards. When Rizzoli and Isles walk in, they deal with these gruesome crimes; this is just a day in their lives. It's what they do. It's work. There has been violence, but they are replaying it in their own minds. I try not to take any pleasure or sadistic pleasure in watching people suffer.'

The 'less is more' method is something Sara Paretsky favours when addressing violence in her books. In her 2018 novel, *Shell Game*, she drives part of the story through the characters of two young women abandoned on the streets of California who suffered severe exploitation and abuse. 'I don't describe it except indirectly,' she said. 'But the scenes make it obvious what has happened, and the force is there.'

Paretsky's fellow American Meg Gardiner tries never to make any violence gratuitous or titillating. 'I do not think there is an appetite to read about women being harmed, that is not what readers are after,' she said. 'They are not saying, where can I find the most vicious, disgusting version of women being destroyed because I want to revel in that. That is absolutely not what I think readers are doing. I think there are a few writers out there who try to go to the far edge, to see how creatively they can come up with new, fresh ways to fling the blood. That doesn't interest me at all, as a reader or as a writer. I think people read fiction to explore their own fears in a way that is safe.'

Emma Kavanagh says she does not like graphic violence in novels and that there are things she will not write about, because she doesn't like to read about them. 'In my own personal point of view, you have to be extremely aware of why you are using violence,' she said. 'What is it there to do? If it's there for a cheap thrill, it shouldn't be there. Me personally, when I am telling a story, if violence is needed or occurs, it's very rare I will give a graphic description of it because I very rarely feel like that adds value to what I am trying to do. Generally, I am focused on the characters and their psychological survival. Personally, I think violence is something that has to be considered *carefully*. I'm not saying there should be no graphic descriptions of violence, but if they are there, they need to be there for a reason other than upping the body count or making it more exciting.'

Anna Mazzola believes women's experience of sexual violence helps them write well about it. 'Most women writers I know have either experienced some form of violence or been close to someone who has,' she said. 'It's easier to write about something you know about, something that concerns you deeply. There are also many male authors doing excellent writing on this subject, but perhaps they write in different ways. Certainly, the novels that I've read that explore sexual violence very well are written by women. All of the women I know and have discussed it with are very conscious that it's important to focus on how violence against women is portrayed and how the victim or the survivor is portrayed.'

Denise Mina, whose 1998 debut novel *Garnethill* was awarded the Crime Writers' Association John Creasey Dagger for Best First Crime Novel, has said: 'If you want abused women to be anything other than passive then you need to tell stories about them as active characters.'[44] Zoe Sharp agreed. 'There is a big difference between graphic and gratuitous,' she said. 'And sometimes you need something that's graphic in order to really illustrate a point in a story. The female character in my book gets her share of violence done towards her, but she is as capable of fighting back as anybody else.'

Katherine V Forrest summed up the opinions of her fellow writers, and the ethos of many of the crime books written by women, by saying it is important for fiction to explore the tragic consequences of violence and murder and the disturbing ways violence is often portrayed in crime fiction. 'The one thing urgently important to me in mysteries is to convey the damage that murder produces,' she said. 'It is literally a nuclear bomb in people's lives. It damages the police officers. It damages everybody that it happens to. An objective of mine has always been to make it as realistic as possible, which will include violence. It will also show the disturbing fact you know about in real life, and you see on the television all the time now, that the victims of this violence are almost always women.'

Melanie McGrath believes violence is a reality that needs to be talked and written about. 'We have to accept violence is a reality,' she said. 'Crime fiction gives writers the opportunity to explore violence. Although men might be more likely in reality to be killed', she added, 'women face a deeper, psychological fear in their everyday lives and need to be conscious constantly to the potential for violence.'

Karin Slaughter has often been challenged about the level of violence in her novels. After her 2001 debut novel *Blindsighted* and the 2002 follow-up *Kisscut* came out, her books were categorised as 'masculine' thrillers. 'I was constantly questioned about why I was writing about stuff men usually wrote about,' she said. 'As if it was abnormal for women to be interested in crimes that happen predominantly against women. From the beginning, I felt it was important to openly describe what that violence actually looks like, and to explore the long-lasting effects of trauma in as realistic a way as possible. Rape is not titillating. Domestic violence is not a private matter. Sexual harassment is not a victimless crime.

'When I think about the next 20 years, I'm under no delusion that violence against women will be eradicated, but we as a society can come to a place where it is not tolerated and we ostracise or imprison the people who think it's okay. My part of that quest is to keep telling honest stories we do not often hear about survivors, fighters, mothers, daughters, sisters, wives, friends and rogues.'[45]

12

Criminal Justice, Reviews and Status

A number of high-flying female members of the criminal justice system have made the bold move either to change professions, or take on an additional and completely different career. These criminal justice professionals have become equally successful crime writers.

They include a trial lawyer in the American civil litigation field, a former US district attorney, a human rights lawyer who dealt mainly with criminal justice-related cases, a British lawyer who worked for the Director of Public Prosecutions, a trainer for international police hostage negotiators and two former British probation officers.

I was interested in why these already high-achieving and successful women decided to change careers, what specifically appealed to them about crime writing and what challenges they had faced.

Meg Gardiner was a well-established American trial lawyer. Her twin fields were commercial litigation and civil litigation. To become a top lawyer, she would have had to undergo seven years of study at university, followed by several years' post-graduate study and research at law school, before she would be able to argue a client's case in court. Women lawyers in the US comprise around 36 per cent of the legal profession, but women are still very under-represented in lead trial lawyer positions. In civil cases, around 76 per cent of the lead counsel are men and in criminal cases that go to trial, almost 80 per cent of lead counsel are men.

All this means that Meg Gardiner, who has also taught writing at the University of California, held a very high status and was in a very well-paid role, one she had worked hard for many years to achieve. Giving it up to become a storyteller can't have been an easy decision to make. 'Except that all lawyers are storytellers,' she said. 'And most of them love to write. I knew when I made the decision to become a crime writer that my legal career would strengthen my books.

'As a lawyer, you train to become a persuasive storyteller. Because every case that goes to court is a narrative about something that has broken down between the two parties to the litigation. Your job is to identify and frame the story and the facts of your client's case in as persuasive a manner as possible, to present it to the judge and jury so they will see the justice in your client's cause. Also, when I switched to writing, I knew that if I botched a scene in the novel, nobody could actually have a judgement rendered against them as a result. There's a lot less stress that way.'

In her debut novel *China Lake* (2002) Gardiner made her lead character a lawyer – the spirited, committed and quick-witted Evan Delaney. Having been a top-grade lawyer naturally gave her stories and her characters real authenticity. 'I know the court system from the inside out,' she said. 'I know how it works. I felt confident I could build on that. I understood Delaney's work-life, the system that she was both working within and trying to escape from at the same time. These things I knew about.'

Fellow writer Alafair Burke was a former US deputy district attorney, during which time she prosecuted domestic violence offences and served as an in-precinct adviser to the police department. She is currently a professor of law at Hofstra University School of Law. Her father is fellow crime writer, *New York Times* bestselling author James Lee Burke, although

Burke, as we have seen, traces her initial fascination with crime back to the hunt for the serial killer Dennis Lynn Rader, who murdered ten people in her home town Wichita, and in Park City, when she was a child. She was finally motivated to write her first crime novel because she was so frustrated with the way fictional district attorneys were portrayed in the crime novels she was reading.

'Whenever they got to the part that had district attorneys in it, I'd get so mad,' she said. 'That's not what the job is like. I thought, I should write a book that features a prosecutor and shows what they actually do and what the job is like. The story just came to me, because I was already carrying it around. I think when you are immersed in that world, as I was for so long, you don't have to make it up. And I can use that to my advantage to give a pulse to the book.'

Burke's debut novel *Judgment Calls* (2003) features deputy district attorney Samantha Kincaid as her lead character. Kincaid is a strong, stubborn and complex woman with a powerful sense of justice and the courage and conviction to take on the police and her colleagues in what is very much a man's world. 'Knowing the procedural stuff, even if it is not on the page, helps me to be able to direct the story in the way I want it to go, without letting stuff get in the way,' Burke said. 'When you are part of that world, it also helps to know and understand the dialogue, the way people talk in law enforcement. And you are hardened a bit to violence and darkness and you understand that people deal with that differently. I am able to capture those characters, given that I knew them.'

Samantha Kincaid's law training and professional experience is very much based on Burke's own. Both studied law at Stanford and both turned down more lucrative job offers to work as a state court prosecutor in Oregon. The writer gave her main protagonist the professional and personal characteristics she most admires: a very moral backbone and an almost obsessive determination to stand up to injustice and do what is right. 'These are the qualities I saw among the people I was fortunate enough to work with,' Burke said. 'These are some of the finest people I have known. I wanted Kincaid to embody their diligence, conviction, determination, fortitude. I hope the reader sees all that in her.'

Kincaid gave Burke the opportunity to write a crime story from the point of view of the prosecutor; one she felt is rarely employed in fiction, at least accurately and authentically. A prosecutor has an enormous amount of power and responsibility and one mistake, whether through ineptitude, apathy or being over-zealous, can blow a case. As a lead character, Kincaid is able to be involved in both the investigation process and the trial, which provides an interesting perspective on each case.

Burke, who grew up watching her father work a full-time job and then come home and write every single evening, followed his example when she started writing. That first novel took a few years to complete. She never imagined how many others would follow. Burke has written fifteen novels to date, including three Samantha Kincaid titles and a further series featuring NYPD detective Ellie Hatcher. She has also co-authored a third *Under Suspicion* series with suspense writer Mary Higgins Clark and has written seven standalone novels, the most recent of which, *Find Me* (2021), also features among its cast of characters a dedicated Manhattan defence lawyer, Lindsay Kelly. 'I thought I was one of those lawyers who would think, oh, it would be nice to write a book and have it on my shelf and say I wrote a book one time,' Burke recalled. 'When I wrote my first book, I never thought I would keep doing it.'

Burke often gets requests from fellow writers wanting legal advice for their own crime novels. 'They sometimes call me or email me with questions,' she said. 'Would the police need a search warrant in a particular instance, for example? They want their books to be authentic. But I tell them, what should come first is your story. What do you want to have happen? Do you want them to have an obstacle or do you want to move quickly? What are you trying to do with that scene? And then what I can do, because I know the law, is tell them the way they can make it so that they do have to go get a warrant, if they need an impediment. Or, what to do if they want them to be able to kick the door in right now.' Why does she think so many women from the criminal justice system have become writers? 'I think lawyers and journalists, a lot of them, wind up being novelists,' she said. 'They are used to writing in non-precious ways. They're used to being under a deadline.'

Unlike her American colleagues Gardiner and Burke, crime writer Anna Mazzola has kept her British legal job. Since qualifying as a lawyer, she has represented clients on both sides of the fence. 'I started in government legal service, doing mainly public law cases,' she said. 'I was doing quite a lot to do with prisons, but also to do with Home Office decisions. Then I decided I was on the wrong side. I started working for a human rights firm and have been working on and off ever since for human rights. Discrimination and immigration and so on, but mostly criminal justice-related cases. In particular in relation to victims of crime and women's justice.'

Mazzola's interest in justice for women and how the justice system has treated them through the ages runs through both her novels. Her debut *The Unseeing* (2014) is set in Victorian London and tells the story of Sarah Gale – the seamstress who was convicted and sentenced to hang for her role in the real-life murder of bride-to-be Hannah Brown – and the idealistic attorney charged with finding out whether justice has been done. Her second novel, *The Story Keeper* (2018), is another period piece set in the mid-nineteenth century on the Isle of Skye in the days following the Highland Clearances. 'There is also a sub-plot about abuse of girls and the inability of women in that era to get justice for crimes they have suffered. It's not surprising really that a lawyer with an interest in victims' rights would go on to write.'

Why does Mazzola think so many women lawyers have become novelists? 'I think if you've got a creative mind, then the law, although it's fascinating, is very stymying in that your style has to be very formulaic and archaic,' she said. 'Certainly, if you're a solicitor, with instructions to counsel, it's a very regulated style. And it was lovely for me to be able to write about the things that I cared for in a more creative way. That might be part of it. I don't really know why criminal justice professionals would take to fiction. I guess it's more that, if you are going to write a novel, then it makes sense to write about something you know about.' Mazzola's background gives her writing authority and makes her work easier to sell and to publicise. Although one of her biggest challenges is being able to move away from the facts in order to write a more interesting story. 'Certainly, for me it was recognising that writing a novel is just an entirely different process to creating legal texts,' she said.

Frances Fyfield is the pseudonym of Frances Hegarty, another lawyer. After graduating, she took a course in criminal law and went on to work for what is now the Crown Prosecution Service. The law, and its many ramifications, is a theme that runs through much of her writing work. The lead characters in her two series – Helen West and Sarah Fortune – are both lawyers. 'I always wanted to be a novelist,' Fyfield said. 'I didn't particularly want to be a crime writer, but that was the subject matter I had near to hand. In that way, the law influenced me.'

During her work for the Director of Public Prosecutions, Fyfield became fascinated by the mechanics of the trial, which she believes is 'wonderful in its storytelling powers. You can have all the evidence during trial and the whole thing can unravel,' she said. 'In the old days, when I would be briefing counsel, I had to take all the documents and do a sort of analysis of the evidence and say what the pitfalls were. The briefs to counsel were quite important things, to get them going. I always thought I had to get the person interested. It wasn't just my job to list what there was; I had to tell it like a story. Which is very good because you would then get the barrister interested.

'So, I was used to telling it like a story,' she added. 'When you're presenting things in court, it's got to have some narrative drive in order to keep the jury on side. So, I suppose what the law taught me was the importance of story.' Fyfield said one of the greatest challenges as a writer was to not be over-influenced by real cases. 'I didn't want to write about real crime. I had to resist doing that,' she said. 'So the biggest challenge was to stop myself being over-influenced by being a lawyer and writing like a lawyer, so that I didn't lose out on the magic of just writing.'

Fyfield admits that part of the motivation for writing was to try to make some sense of the things she has witnessed during the course of her work. 'We have awful, tragic cases and murder cases, and I thought perhaps if I wrote the story I could change the ending,' she said. 'Instead of the burglar coming in and seeing the old man in the library and not realising anybody was there, in my story he would just retreat. Whereas, in the real case, he picks up a piece of piping and hits the old man over the head. The idea would be, you could put reality in there and, not sanitise it, but give it a happy ending. At least for somebody.'

Emma Kavanagh was a police and military psychologist for many years, providing training for police hostage negotiators, and was deeply embedded within the criminal justice system, in particular the area of kidnap and ransom. 'I saw things most other people are never exposed to,' she said. 'My entire adult life was being in these really uncommon situations. I don't think you realise quite how uncommon they are until you are with normal people. And then you go, oh yeah, this isn't normal.'

Kavanagh has to date written four standalone novels, the first of which *Falling* (2014), since renamed *After We Fall*, is the story of a tragic plane crash and the aftermath. Kavanagh's background and training were invaluable in crafting the characters and exploring the short and longer term consequences of tragedy. Her third book, *The Missing Hours* (2016), is the story of a mother who goes missing for 20 hours, and the workings of the kidnap and ransom consultancy she ran with her husband before he died.

'Kidnap for ransom is big business around the world,' Kavanagh said. 'Up to 30,000 cases are reported each year. There must be many more that go unreported.' Because of the strict privacy surrounding the kidnap and ransom industry, Kavanagh found the book very difficult to research, in spite of her experience in the field. Research has been crucial for Kavanagh's writing. 'I think that comes from my background,' she said. 'I know what happens if you do a television series or a book that isn't accurate in terms of policing practice,' she said. 'I know what police officers say about that.' Being able to draw on her work for her fiction gives her novels vital authenticity, but taking her knowledge and experiences into her novels also helps her to make sense of the things she has witnessed or heard about.

She thinks this helps explain why so many people who have worked in or on the fringes of the criminal justice system turn to writing crime fiction. 'Obviously I can only approach it from my own experience,' she said. 'But I think having done these things and being in these situations – especially when I became a mum and my life took on a very different shape – I think for me there was always a sense of wanting what I had done to have a continued meaning. I got to see a part of the world and part of society that a lot of people don't get to see. I think that's even more true of police officers. Those who are still embedded within the criminal justice system, we see things that a lot of people aren't exposed to.'

Bestselling writers Ann Cleeves and Mari Hannah were both probation officers early in their careers. 'Many former cops have become crime writers and that is not surprising,' Hannah said. 'But a great number of today's popular mystery writers were, in their past careers, probation officers and that is perhaps more surprising.' Hannah's own career in the probation service was cut short when she was assaulted on duty and let go on a medical pension. 'Obviously my background informs what I write,' she said. 'I knew a lot about the world in which I was writing. I was in the probation service for about 15 years. And I have worked in and out of prisons. My partner is an ex-murder detective so, in this house, over the coffee table, we have shared very many stories.' This background and knowledge mean that it's easier for Hannah to get the procedure right in her novels, something a lot of people who write crime struggle with.

Ann Cleeves says her former career as a probation officer gave her an insight into the criminal justice system, and also the criminal mind. 'I've been into prisons. I have worked with murderers,' she said. 'I was based in Birkenhead and Wallasey in the 1980s. Just at a time when heroin was flooding the market. People were selling heroin very cheaply outside school gates. And then, once they were hooked in, there was no escape for them. And that was a really despairing, dreadful time.

'Because I wrote pre-sentence reports for people who had been found guilty, we would go and do a report for the court explaining something of the offender's background and education. You go into these homes and ask the most intrusive questions, about what might have led to the offending. And just that contact with people – that most people never ever meet – that was great for my writing. I didn't use anything specific. It was just the different worlds colliding really.'

Cleeves had lifers on her caseload and says that, in real-life, murderers are often sad, pathetic and inadequate. One of the men she met had killed a prostitute because she laughed at him. 'And they'd all either been drunk or high when they committed their crimes and were just not very bright, not very intelligent,' she said. 'Not interesting really. So, fiction, I think, fictional murder, is much more interesting generally than real murder.

'I don't want to write about monsters,' she added. 'That's not something that interests me. I don't want to write about psychopaths or about serial killers. In fact, the murder is probably the least important bit in the story. It is much more about looking at what interests me, which is about fractured families and I got lots of that in my work. I didn't stick it for very long.'

These are just a few of the women writers who are using their experience of the criminal justice system, not only to bring authority to their work. Their novels also take a candid and clear-eyed view of the criminal justice world from many different perspectives and can expose its flaws and shortcomings and, essentially, women's real-life experiences within it, as professionals and as victims.

Throughout this book I have mentioned the Sisters in Crime organisation, which was founded in America in 1986 by writer Sara Paretsky, and deserves further attention here. Only four years after writing her debut crime novel, *Indemnity Only* (1982), Paretsky, already a highly political feminist, surveyed the scene facing female mystery and crime writers in the US and recognised some major challenges. These women were being heavily discriminated against in a variety of pernicious ways. At a conference at Hunter College on 'Women and Mystery' in 1986, Paretsky spoke of the growing use of graphic sadism against women in fictional mysteries. Her remarks initiated a flood of calls from writers all over the country who wanted to share with Paretsky their own stories of mistreatment. Fellow American mystery writer Phyllis Whitney stood side by side with Paretsky. She wrote a letter to the organisation Mystery Writers of America, pointing out that women writers were not being nominated for prizes and awards. Later that year,

Paretsky convened the Bouchercon World Mystery Convention in Baltimore, during which the pitifully low number of women crime writers being nominated for literary awards was discussed. Sisters in Crime was officially formed at a third meeting held at crime writer Sandra Scoppettone's loft during the annual Edgars prizes week.

This was the Sisters in Crime 1986 mission statement: 'To combat discrimination against women in the mystery field, educate publishers and the general public as to inequities in the treatment of female authors, raise the level of awareness of their contributions to the field, and promote the professional advancement of women who write mysteries'.

Sisters in Crime never went out of business. At the time of this study in 2020, the organisation has 3600 members in 48 countries worldwide. The group offers networking advice and support to female mystery writers. Former and existing members include writers, readers, publishers, agents, booksellers, librarians – all of whom support women who write mysteries and are bound by their close affection for the genre. But is the organisation needed today? How many of those original objectives have been met? Has the position of women crime writers radically improved over these last 34 years?

'Women crime writers are still getting very little review space in the States,' Paretsky said. 'As is similar to the *Guardian* in Britain, the *New York Times* has a round-up of crime novels. It is published bi-weekly, a single page, and that is the only possible place to get the smallest possible review , even if you have been publishing for 30 years as I have and have brought out more than 20 novels. If, however, someone who is regarded as a mainstream literary writer, like Kate Atkinson, writes a crime novel, then everybody is falling over themselves. There are big reviews. But for people like me, no, never. I am never reviewed outside the small crime round-ups.

'I don't think it's changing at all,' Paretsky added. 'Partly because the papers are mostly owned by the big conglomerates. And the reviews are fed through Associated Press, or a similar central figure who sends out reviews which people can run or not run as they choose. Book review space is smaller and smaller for every writer, and for crime writers it is as hopeless as it used to be.'

Katherine V Forrest says it's hard for women to get as much review space as men. 'I am so glad I had the bulk of my career when I did,' she said. 'Because now there is just so much noise out there. My books used to be a publishing event. Now hundreds of books come out every month. It is very hard to get noticed.'

Alafair Burke acknowledges the lack of newspaper review space is partly to blame. 'The lack of quality review space is definitely a problem and it does make a difference,' she said. 'Publishers are reliant on publicity to sell books. Only a handful of media outlets that do their own reviews are left, and they can make or break you. It is not about good or bad reviews; it's about telling readers you exist.

'In terms of adaptations, people in Hollywood are not sitting around reading hundreds of books per year,' she added. 'They read the reviews. If you have a Janet Maslin, you're going to get a movie option. (Janet Maslin is a *New York Times* film and literary reviewer). Several influential reviewers really can change people's careers.'

Her fellow American Kathy Reichs agrees that, while women have carved out a big chunk of the real estate of crime writing, they are still not equally reviewed. 'One small but important example is that women crime writers are much less likely to be on the cover of the *New York Times* book review section,' she said. 'There are definite problems in this area.'

Tess Gerritsen believes the situation is beginning to improve in the States. 'When it comes to review coverage, it used to be terribly unequal,' she said. 'I am hoping it is becoming more equal. But I think there are surveys that show female novelists still lag behind males when it comes to reviews.' Gerritsen acknowledges that, in America today, around 50 per cent of published authors are women, and this has certainly meant a degree of improvement for review coverage for the female writers in the mystery genre.

Frances Fyfield pointed out a quirky but probably accurate reason men do better with review coverage. 'I think men have it easier with reviews because they are more "clubbable" in that regard,' she said. 'You see some male fiction writers who always get the same very good blurb on the back jacket, almost as if there is a "Boys' Own" club. And they get passed around.'

Jane Casey found herself in hot water recently for comments she made about Washington-born George Pelecanos, a crime novelist, and writer and producer of the hit HBO television series *The Wire*. In a 'By the Book' interview in the *New York Times*, Pelecanos talked about the novels and writers that had influenced him, and that he would recommend to family and friends. Of the 26 authors he mentioned, not one was a woman.

Drawing attention to this imbalance, Casey caused a furore among male writers who defended Pelecanos' right to exclude women – and to mainly exclude crime writers of both sexes from his list. 'He's being quite literary in his take,' Casey said. 'But every single one on his list is a man. And he's not the only person who's ever done it. For a crime writer to not manage to mention a single woman… and he works with Laura Lippman and Megan Abbott. I mean, they are two of the best female crime writers out there. I found that very difficult. But I found the reaction of men very interesting.'

A study of the 'By the Book' series has shown that, when writers were asked to talk about their own world of books or their recommended authors, 51 per cent of the novels mentioned by women were written by other women and 49 per cent were written by men. With men, the split was 80 to 20 in favour of fellow male writers. 'So, you have this thing where the women are sort of equally interested and reading across the genre, not really thinking, that's not for me because it's by a man,' Casey said. 'But men are reading men, and talking about men, blurbing men, recommending men, being on panels with men. It is an issue. And it bubbles under the surface.'

Bringing this issue to light though landed Casey in trouble. 'The men were livid,' she said. 'That anyone would be pulled up for not mentioning women. Because if those are the people that are influencing him, then those are the people who influence him and why *should* he mention women? And they grouped women together with other minorities which, I pointed out, is not quite accurate.'

'There is a bias, a male bias, in getting reviewed,' Mari Hannah said. 'There are many successful writers, male and female, but the statistics speak for themselves. Men's advances are greater, and their books are reviewed more frequently. Two years ago, the women's dominance in the genre was estimated at 80 per cent and men were adopting female pseudonyms to keep up. Not now. In the recent *Sunday Times' 100 Crime Novels and Thrillers to Love*, only 28 were by women.'

Sarah Hilary sums up the findings of her organisation, Killer Women. 'There is a general acknowledgement that there isn't enough recognition or opportunities for women crime writers to appear on panels or to be reviewed,' she said. 'There is definitely the sense that if we all joined forces, perhaps we could get things moving. I hope there is an element of strength in numbers.'

Leigh Russell has a different take, suggesting reviews no longer carried the weight they used to and that this has changed the landscape for crime writers. 'There was a time when reviews in the press, the quality press, were hugely influential,' she said. 'But not nowadays. Bloggers are very influential now. The press is able to review fewer and fewer books, although if there is a big name – a big author with a new book – then that will get reviewed.'

Many readers today do rely on websites such as Goodreads and Amazon for recommendations, an online form of word-of-mouth. Sophie Hannah agrees, recalling how a fellow crime writer complained that she could not get big reviews for her books in the quality press. 'I told her, no you won't, you probably won't,' Hannah said. 'But on the other hand, you're writing in the most popular and most commercial genre. Instead of feeling like a victim and getting steamed up, look on the bright side and say, yes, I am writing in the most commercial sector and who cares if newspapers review me? Also, all the literary blogs review crime endlessly. So, the landscape is changing. What a newspaper does is not as influential as it used to be.'

Anna Mazzola is one of the few crime writers who repeatedly receive excellent reviews in prestigious journals. 'I was lucky to get my books reviewed in the quality press, but I think it may be because they are historical as well as crime,' she said. 'In *The Guardian*, there is this short round-up, but if you want big reviews for crime they won't give you that. It's also hard to get big quality prizes. I don't think it matters much in terms of your writing. I won an Edgar in the US, but it hasn't made much difference to my career. Those awards only make a difference if the publisher gets on board and uses it and does a great deal of marketing. Although it does help your own self-regard and your ability to keep going.'

Winning prizes does seem to be one way of achieving review space. 'I haven't won a big literary prize,' Stella Duffy said. 'The only prizes I have won have been specifically crime prizes. So that does make a difference. I have been longlisted for the Orange Prize twice, but I didn't win it. I think you need to be a prize winner for your literary fiction for them to then up your crime attention.'

Zoe Sharp feels there is a similar resistance to women getting prizes as there is to women getting long, quality page reviews. 'I recall Jake Kerridge did a "Top 100 Thrillers" list and there were less than half a dozen women on it,' she said. 'There is still resistance to women getting prizes and awards. That resistance might be behind the choice of some female authors to use initials. It is almost a given now if you see initials on the cover, that the author is a woman.

'I would rather do it by reputation, but that is the hard way,' Sharp added. 'I am not sure if I want to be nominated for a literary prize. In a recent article about what makes readers buy books, the fact that a book had won an award was very low on the list.'

Sara Paretsky has suggested the general discrimination against women in the mystery field, and the lack of professional support for the advancement of female crime writers, was partly because there is still a crucial divide between the significance readers, publishers and critics give to so-called literary fiction and that given to crime fiction. Literary fiction is given much greater status, meaning books that fall into that category are eligible for awards and prizes, whereas crime books are given precious little status, and this means the linked world of classical reviews, literary prizes and mainstream awards is closed off from them. In April 2019, the British *Sunday Times* published its *100 Best Books of the 21st Century*. The list did not feature a single crime novel.

Alison Joseph believes that if something is written by women, it is often dismissed and not taken seriously. 'If you call something chick-lit, you certainly don't have to take that seriously,' she said. 'There are some very bad male writers who should be put in some pigeonhole of their own, but then they win Booker prizes and are terribly well thought of. And actually, they are writing about the experiences of a very tiny group of middle-class chaps. And not doing that terribly well either. But you know, the world is set up to treat that as serious and good. Many battles haven't yet been won.'

In Britain today this situation is beginning to change, albeit slowly and negligibly. In 2018, accomplished crime writer Belinda Bauer did what no other British crime writer had done before her. She managed to secure a place in the longlist for the most prestigious literary award: the Man Booker Prize for Fiction. Her novel was *Snap,* a dark yet deceptively simple story about a young boy who has to look after his two younger sisters after his mother is murdered – and find out who killed her. The book was inspired by the real-life murder of pregnant woman Marie Wilks on the M50 in 1988, a case that has never been solved. The story is edgy, dark, tense and unsettling, with a rare blend of humour. The judges described it as 'an acute, stylish, intelligent novel about how we survive trauma', which 'undermines the tropes of its own genre, and leaves us with something that lingers'. Although it is the first mystery thriller to be placed on the Booker list, like all good literature, it disregards classification.

It's a fact that a lot of critics and writers continue to view so-called literary fiction as a form of writing that is superior to genre fiction, which, in turn, is considered to be 'low-brow' entertainment with little or no literary merit. The website *Goodreads* defines literary writing as 'serious' fiction: 'which is a work that claims to hold literary merit, in comparison to genre fiction and popular fiction'. In an article for *The Huffington Post*, journalist and editor Steven Petite said the main reason for a person to read genre fiction is for entertainment, 'for a riveting story, an escape from reality. Literary fiction separates itself from genre because it is not about escaping from reality,' he said. 'Instead, it provides a means to better understand the world and delivers real emotional responses.'

Petite acknowledges that this doesn't mean all genre writers are poor writers, but added: 'Do these types of writers sweep a reader down into their fictionalised world? Yes. But do they provide a means to stay inside reality, through the trials and tribulations of everyday life, and deliver a memorable experience that will stick with you emotionally for the rest of your life? In my opinion, no.

'In essence, the best genre fiction contains great writing, with the goal of telling a captivating story to *escape from reality,*' he said. 'Literary fiction is comprised of the heart and soul of a writer's being and is experienced as an *emotional journey* through the symphony of words, leading to a stronger grasp of the universe and of ourselves.'[46]

In 2016, writer Ottessa Moshfegh said her Man Booker-shortlisted novel *Eileen* (2015) was a deliberate exercise in playing with the format of commercial fiction to get the attention of a big publisher. Although her short stories and her first novel *McGlue* (2014) have earned her a variety of awards, she wanted to produce a novel that would give her a career where she could live off her writing. 'That was my prime motivation for writing *Eileen,*' she said in an interview for *The Guardian.* 'I thought, fine. I'll play this game.' Moshfegh didn't want to keep her head down and wait 30 years to be discovered. 'Because there are all these morons making millions of dollars,' she said. 'So why not me?'[47]

Her response suggests there remains an assumption that writing genre fiction is 'easy', especially for someone who considers themselves a literary writer. But Alafair Burke points out that some 'literary' writers have tried it with 'terrible' results. 'They think they know the genre, but actually they don't,' she said. 'What they think is a plot twist, can be seen from chapter one by an experienced crime writer or reader.'

Anna Mazzola dismisses the dividing line between genre and literary fiction as 'foolish'. 'When I wrote *The Unseeing*, which is historical, I didn't think, this is a crime novel or, this is an historical novel,' she said. 'I just wanted to tell one woman's story. I wasn't thinking about where it would be placed in the market. Once my publishers got hold of it, they decided it fit into the crime genre.

'I don't think there *should* be a dividing line between literary and crime fiction. My favourite books have a crime in them, but they are not termed crime fiction. Think *of Alias Grace* (1996) by Margaret Atwood, *Gillespie and I* (2011) by Jane Harris or *Fingersmith* (2002) by Sarah Waters. I generally describe myself as a historical crime novelist. I don't like to be pinned into a genre. The crime writing community is lovely, but there is a huge amount of snobbery towards it.'

Jane Casey considers herself foremost a crime writer who is primarily doing her job to entertain people. 'The division between the two categories of crime and literary fiction doesn't annoy me,' she said. 'I feel literary fiction is such a tiny world and has such tiny sales, and I know they have to be very protective of that world in terms of its status. Crime sells very well, it's very popular and I get a lot of support from my readers. If I'm going to write crime fiction, I'll write it to the absolute best of my abilities.'

'Somebody like Tana French,' Casey added. 'Her book *Broken Harbour* (2011) begins with about 200 pages of the detectives going around a crime scene, and it's the most extraordinary thing. And she shouldn't have been allowed to get away with it in terms of genre conventions. So that, to me, is a literary crime novel. I really respect her for doing it. Because publishing has done extraordinarily well for crime writers for more than five years, crime has been *the* genre that people wanted to write. This has inspired a lot of the literary writers to sideline into crime for fun and also for money.'

Alison Bruce thinks part of the problem is the labelling and categorisation. 'I think it is a shame books have labels,' she said. 'But that literary versus crime argument is ongoing. It stretches into covers. Often the jacket tells you it is crime, so it's the publisher who decides how each book will be packaged and presented. It's a shame the playing field is not even. Some crime novels are very thought-provoking and very character-driven, which should mean they can be judged just like literary fiction, but they're not.'

Frances Fyfield said she might have resented that line when she was a younger writer. 'I no longer resent it,' she said. 'I have got a clearer route to the bank. And I don't think true literary novelists feel that distinction. I never knew there were any rules. I was just writing. I was simply delighted to have a book published. The older I grow, the less I want violent crime in my books, but my publisher ticks me off and says I have to toughen it up a bit. But I don't see myself as a literary fiction writer either. I think of myself as a writer. A storyteller.'

Stella Duffy points out that, while status goes to literary fiction, the money goes to crime and that so-called literary novelists would do well to remember that. 'Weird,' she said. 'You hear literary novelists slagging off crime, when the truth is those literary novelists are only getting *any* money from publishers because the crime writers – and the romance writers and the chick-lit writers – are bringing money into publishing. People say, oh no, I don't read crime. They don't say that about Greek tragedies or *Crime and Punishment* or *Macbeth* or *Medea*. How stupid to limit yourself to reading one particular type.'

Katherine V Forrest invoked some classical crime writers to her cause. 'Margaret Atwood has written science fiction and Norman Mailer has written a mystery,' she said. 'The genres are still stepchildren, they really are. Thank goodness for P D James and Ruth Rendell. They definitely fit into the literary category, and no one can argue with that.'

Mari Hannah does recognise there is a dividing line but feels the row over literary merit is foolish. 'I don't read much literary fiction and I certainly don't take four, five, six or seven years to produce a book,' she said. 'It is rubbish that people like me, who write for a mass market, are seen as second class.'

Nicola Upson was present at the Harrogate Crime Writing Festival in 2009 when Booker prize-winner John Banville betrayed the prejudice many writers and critics have against crime fiction. Banville was appearing at the festival as Benjamin Black, his crime writing pseudonym. When asked to describe the difference between his crime and literary work, he said that when he was writing as Black, he produced around 2,000 words a day; when he was Banville, he wrote about 200. 'The gist of that was that words were more important when he was Banville,' Upson said. 'The whole audience got it and were appalled. I don't think that attitude exists among readers, or among booksellers. It exists among prize-givers, reviewers, and, patently, among some writers. I think it is disrespectful. It is also a question of, where does a crime writer start? If they start inside literary fiction then move to crime, they bring their reputation with them. It is rarer the other way around. I am proud to be a crime writer,' she added. 'But that whole literary line idea is becoming increasingly debased. The women I spoke to take pride in being genre writers. The term literary fiction is now shorthand for a novel about a middle-class, middle-aged white man having a breakdown of some kind in his marriage, and how he deals with that. Whereas some of the so-called literary classics are actually crime novels, all the way back to Shakespeare and to the Greek myths. We are a lovely community, crime writers. We would welcome anybody and everybody, but not if you take a cheap swipe at us. I don't think that helps anyone.'

Tess Gerritsen sees the root of the problem as being the publishing industry. 'The founders of this artificial line are the publishers,' she said. 'Literary fiction is defined by what they decide is literary fiction and how they package it. I don't see much difference. There are some beautifully written crime novels that only the packaging has determined its genre.'

New England writer Elizabeth Edmondson (also known as Elizabeth Aston) wrote more than 30 novels, including a series of vintage mysteries set between the 1920s and the 1950s. Writing in 2014, two years before she died, she described genre fiction as a 'nasty phrase', clever marketing by publishers to set certain contemporary fiction apart and declare it literature, suggesting it is more important and better than other writing. 'Jane Austen's works are described as literary fiction,' she said. 'This is nonsense. Can anyone think for a moment that were she writing today she'd be published as lit fic? No, and not because she'd end up under romance or chick lit, but because she writes comedy.

'For me, in good fiction of whatever kind, the imagination of the writer speaks directly to the imagination of the reader. I want and expect to be entertained, enchanted, transported into the world of the writer, lost in a good book. I don't want to be lectured, have issues thrust down my throat or, dare I say it, be called upon to admire the beauty of the language. If a writer writes well in addition to being a great storyteller, I'm grateful and delighted. If they write well but there's no story, I don't want to read it.

'Remember,' she added, 'that profundity has a dark twin called pretentiousness. Good fiction is good fiction, good writing is good writing and the old, old desire of the literati to cast readers with different tastes into pits labelled 'middle-brow' and 'low-brow' is judgmental and arrogant.'[48]

Women writing crime today understand that readers make up the most important audience, and not only because of the financial rewards a bestselling novel brings with it. 'I have heard a few arrogant writers say they don't care about readers at all, or that readers are not important,' Nicola Upson said. 'How ridiculous. The best writers are writing to connect with other human beings. That is the whole point of writing. I write to touch other people with my story and my characters. I don't want a big literary award that is simply a compensation for lack of sales.'

Crime writers are saying something important, and to an increasingly large audience. The best crime stories dig deep into the complexities of the human soul and the human experience and hold a clear and often unforgiving mirror up to human morality, love and pain, and the society in which they are set. It's not always easy to read. And, in spite of the snobbishness of some of those in the literary world, it is not easy to write.

This is the first book to examine what female crime writers as a group think and feel about crime writing and about fellow crime writers. I have talked to many writers in the US, Canada and Great Britain and discussed the issues raised in this study with women of many colours and ages; those who identify as lesbian, bisexual, heterosexual, able-bodied, disabled, feminist and right or left wing; those who have experienced violence, sexism, homophobia, or racism; and those who come from big cities or small country villages. What they have in common is that they all write crime, and a great many of them read crime.

I have explored the complex and fascinating question of why women, who face and fear violence in their daily lives, should be so addicted to crime novels, many of which feature extreme violence. I was interested in the issues that preoccupied these writers, and the issues they choose to portray in their fiction – and how they create their characters. I noticed very quickly there were some, but not a great many, elderly, gay, disabled, black and ethnic leading protagonists in mainstream crime fiction. All of the interviewees were aware of the dangers of stereotyping, but some admitted to not taking enough care to avoid this.

I have looked at the new women's groups which have joined the traditional crime writing group, such as the media-oriented Killer Women collective, and the criminal justice system professionals – the police officers, forensic scientists, probation officers and lawyers – who have turned to crime writing.

I looked most particularly at the explosions of crime writing by women between 1930 and the present day and have highlighted several key groups: the Golden Age women writers in the UK, the 1950s American women novelists, the experimental and exciting trio, Marcia Muller, Sara Paretsky, and Sue Grafton, who created the first female private investigators in America in the 1980s, and the important emergence of female police protagonists throughout the US, Canada and the UK, as well as those central characters who are lesbian, disabled, black or ethnic minority. I have also examined the significant explosion of domestic noir thrillers and the smaller but highly significant forensic science writers.

Many women writers have taken to crime in order to reflect upon and comment on the social and political landscapes they see around them. In their novels, many of them are exploring highly creatively the significant issues facing women today.

Everyone I spoke to is aware of the mythical divide between fiction labelled 'literary' and fiction labelled 'genre', and the indisputable fact that higher status is given to one over the other. No one in this study approved of the line. Nor does the writer of this study. I believe that first-class crime writing is not merely entertaining, it provides a crucial look at society's moral issues and crucial values. The best of it warrants good critical attention. And it should be taken seriously – and given the credit it so richly deserves.

References

1. Sally Cline, *Dashiell Hammett: Man of Mystery,* Arcade Publishing, New York, 2014.

2. Julia Crouch, *Notes from a Genre Bender in Domestic Noir: The New Face of 21st Century Crime Fiction* (Foreword) (ed) Laura Joyce and Henry Sutton, Palgrave Macmillan, 2018.

3. Melanie McGrath, *Women's appetite for explicit crime fiction is no mystery,* Website: theguardian.com, June 2014.

4. Melanie McGrath, *Is reading crime fiction written by women a feminist act?* Website: nationalpost.com, May 2019.

5. Caroline Crampton, *Playing by the Rules: Christie's Unconventional Crimes,* Website: agathachristie.com, April 2019.

6. Agatha Christie, *Mrs McGinty's Dead,* Dodd, Mead and Co (US) 1952, Collins Crime Club (UK) 1952.

7. Agatha Christie, *The Body in the Library,* Dodd, Mead and Co (US) 1942, Collins Crime Club (UK) 1942.

8. Agatha Christie, *The Murder at the Vicarage,* Collins Crime Club (UK) 1930, Dodd, Mead and Co (US) 1930.

9. Ernest Mandel, *Delightful Murder: A Social History of the Crime Story*. Pluto, London, 1984.

10. Val McDermid, *The Brilliant Unconventional Crime Novels of Josephine Tey*, Website: telegraph.co.uk July 2016.

11. Alexander McCall Smith, *True Detective*, New York Times Book Review. September 2014.

12. Sophie Hannah, *Inspector Alleyn Returns*. Website: theguardian.com. March 2008.

13. Steve Walker, *Money in the Morgue by Ngaio Marsh and Stella Duffy*, Website: stuff.co.nz. April 2018.

14. Marcia Muller, *Games to Keep the Dark Away*, St. Martin's, New York, 1984.

15. Sue Grafton, *J is for Judgment*, Henry Holt and Co, New York, 1993.

16. Sue Grafton, *A is for Alibi*, Bantam New York, 1982.

17. Sue Grafton, *M is for Malice*, Henry Holt and Co, New York, 1996.

18. Val McDermid, *Book of a Lifetime: Indemnity Only by Sara Paretsky*. Website: theindependent.co.uk. September, 2009.

19. Barry Forshaw, *Brush Back by Sara Paretsky – Book review: Warshawski is back, as bloody-minded as ever*. Website: theindependent.co.uk. July, 2015.

20. Penny Perrick, *Crimes of Dispassion*. Website: thetimes. co.uk. August, 2006.

21. Emma Brockes, *Murder She Wrote*. Website: theguardian. com. March, 2001.

22. Elly Griffiths, *The Crossing Places*, Quercus, 2009.

23. Ann Cleeves, *The Crow Trap*, Pan Macmillan, 1999.

24. Kristen Lepionka, *Top 10 female detectives in fiction*, Website: theguardian.com, July 2017.

25. Dan Bilefsky, *An Affable Canadian Author with a Penchant for Murder*, New York Times, May 2018.

26. Elizabeth George, *A Great Deliverance*, New York, Bantam, 1988.

27. Alexandra Alter, *The Wall Street Journal Bookclub: Gillian Flynn on Patricia Highsmith*, Website: wsj.com, April 2014.

28. Dennis Lythgoe, *Ace crime writer struggles with fears her books won't sell*, Website: deseret.com, July 2006.

29. Q & A with Laurie R King, Website: goodreads.com, September 2012.

30. Brian Skupin, *What's Happening with... Abigail Padgett*, Website: mysteryscenemag.com, 2007.

31. Angela Neustatter, *I was guilty. I did my time*, Website: theguardian.com, November 2003.

32. *About Cormoran Strike,* Website: Robert-galbraith.com

33. Robert Galbraith, *Career of Evil.* Sphere. 2016.

34. Katharine Quarmby, *Bringing down the Wall. What to do about disability representation in literature,* From a speech at Nottingham Festival of Literature, November 2016.

35. Dave Corbett, *Changing the Face of Crime Fiction: 6 Writers of Color on Writing Mysteries, Crime Novels, and Thrillers,* Writer's Digest, January 2019.

36. John Fram, *How White Crime Writers Justified Police Brutality,* New York Times, January 2020.

37. Elaine Lies, *Book Talk: Tess Gerritsen turns to her Asian-American roots,* Reuters' Lives, Website: reuters.com, July 2011.

38. Maureen Reddy, *Women Detectives.* In *The Cambridge Companion to Crime Fiction* by Martin Priestman, Cambridge University Press, Cambridge, Massachusetts.

39. Kellye Garrett, Rachel Howzell Hall, speaking at: *It's Up to Us: A Roundtable Discussion,* Website: Los Angeles Review of Books, November 2018.

40. *EA Aymar, Crime Writers of Color, Website: thrillbegins.com*

41. Patricia Cornwell, In conversation with Tina Brown as part of the Women in the World Summit, San Antonio, 2016.

42. Fiona Peters, *Domestic Noir: The New Face of 21ˢᵗ Century Crime Fiction,* In *The Literary Antecedents of Domestic Noir,* Laura Joyce and Henry Sutton (eds), Palgrave Macmillan, 2018.

43. Rebecca Whitney, *Domestic Noir is bigger than ever: top ten releases for 2015*, Website: theindependent.co.uk, January 2015.

44. Libby Brooks, *Denise Mina: I don't think there's any such thing as an apolitical writer,* Website: theguardian.com, April 2019.

45. Karin Slaughter. *Karin Slaughter Was 20 Years Ahead of Our True Crime Obsession,* Website: bustle.com, August 2020.

46. Steven Petite, *Literary Fiction vs Genre Fiction*. Website: huffingtonpost.co.uk April, 2014.

47. Paul Laity, *Ottessa Moshfegh interview: 'Eileen started out as a joke – also I'm broke, also I want to be famous.'* Website: theguardian.com. September, 2016.

48. Elizabeth Edmondson, *The genre debate: 'Literary fiction' is just clever marketing.* Website: theguardian.com. April, 2014.

Acknowledgements

This book has been delayed by two spells in hospital, followed by more than five months shielding from Covid-19. It would have been hard to achieve without the mighty help of three people: Vic Smith, who came regularly and kept my garden invigorated and my spirits upbeat, Kim Rayson, who offered neighbourly support and much fine baking and, most especially, Angie North, who posted letters, sorted admin, and kept me stocked up with painkillers, white bread and marmite.

My most important professional acknowledgement goes to Elaine Bishop, who transcribed dozens and dozens of taped interviews, read more than 90,000 words, edited every chapter and hugely improved the content.

Thank you, Laura Morris, my agent and long-term friend who, during her own hard time, breathed confidence in me all the way. Thank you, Ion Mills, my delightful publisher, whose patience was amazing. Thank you to the whole Editorial Team at No Exit Press who are a joy to work with.

Thank you, Tracey Bagshaw, my responsible, imaginative and original researcher for keeping the guts of the book on track.

Thank you, Glenn Jobson for three years' computer and high-tech skills and unceasing comradeship.

Thank you, Barbara Levy, my former agent and good friend, for talking through the book as soon as it hit the machine.

Thank you, Steve Cook and Eileen Gunn at the wonderful Royal Literary Fund, for not only keeping me afloat through some difficult months, but having faith that I would finally finish this book!

Thank you, Richard Reynolds at Heffers Bookshop, Cambridge (who knows more about crime than I do) for your invaluable help. Thank you, Barry Forshaw for that early encouragement.

I had several years' excellent retreats at Tracy and Richard Baker's Sunset Lodge in Sennen Cove, Cornwall; at Susan and Larry Gilg's high-in-the-sky apartment in Austin, Texas, and at Carol Jones' and Cheryl Day's peaceful white house and extensive gardens in Newlyn, Cornwall.

Thank you, Dr Tom Alderson, whose skills and kindness helped me get through the very hard health bits. At Addenbrooke's Hospital, Cambridge, I appreciate the work of the heart, kidney, lung and trigeminal teams; in particular the flexibility and open-house approach of Professor Paul Flynn, a good friend as well as a fine consultant.

Thank you, to the Cambridge Women's Book Club: Michele Hamilton Dutoit, Frances Ward, Angie North, Sam Pearson and Judith Boddy.

In the UK, I want to thank – for their generous support – my friends Sally Lawrence, Marion Stewart, Frankie Borzello, Michelle Spring (who helped get me started), Kathy Bowles, Alan French, Chris Rayson, Miranda Forward, Mandy Bryant, Katharine McMahon and, for special help, Colette Paul and John Gardner.

Further afield, thank you Bjorn Ribers, Davina and Larry Belling, Martha Campbell, Anne Helmreich – who telephoned and emailed and once wonderfully flew to England – and Annie Gurnett who, despite going through the hardest time of her life, offered me constant and cheery support every Saturday night.

Thank you most of all, to all my interviewees without whom there would have been no book. My special gratitude goes to Stella Duffy, whose close friend died a day before we spoke, and to Alison Bruce, Nicola Upson and Melanie McGrath, for many conversations about crime, to Lee Child, for a very long, very creative talk, and to Maggie Griffin, Lee's publicist and administrator, whose kindness and efficiency made all things possible. And, above all, to Sara Paretsky whose husband and best friend for more than 40 years – the late physicist Courtenay Wright – had just died. In spite of her terrible grief, Sara insisted on our interview going ahead.

Jill Dawson, a writerly inspiration to me, has been there from the first dawning of this book, with imaginative suggestions, a listening ear and fine red wine.

As ever, my extended family have been stalwart, strong and absolutely to be relied upon. Marmoset Adler, my daughter, who is always caring, always alert, this year sent for the marvellous paramedics who rescued me so I that could write the last five chapters. Thanks also to Vic Smith, for all your positive laidback, funny calls and visits, Coz Jane (who offered clever feedback on several chapters) and Coz Kath (who phoned every week with optimism and a patient ear). And, for their rock-hard support, Ric Wilson, Esme Ashley-Smith, Soren Ashley-Smith, Coz Joan Harris, Coz Paul Shackman, Coz Tony Cline, Coz Danya Harris and – before Covid-19 made supper visits impossible – Coz Jonathan Harris for his incredible cooking.

Two young people, Arran Adler-Williams and Theo Adler-Williams, my grandsons, were remarkable, smart, helpful and innovative.

Most of all Ba Sheppard, for the forty-second year, provided a daily dose of sanity, love, and care in a world of political shambles and literary uncertainty. Thank you.

Awards

Currently prizes and awards must be virtual. So, here are the two After Agatha Awards, 2020.

The first: the After Agatha Award for Excellence in Crime Prose goes to Frances Fyfield.

The second: the After Agatha Award for Creation of the Genre's Most Significant Private Eye goes to Sara Paretsky.

Index

⬤LDCASTLE BOOKS

POSSIBLY THE UK'S SMALLEST
INDEPENDENT PUBLISHING GROUP

Oldcastle Books is an independent publishing company formed in 1985 dedicated to providing an eclectic range of titles with a nod to the popular culture of the day.

Imprints vary from the award winning crime fiction list, NO EXIT PRESS, to lists about the film industry, KAMERA BOOKS & CREATIVE ESSENTIALS. We have dabbled in the classics, with PULP! THE CLASSICS, taken a punt on gambling books with HIGH STAKES, provided in-depth overviews with POCKET ESSENTIALS and covered a wide range in the eponymous OLDCASTLE BOOKS list. Most recently we have welcomed two new digital first sister imprints with THE CRIME & MYSTERY CLUB and VERVE, home to great, original, page-turning fiction.

oldcastlebooks.com

OLDCASTLE BOOKS		KAMERA BOOKS		HIGHSTAKES PUBLISHING
POCKET ESSENTIALS		CREATIVE ESSENTIALS		THE CRIME & MYSTERY CLUB
NO EXIT PRESS		PULP! THE CLASSICS		VERVE BOOKS